Cistercian Studies Series: Number Sixty-one

SIMPLICITY AND ORDINARINESS

CISTERCIAN STUDIES SERIES: NUMBER SIXTY-ONE

SIMPLICITY AND ORDINARINESS

STUDIES IN MEDIEVAL CISTERCIAN HISTORY IV

JOHN R. SOMMERFELDT, *editor*

§

CISTERCIAN PUBLICATIONS
Kalamazoo, Michigan
1980

Available in the Commonwealth and Europe from

A. R. Mowbray & Co Ltd
St Thomas House Becket Street
Oxford OX1 1SJ

Library of Congress Cataloging in Publication Data
Main entry under title:

Studies in medieval Cistercian history, IV.

  (Cistercian studies series ; no. 61)
  1. Cistercians--Addresses, essays, lectures.
I. Sommerfeldt, John R. II. Title: Simplicity
and ordinariness. III. Series.
BX3402.2.S784   271'.12'04   79-27197
ISBN 0-87907-861-8

This volume is gratefully dedicated

to my mother and father,

Virginia and Hans Sommerfeldt,

whose interest and love and care

enabled me to begin my own

Cistercian studies.

INTRODUCTION

Most of the papers in this volume were presented at the Fifth and Sixth Cistercian Studies Conference, sponsored by the Institute of Cistercian Studies of Western Michigan University in 1975 and 1976. At these meetings, some thirty-six papers were presented on diverse facets of Cistercian life: the Cistercian Fathers; the predecessors and diffusion of Cistercian life and thought; Cistercian liturgy, art, and architecture; and the institutions which expressed and modified Cistercian values.

From this rich fare we have chosen for this volume a sample of papers centering on intellectual history, especially the spirituality of the Cistercian Fathers. The theme--and title--of this volume derive from the first article, Father Chrysogonus Waddell's fine paper on Simplicity and Ordinariness among the early Cistercians. All the papers in this volume do not address this question directly. Rather, this theme is the measure by which we can judge the authenticity of Cistercian life and thought reflected in the other papers. This standard justifies the inclusion of the one paper not devoted to spiritual or to intellectual questions: Father Columcille Ó Conbhui's informative paper on Cistercian abbots in medieval Ireland.

Father Columcille's paper was not presented at the Cistercian Conference. It was given to a delighted audience of monks and lay scholars from Europe and America at the third meeting of the Associa-

tion for Cistercian Studies at Holy Spirit Abbey in Conyers, Georgia.
Abbot Augustine Moore, Father Thomas Fidelis, and the community were
warm, gracious hosts to this informal meeting. At the time, Father
Louis Lekai was searching for a title for the successor to his de-
servedly popular book The White Monks--subsequently to appear as The
Cistercians: Ideals and Reality. After hearing Father Columcille's
presentation of the lives and loves of Irish abbots--and the offspring
who sometimes succeeded them--one of the Conyers community suggested
that the proper title of Father Louis' book would be Son of the White
Monk. Of such stuff is Cistercian scholarship--and good humored Cistercian simplicity--made.

As I have said, not all the papers presented at the 1975 and
1976 Cistercian Conferences have been--or could be--included in this
volume. Many of them will appear in subsequent volumes in this series.

John R. Sommerfeldt

The University of Dallas

TABLE OF CONTENTS

ABBREVIATIONS

(Medieval texts cited by English title appear in translation in the Cistercian Fathers Series.)

Apo	Bernard of Clairvaux, *Apologia to Abbot William of St Thierry*
ASOC	*Analecta Sacri Ordinis Cisterciensis.* Rome, 1945– .
CF	Cistercian Fathers Series. Cistercian Publications, 1969– .
CS	Cistercian Studies Series. Cistercian Publications, 1969– .
Csi	Bernard of Clairvaux, *Five Books on Consideration.*
Div	Bernard of Clairvaux, *Sermones de diversis.*
EM	Conrad of Eberbach, *Exordium magnum Cisterciense.*
Ep(p)	*Epistola(e)*
Hom.	Homily
Letters	Bruno Scott James, *The Letters of Saint Bernard of Clairvaux.* London–Chicago, 1963.
Nat	Bernard of Clairvaux, *Sermo in nativitate domini.*
Op. S. Bern.	Jean Leclercq, H. M. Rochais, C. H. Talbot, *Sancti Bernardi Opera.* Rome, 1957– .
Palm	Bernard of Clairvaux, *Sermo in ramis palmarum.*
PL	J. P. Migne, *Patrologia cursus completus, series latina.* Paris, 1844–64.
RAM	*Revue d'Ascétique et de Mystique.* Toulouse, 1920– .
R Ben	*Revue Bénédictine.* Maredous, 1884– .
RTAM	*Recherches de Théologie ancienne et médiévale.*
S(S)	Sermon(s)
SC	Bernard of Clairvaux, *Sermons on the Song of Songs.*

SCh   Sources chrétiennes. Paris, 1941- .

VA   *Vita venerabilis Amedaei Altae Ripae.*

VP   *Vita domni Petri abbatis Claravallis.*

SIMPLICITY AND ORDINARINESS:

THE CLIMATE OF EARLY CISTERCIAN HAGIOGRAPHY

CHRYSOGONUS WADDELL, O.C.S.O.

In early December of 1942, a young Columbia graduate who had
majored in English literature entered the Trappist monastery of
Our Lady of Gethsemani. The newcomer was an excellent linguist.
He had a special proficiency in French, which he even spoke with
a slight toulousain twang. The abbot, Dom Frederic Dunne, was delighted. There were any number of French books which he wanted
to see made available to the English-reading public. Dom Frederic's
choice of material to be translated was not particularly inspired;
but young Frater Louis proved to be a highly gifted translator--and,
indeed, more than a translator. He had a special gift for quickly
assimilating large amounts of material, sorting out the essential
from the trappings, and developing it further with the help of
his own insights. The Valley of Wormwood, which has survived only
in scraps, is an early example of this. Frater Louis, who was
later to become better known under his secular name, Thomas Merton,
first devoured most of the early Cistercian hagiographical literature to be found in the huge folio tomes of the Bollandists' Acta
Sanctorum. Then, making a careful choice of the material best suited

to his purpose, he translated/paraphrased the Latin texts, adding his own insightful reflections.

In 1945, Frater Louis, at the request of Dom Frederic, wrote a biographical sketch of the thirteenth-century Cistercian Flemish mystic, Lutgarde of Aywières. Originally meant to appear as an anonymous pamphlet, it was actually printed only in 1948, in the wake of the great popularity enjoyed by Thomas Merton's autobiographical Seven Storey Mountain. Frater Louis was later to look upon his What Are These Wounds? as one of the literary sins of his monastic youth. He was, I think, a bit harsh on himself. Granted that the literary genre which he adopted--that of the edifying biography written to be read in monastic refectories-- has a limited reader appeal, the book is shot through with occasional flashes of deep insight. One of these appears in the final section of Frater Louis' discussion of Lutgarde's school of mysticism. He writes:

> But all that has been said so far must not obscure
> the fact that these thirteenth-century Cistercian
> mystics with whom we have mostly been dealing do
> not represent the pure Cistercian spirituality that
> characterized the first century of the Order's history.
> In St. Lutgarde we find practically nothing of that
> beautiful and simple zeal which was the very founda-
> tion stone of the Order--the zeal for the Rule of St.
> Benedict in its purity, the zeal for labor in the
> fields, silence, solitude, community life, monastic

simplicity, and that concern with doing ordinary
things quietly and perfectly for the glory of God,
which is the beauty of pure Benedictine life. Of
course, St. Lutgarde was Cistercian and Benedictine
in her spirituality, in her love of the Divine Office,
in her love of Christ above all else; but she lacks
this Benedictine <u>plainness</u>, and this Cistercian tech-
nique of humility which consists in a kind of protec-
tive coloring, by which the monk simply disappears
into the background of the common, everyday life,
like those birds and animals whose plumage and fur
make them almost indistinguishable from their
surroundings.[1]

A year or so later, Sr Simone Roisin, in the introduction to

her fine study of Cistercian hagiography in the diocese of Liège

in the thirteenth century,[2] was also finding something "different"

about Lutgarde, the Cistercian milieu, and the thirteenth-century

hagiographical scene in general. The thirteenth century, she ex-

plains, inaugurates a new method of hagiographical production. The

Acts of Martyrs went out with the end of the era of persecutions.

The age of the great missionary bishops is likewise past. Columban

and the Irish monks are no longer launching out on their pilgrimages

<u>propter</u> <u>nomen</u> <u>Domini</u>. The thirteenth century is characterized, then,

by preoccupations of a higher nature. And on what do these pre-

occupations center? On the intimate relationship of the soul with

God. <u>C'est</u> <u>le</u> <u>triomphe</u> <u>de</u> <u>la</u> <u>biographie</u> <u>mystique</u>, she writes. And

she goes on to refer to an impressive list of experts who say the

same.[3]

In brief, Fr Louis, who knew, and knew well, the available
Cistercian hagiographical literature of the twelfth and thirteenth
centuries, finds in the twelfth century an element of "ordinariness"
which contrasts with the mysticism of the thirteenth-century Flemish mystics; and Simone Roisin (among others), discerns the "mystical preoccupation" of the thirteenth-century hagiographers as
something rather specific to this century.

My own impression is that the "invasion of mysticism" was
already a _fait_ _accompli_ in Cistercian hagiographical literature
of the twelfth century, but that it was a mysticism which sprang
up and flourished in an environment characterized by extreme
simplicity, plainness, ordinariness. My preference, then, is not
so much to oppose twelfth-century Cistercian ordinariness with
thirteenth-century mystical preoccupations, as to note, in the
course of the thirteenth century, the gradual diminution of that
note of simplicity so characteristic of the experience of the holy
monks and nuns of the first Cistercian century. The mystical element was, it seems to me, common to both centuries; only its outward form differed. Though, even here, I do not wish to speak of
this discernible differences in terms of an extreme opposition.

SOURCE MATERIAL

Anyone interested in Cistercian hagiography of the Middle

Ages has ample source material at his disposal. The most helpful
work instrument in this area of research is surely the material prepared by Fr Seraphin Lenssen, O.C.S.O., under the auspices of the
Liturgy Commission of the Cistercians of the Strict Observance, in
preparation for a reform of the Order's Menology (containing brief
biographical sketches of Cistercian monks and nuns, arranged for
day by day reading in refectory). The first publication appeared
as early as 1937--<u>Actes</u> <u>de</u> <u>la</u> <u>Commission</u> <u>de</u> <u>Liturgie</u> <u>concernant</u> <u>le</u>
<u>Ménologe</u> <u>cistercien</u>.[4] The bulk of the material is devoted to a
lengthy catalogue of 1,215 names of Cistercians (and a few others)
who might conceivably have a right to a place in the revised Menology.
Each entry includes essential dates, reference to the <u>cultus</u> (if any)
hitherto accorded the person in question, and a schematic bibliography
of source material pertinent to this eligible candidate for the Menology. Even more ambitious was the same Fr Seraphin's <u>Hagiologium</u>
<u>cisterciense</u>, which appeared in three polycopied volumes, beginning
in 1948.[5] The emended catalogue of 1937 was fleshed out enormously
with lengthy biographical sketches of each person, with detailed
notes on the <u>cultus</u>, and with up-dated, much expanded bibliographies.
Since 1948, of course, one has only to follow the bibliographical
<u>indices</u> of <u>Analecta</u> <u>Bollandiana</u> to note that each year brings forth

new source material, or at least new editions of source material.
But Fr Lenssen's _opus magnum_ remains, to date, the irreplaceable
work instrument.

I have no intention of trying to prove anything in this paper.
I simply wish to reflect on a few--a very few--texts by way of illus-
trating my general impression that simplicity is the characteristic
climate of early Cistercian hagiography. In choosing from the
embarrassment of riches at my disposal, I straightway eliminated a
whole category of hagiographical texts--the biography written with
a view to the canonization of the holy monk or nun in question.
The conventions of the official biography-with-a-view-to-canonization
are such that we are not always sure whether the biographer captures
his saint in his most characteristic attitude. I have forsworn, then,
any reference to the rich hagiographical literature shaped up with
a view to the canonization of St Bernard. Besides, Bernard, who
was certainly one of the greatest of the Cistercians, in some ways
was the least typical--as he himself humbly protested on more than
one occasion. Eliminated, too, were Geoffrey of Clairvaux's canon-
ization-biography of the imcomparable Peter, bishop of Tarentaise,
and the anonymous _Vita_ of William of Bourges, prepared for the same
purpose. In general, too, we should eliminate from our consideration
the hagiographical narratives concerning other monks who, like Peter

and William, were perforce wrenched from their Cistercian milieu
and promoted, protesting, to episcopal and cardinatial dignities.
We are concerned here, not with accounts about great and ideal
bishops, but with accounts about typical twelfth-century Cistercian
holy men and women. Originally I had decided to include in my
dossier the lengthy Vita sancti Stephani Obazinensis, which only recently became accessible in its integral version in a fine Latin-
French edition;[6] and also the text of the Vita Christiani monachi,
which at last, through the sleuthing skill of Fr Jean Leclercq,
osb, is now accessible in its complete form.[7] But, having looked
over my preliminary notes, it seems to me that most of what I want
to say can be said with reference chiefly to two works of more
modest dimension--the anonymous Vita venerabilis Amedaei Altae Ripae,
written around 1160 by a confrère of Amedeus the Senior, monk of
Bonnevaux (died around 1150); and the Vita Domni Petri abbatis
Claraevallis, written by a close friend and admirer of Peter the
"One-eyed" in 1204, almost two decades after Peter's death in 1186.
True, this takes us into the first part of the thirteenth century;
but the Benedictine author, Thomas of Reuil, is writing as an old,
old man, who belongs more to the twelfth than to the thirteenth
century; and most of his source material comes from witnesses who
speak and write as monks of the same twelfth century. Also, I have

drawn from a few pages of the great collection of <u>cisterciana</u>, the <u>Exordium</u> <u>magnum</u>. I first fell in love with this compilation of edifying (and not so edifying) stories when, as a young novice, I opened up Tome 185 of Migne's <u>Patrologia</u> <u>latina</u>, and hit at random upon the account of Lawrence, the laybrother who was sent on an errand from Clairvaux to the king of Sicily, and returned to Clairvaux driving a herd of some ten buffalo.[8] Even the sketchiest essay on Cisterican hagiography should pay at least a token tribute to this important monument to the spiritual experience of the first generations of White Monks.

SIMPLICITY AND ORDINARINESS

By "ordinariness" I mean to denominate the sense in which I shall be using the term "simplicity" throughout most of the following pages. In the context of Christian literature, few terms offer so many complexities as does <u>simplicitas</u>; and a word should be said about this before proceeding further.

The Greeks provided the translators of the Septuagint with relatively meagre material when it came to the vocabulary of childhood and simplicity. In spite of the admirable Greek sensitivity to the exigencies of the various stages of growth from the womb to hoary old age, and in spite of their concern for every aspect of <u>paideia</u>, Greek writers tend more often than not to use nēpios (simple) in a

somewhat pejorative sense. We find it constantly associated with
other terms belonging to the vocabulary of childhood, and it would
seem that the thrust of contemporary scholarly opinion moves in the
direction of a derivation of the adjective from the Ionic verb
nēpeléō, "to be without power."[9] More often than not, however,
"simple" is used as convertible with "foolish" and "inexperienced."[10]
The "simple" man is the man unable to base his actions on reality.

The Greek and Hebrew versions of the Old Testament are prodi-
giously rich in the terminology of childhood, and one has only to
thumb through the several pages devoted to the Septuagint usage
of nēpios in Kittel's Wörterbuch[11] to be convinced of the fact.
New Testament usage inherits the same complexities of "simple"
understood in terms of the weak, innocent child helplessly affected
by the world's condition, and "simple" understood in terms of the
righteous who, depending wholly on God, are "simple," out of contact
with reality as the world sees it. "Simple" as applied to a person
who refuses to grow out of childhood is, of course, blameworthy in
the extreme. Maturity is the ideal, and the simplicity of those
Cistercians unable to discern the true from the counterfeit, the
specious from the substantial, is quite simply stupidity.[12]

But the essential New Testament usage which Christian tradition
was to develop with such incredible richness is found in Mt 11:25 and

Lk 10:21, where Jesus praises the Father, Lord of heaven and earth,
for having hidden "these things from the wise and understanding and
revealed them to babes" (n<u>ēpíois</u>, <u>parvulis</u>); and in Mt 21:16, where
Jesus enters Jerusalem, and defends the children who rejoice at his
coming, by citing Ps 8:2: "Out of the mouth of babes (n<u>ēpíōn</u>, <u>in-</u>
<u>fantium</u>) and sucklings thou hast brought perfect praise." It is the
helpless man, the poor man, wholly dependent on God, who recognizes
Jesus, and breaks into perfect praise. Evidently, the Latin word
<u>simplex</u> is here not used. But <u>simplex</u>, along with <u>parvulus</u> and <u>in-</u>
<u>fans</u>, belongs so much to the vocabulary of childhood, that the
shift from one term to another is made without any perceptible dis-
continuity. In brief

> Those whom the world does not notice, children, the lowly,
> the disciples and the masses bear witness to Jesus.
> They acknowledge Him to the praise and glory of God.
> Flesh and blood did not reveal this to them any more
> than to Peter, but God Himself. To them is given under-
> standing of the <u>mustēria</u> <u>tēs</u> <u>basileías</u> <u>tōn</u> <u>oúranōn</u>.[12a]

And this is where the real complexity begins; for, obviously
this evangelical <u>simplicitas</u> is of one piece with such fundamental
biblical notions as humility, poverty, meekness, gentleness.

Patristic usage, tributary to so many different sources of influence, was to admit of even further developments. <u>Simplex</u>, <u>sim-</u>
<u>plicabilis</u>, <u>simplicitas</u>, <u>simpliciter</u>, <u>simplitudo</u>, <u>simplo</u>, <u>simplus</u>--

these words are treated by one of the finest lexicographers of Christian Latin, Albert Blaise,[13] who notes at least six distinct uses of <u>simplicitas</u>: 1. simplicity as the state of that which is not compound in nature; 2. simplicity in the sense of unaffectedness; 3. simplicity as meaning absence of complication; 4. simplicity as integrity, that is to say, the integrity or purity of faith; 5. moral simplicity, frankness, straightforwardness; 6. simplicity as naïveté.[14] Even more of the complexity of the term can be seen in a study such as Fr P. Antin's article, "<u>Simple et simplicité</u> chez saint Jérome,"[15] where, after ten pages of fine print written in telegraphic style, the author ends on a somewhat apologetic note: Jermone's use of the term does not extend to its metaphysical and theological aspects.

Jerome might have avoided the use of "simple" and "simplicity" in their metaphysical and theological aspects, but not so Augustine, Gregory, and others among the Fathers of the Church. By the time we arrive at the century of the great Cistercian writers, our terms are rich with resonances and even specific meanings of many different sorts, and one must distinguish the exact nuance of "simplicity" according to the context. A series of monographs on "Simplicity in the Writings of Bernard of Clairvaux," "...of William of St-Thierry,"

"...of Isaac of Stella," etc. would be a valuable contribution in
the field of Cistercian studies.

To date, perhaps the most interesting study of "Cistercian
simplicity" is to be found in a book which ought not to be neglected
by anyone interested in the Cistercian-Trappist renaissance of the
twentieth century. The Spirit of Simplicity: Characteristic of the
Cistercian Order[16] is a translation with commentary on an official
report asked for and approved by the General Chapter of the Order.
The author is anonymous, but it is really the great and saintly abbot
of Sept-Fons, Dom Jean-Baptiste Chautard; the translator-commentator
is also anonymous, but it is Fr Thomas Merton of Gethsemani. The
original report dates back to 1925/1926; the translation to 1948.
In his five chapters of the lengthy report, Dom Jean-Baptiste had
devoted the first to a discussion of "interior simplicity" as the
principle from which exterior simplicity derives. St Bernard is
here represented by a single citation; the Rule of St Benedict is
better represented, as also St Thomas Aquinas, Augustine, and
Pseudo-Denis the Areopagite. In the subsequent chapters, however,
the tone was set by a wearying catalogue of particular instances
of Cistercian legislation concerning exterior simplicity. "In
1240 the Chapter suppressed all pictures on altars....At this
Chapter permission was granted for a second candle at the high

altar....The Chapter of 1207 specifies that chasubles are to be of one color only...." etc., etc., etc. Fr Louis, who at this time was deep into Bernard, and who had profited enormously from his careful study of Gilson's seminal <u>The Mystical Theology of Saint Bernard</u>,[17] was appalled by the non-mystical dimension of the General Chapter report. So he supplemented it with a collection of Bernardine texts excerpted, translated, and exegeted by himself. In this section, "St Bernard on Interior Simplicity," Fr Louis studies the mystical ascent in terms of a gradual simplification and unification of the spiritual faculties. Though this essay lays not the slightest claim to any kind of literary pretensions, it remains to this day the best treatment of "simplicity in St Bernard."[18] Still, this metaphysical-theological simplicity, though obviously rooted in revelation, represents a refinement of patristic thought several times removed from the simplicity of the poor, the humble, the lowly who are the bearers of the Gospel revelation.

In the early Cistercian hagiographical literature, one finds, in point of fact, almost every possible use of the term <u>simplicitas</u>. But my impression is that the really central aspect which provides the context for other uses of the term is the aspect of that evangelical humility and poverty and childlikeness such as Jesus rejoices over in his great cry of exultation, "I thank you, Father, Lord of

heaven and earth, for you have hidden these things from the wise
and understanding and revealed them to babes..."[19] In no way,
of course, do I wish to oppose any one use of the term to another,
for most of them are inter-connected and closely related. But to
the extent that "simplicity" becomes removed from the climate of
its gospel context, to that extent it loses something of its
applicability to the Cistercian experience.

What we find in early Cistercian hagiography, then, is an
evangelical simplicity characterized by childlikeness, unpreten-
iousness, plainness, ordinariness.

It is time to look at a few texts.

THE VITA VENERABILIS AMEDAEI ALTAE RIPAE

One of the most remarkable of all the twelfth-century Cistercian Vitae is that of Amedeus the Senior, monk of Bonnevaux.[20]
Amedeus Senior has been eclipsed by his son, Amdedeus Junior, who
was important both as bishop of Lausanne and as a Cistercian writer.
But Amedeus, lord of Hauterive, was, as St Bernard had been, the
catalyst of a conversion en masse. The catch included, besides
himself, sixteen companions recruited from the higher ranks of the
nobility, as well as Amedeus' young son, who bore his father's name.

I say that there is something quite remarkable about this biography written around 1160 by an anonymous monk who had been Amedeus' companion for a number of years. In spite of the author's heavy debt to all the conventions of hagiography, he records not a single instance of a miracle or a revelation. This is quite unusual. True, the Cistercian hagiographer, like the anonymous author of the <u>Vita</u> <u>Sancti</u> <u>Stephani</u> <u>Obazinensis</u>, might lament the fact that people nowadays are more interested in signs and mrracles than in examples of solid virtue.[21] But, for all their protests, the hagiographers are as interested in signs and miracles as anyone else. If there are no signs and miracles in the <u>Vita</u> <u>Amedaei</u>, it is because there were no signs and miracles in the life of Amedeus. No miracles? No revelations? Then what is there to write about?

Amedeus' humility. <u>Humilitas</u> is, indeed, the very first word of the prologue to the <u>Vita</u>; and in this word the author finds the term best suited to express Amedeus' concrete living out of the Cistercian way of life. Our author indulges in the usual <u>nomen-omen</u> routine. "Amedeus," he tells us, means "God-Loving"; though we, who have read the foot-notes to Fr Dimier's edition of the text, know that the name more likely derives from the barbaric <u>Hama-deoh</u> borne by the wild and distant ancestors of Amedeus in centuries now long past. As for "Hauterive"--<u>Alta</u> <u>Ripa</u> in Latin:

<u>alta</u> means "high," of course; and any fool knows that <u>ripa</u>, that
is to say, "river bank" obviously stands for humility, since river
banks generally tend to be lower than the surrounding landscape.
Clearly, then, Amedeus is predestined, in virtue of his name, to be
a model of the highest kind of lowliness. And he chooses the right
Order and the right monastery in which to exercise this charism
of humility.[22]

Having disposed of their women-folk in the convent later to
become Laval-Bressieux, Amedeus and his companions trouped off to
the wretchedly poor and still struggling community of Bonnevaux,
rather near Vienne, on the banks of the river Gère. Founded from
Cîteaux as early as 1117, at the special request of the Archbishop
of Vienne, Guy, who was soon to be pope under the name of Callistus
II, the monastery abounded chiefly in poverty.

Our author is not given to flights of higher mysticism. In
his lengthy description of the life of the brethren of Bonnevaux,
he says next to nothing about their life of prayer (except that they
celebrate the Office with great devotion), nothing about their interior life (though he does mention reading as being one of their occupations). What concerns him most immediately is the rough, heavy
work, and the extreme frugality of the life-style in all its aspects.

Social conventions being what they were in the twelfth century, the sight of a well-born but smoke-smudged, hand-calloused monks chopping down trees and stoking the fires that helped clear the brush wood had something of a morbid attraction about it--a bit like dropping into a London pub, and finding Queen Elizabeth II hard at work washing out beer tankards. "Black as blacksmiths" is the way ˜our author describes them; and his pen-sketch of their refectory fare is painted in colors just as black.[22a]

"When anyone cometh newly to be a monk, let him not be granted an easy admittance, but, as the apostle saith: 'Test the spirits, to see whether they come from God.'" This directive formulated by St Benedict in Chapter 58 of his Rule explains the cool reception accorded Amedeus and his companions. In spite of the genial Abbot John's long catalogue of the _dura et aspera_ of the Cistercian way of life, and in spite of the initial wavering of some members of the group, all eventually remained firm in their resolve. Re-assured of the seriousness of their intention, Abbot John touches on one of the multiple aspects of interior simplicity. _Non corde duplici ad nos venistis, amici_--"You come to us, O friends, with undivided heart."[23] Here we meet with the theme of the _cor simplex_, the undivided heart, the simple heart set on the one thing necessary;

the heart which, being undivided, can reduce the complexities of
human experience to a life-sustaining unity.

At this stage, however, Amedeus' heart was not all that undivided. Breaking with the conventions of hagiography, our honest
biographer describes in a fair amount of detail the great sin of
Amedeus' life. Though too young to be admitted to the novitate,
Amedeus Junior was nonetheless at Bonnevaux. The abbot, assisted
by some of the monks, was to see to the boy's education. As
educators, Abbot John and the monks were total failures, their philosophy of education being that the anointing of the Holy Spirit
had more to teach the boy than could Priscian's rules of grammar.[24]
Unimpressed, Amedeus Senior let his worry over the boy's neglected
education get the better of him, and the day came when he took his
son and set off on horse-back for the great Abbey of Cluny. The
father almost immediately exchanged the white cowl for the black,
and after a few days, young Amedeus was sent off to Germany to be
educated in the manner befitting his noble birth, at the court of
Emperor Conrad.[25]

At Cluny, Amedeus now experiences a second and deeper conversion to the Cistercian form of monastic life. The contrast between
the life-style of Cluny and that of Bonnevaux is borne in upon him
in a crescendo of intensity which reaches its climax in the course

of the solemn celebration of a major feast day. Vested in liturgical splendor, Amedeus thinks of the rags of the brethren at
Bonnevaux; and the sound of the exuberant, modern-style tropes
and sequences of Cluny—so different from the sober, classical
style of Cistercian chant—forms the tonal background against
which Amedeus begins to soliloquize over his lost ideal of
poverty and simplicity. In a dramatic gesture, he throws off his
vestments and storms out of choir, weeping bitterly.[26]

The contrast between Cluny and Cîteaux loses nothing in the
telling, but our author ought not to be understood as intentionally
feeding the flames of the Cluny-Cîteaux polemic which still smould-
ered.[27] Indeed, in the highly rhetorical, clearly fictitious dialogue between Amedeus and the Abbot of Cluny, in which Amedus explains
the reason for his outburst, our Cistercian apostate explicitly ac-
knowledges the community of Cluny as a shining example (praefulget
is the word he uses) of holy living and of devotion of the highest
order. But for Amedeus, the poverty and simplicity of Bonnevaux
marks the sole path to salvation.

Amedeus' re-appearance brought joy to the brethren of Bonnevaux, if we are to believe the biographer: de reditu suo [eos]
permaxime laetificavit.[28] Still, the re-admittance of an apostate
was subject to the conventions of monastic protocol.[29] Accompanied

by several of the brethren, the abbot goes to the monastery en-
trance to meet Amedeus. He lifts him from the ground where he
is lying prostrate, lectures him a bit on the nature of temptation,
and tells him that today and tomorrow he must continue waiting
at the gate of the monastery, before being received back into the
community, in the chapter room on the third day.

And now follows one of the really great pages of Cistercian
literature. Amedeus takes his place with the beggars fed by the
monastery alms. Though he receives each day the same fare served
the brethren in the refectory, he gives this to the poor, and himself eats only from the food distributed to the poor at the end of
the community meal, consisting mostly of leftovers from the monk's
repast. Each time a monk enters or leaves the enclosure gate,
Amedeus is there lying prostrate, begging for forgiveness and
promising amendment. Only, for Amedeus, this is to be more than
a two-day penance. He insists that he is too unworthy to re-enter
the community. A week passes, and the abbot comes out again to
re-assure Amedeus that he has made sufficient satisfaction for his
misdeed. He pleads with Amedeus to come back into the community.
But, no, Amedeus is still too unworthy. In time, Amedeus' ritual
prostration begins wearing a bit thin. The brethren try to avoid
him by using a different door to enter and leave the enclosure.

But Amedeus finds them out, and perseveres unabated in his aggres-
sive prostration-routine. The abbot begins complaining that
Amedeus, lord of Hauterive, has the monastery under siege. Two
weeks pass. Again the Abbot pleads with Amedeus. "You have become a real nuisance to me and the community. You think you are
making satisfaction, but all you are doing is incurring the
guilt of disobedience, and thus turning humility into a vice. So
would you please, PLEASE stop making this kind of satisfaction...."
But, no, Amedeus is still too unworthy. Unfortunately, the ancient
Cistercian usages provided nothing which quite covered such a situation. But the abbot at last hits upon an inspired way of getting
Amedeus back inside the cloister. He joins Amedeus in his prostration ritual, and tells him that he intends to keep it up till
Amedeus agrees to let himself be received once more into the community in keeping with the Order's custom. The abbot wins out.[30]

Scholars really serious about understanding the twelfth-century
Cistercian experience should not neglect the evidence of pages
such as this one. It is not enough to study the mystical theology
of St. Bernard, or the spirituality of a William of St-Thierry. It
is not enough to study Cistercian architecture, Cistercian chant,
Cistercian art. It would be great to recover the exact text of the

earliest form of the <u>Carta</u> <u>caritatis</u>, and a working knowledge of
early Cistercian legislation, of the Order's customary, and of
Cistercian economy and inner polity is important--but still not
enough. These have to be supplemented by contact with sources
of the homelier sort such as we find in these unpretentious
hagiographical writings.

Re-integrated into his community, Amedeus' form of sanctity
now begins to emerge in its characteristic shape. Nothing is said
about his fasts, his vigils, his pious macerations. The predominant
theme, rather, is that of the <u>frater</u> <u>utilis</u> (<u>Rule</u> 7, 18), that of
the monk who spends himself in the quite, simple, unobtrusive service of the brethren.

Three initial vignettes illustrate in a fair amount of repul-
sive detail just what is meant. In the first, Amedeus decides that
priests, whose hands daily come into contact with the sacramental
Body of the Lord, ought not to do their own shoe-polishing--or rather,
the twelfth-century equivalent, which consisted in keeping the leather
well-oiled and greased. Due to poverty, the brethren of Bonnevaux
had had to concoct an inexpensive but particularly foul-smelling
form of neat's foot oil composed of butter fat from alpine sheep,
pork lard, tallow, and ashes. The biographer shows us Amedeus
hard at work polishing the brethren's shoes--sleeves rolled up to

elbow, sweat oozing from every pore, his whole body steaming from
his closeness to the fire and from his bodily exertion. A visiting
uncle who drops in unannounced finds Amedeus hard at his task.
Not yet seen by Amedeus, the uncle silently withdraws. Later,
uncle and nephew have a happy chat together in the guest-quarters.
Uncle and knight companions mount their horses and ride off, edified;
Amedeus goes back into the cloister. And that is all.[31]

    A second vignette. Amedeus is a thief. He steals the filthy
bandages, dirty rags, soiled linens used by the sick brethren in
the infirmary. He washes them, dries them in the sun or by the fire,
and then returns them on the sly. The biographer insists on the
anonymity of this practice: <u>nemine</u> <u>sciente</u>; for, he explains, "Amedeus strove, as much as in him lay, to hide from everyone whomsoever
all the good he did."[32]

    No saint's life of noble-born monks or nuns is complete, of
course, without at least a passing reference to the saint humbly
emptying and scouring the "baser vessels" of the monastery. We
know what is meant. Amedeus goes one better. It is summer. The
Gère river, which ordinarily carries off the sewage, is dried up.
The accumulated waste matter piles up beneath the dormitory. The
stench is noisome, danger to health considerable. During the
after-dinner meridian, while the brethren are dozing in the dormi-

tory, Amedeus dons his work scapular, climbs under the latrine, channels what water he can into the area, and shovels the foul business into the trickling stream as best he can. "He cleaned the jakes right decently," says our biographer, and then breaks into a paean in praise of Amedeus' humility.[33] This picture of the former Lord of Hauterive mucking about in the monastery merde is not a commonplace of conventional hagiography, but it fits in wonderfully well with life in a twelfth-century Cistercian community.

It might be thought that Amedeus was not particularly well endowed with gifts of the intellect, but this is far from being the case. We have already seen that the education of Amedeus Junior was an important enough matter to justify, in a moment of confusion and weakness, Amedeus' apostasy. And now Amedeus, the frater utilis, undertakes the enormous work involved in preparing for and actually carrying out the foundation of four daughter-houses of Bonnevaux. As former lord of Hauterive, Amedeus' prestige was, of course, immense, and members of the nobility were generous in answering his appeals for land-grants and donations. But Amedeus' role went much farther than that of simply securing patronage. Once the essential property had been secured, Amedeus, with a small crew, was sent to undertake the immense task of preparing

things for the eventual arrival of the new community. Woods had to
be cleared, fields rendered productive, grazing lands puts into
order. Necessary buildings and regular places had to be constructed,
and the firm basis of a reliable income had to ensured. Only when
everything was in due order could the new colony of monks--twelve,
plus the abbot and a number of laybrothers--be sent from the mother-
house. The newcomers would arrive, Amedeus would depart. He feared
that, as virtual founder and builder of the monastery, he might be
made too much of by the brethren of the newly founded abbey. So back
to Bonnevaux, back to the humble round of quite ordinary tasks, to
the washing of dirty bandages, and to the polishing of shoes. Four
times Amedeus was involved in setting up new foundations: Mazan,
in 1120; Montpeyroux, in 1126; Tamié, in 1132; and Léoncel, in 1137;
and four times he returned, his task completed, to Bonnevaux and to
the hidden, simple life.[34]

Amedeus must have died as simply and as unobtrusively as he had
lived since his return from Cluny. The biographer makes little to
do about it. He assures us, however--and surely he is right--that
Amedeus reigns now with Christ in heaven, "who, whilst living in the
body here below in this world, disdained not to serve Christ's faithful, whosoever these might be."[35] Not a single miracle; not a single
revelation; not even a memorable word.

THE <u>VITA</u> <u>DOMNI</u> <u>PETRI</u> <u>ABBATIS</u> <u>CLARAEVALLIS</u>

The Benedictine biographer of Peter Monoculus (Peter the "One-eyed") is a much more sophisticated biographer than the biographer of Amedeus. A monk of Reuil, near Paris, in the diocese of Meaux, he wrote, as he tells us in the Prologue, in 1204, as an old, old man, decrepit and with only partial vision. Peter had died almost two decades earlier, on October 29, 1186. And Thomas, who had known and loved Peter, but whose contacts with him were perforce limited, had been waiting all this while for a Cistercian to take up his pen and thus preserve Peter's memory for generations yet to come. He waited in vain. "The philosophers of that Order," he drily remarks, "are more given to silence than to the stylus."[36]

Thomas embarked, then, on his own biography of his friend. His personal recollections of Peter covered, of course, only a small part of Peter's life. He depended then, on sources close to Peter. Their quality varies considerably. Thomas, who despite his protestations to the contrary, was obviously a connoisseur of elegant diction nevertheless did little to blend his disparate material into a smoothly blended unity.

Thomas is not really interested at all in the simplicity and prosaic nature of Cistercian life. He is interested in signs and revelations. "The early Church," he writes in his Prologue, "had

need of signs and revelations, and these she had in fullest measure."[37] No age, of course, was ever so badly off, saint-wise, as
his own. We need, then, signs and miracles. This is hardly an encour-
aging approach for someone who, like myself, is interested rather
in the theme of the ordinariness of early Cistercian saints. Thomas'
witness, then, is all the more impressive, for, against the background of locutions, prophetic insights, visions and revelations,
the portrait of a saint emerges, whose most extraordinary trait is
his unique ordinariness.

There is some dispute about Peter's parentage. Thomas makes
him out to be an Italian of the very highest birth, but there is
other evidence which suggests that Peter, born around 1120, might
well have been the nephew of Philip I of France--though by Bertrada,
who, in 1092, ousted from bed and board Philip's legitimate wife,
Bertha.[38] Caesar of Heisterbach, too, makes Peter a kinsman of Philip
II, "who had such a love for holy simplicity," he adds.[39]
Whatever the precise ancestry might have been, it is quite certain
that Peter's birth was of the highest, and Thomas emphasizes the
point only to insist that Peter always did what he could to hide
the high estate that was his by birth.

Thomas claims Peter came to Reims from Italy, in search of
schooling in higher studies. He found a different kind of educational

institution outside the city--the recently founded monastery of Igny.[40]
There he took the religious habit. He was not much to look at: "Of
average height, but tending toward the short side; light in weight,
if not downright skinny, but sound and wiry in his skinniness."[41]
From the very beginning of his religious life Peter enjoyed the
great charism of the Spirit. Peter had all the virtues of the
good monk, and there is no need here to rehearse this lengthy catalogue. But the virtue he really specialized in was an unpretentious
humility. Thomas quotes St Bernard's statement that the truly humble man does not want the reputation of being humble, but wants to
be seen as someone quite ordinary and commonplace. The word is
vilis. Be careful of this word. Though the primary meaning of our
English "vile" is that of being of "small worth or no account,"[42]
the word usually has overtones of "low, disgusting, contemptible."
In Thomas' Latin vocabulary, however, as in Bernard's and in Benedict's (the sixth degree of humility, in Chapter Seven of the Rule),
the word is best understood as the lexicographer Albert Blaise understands it: "Common, ordinary (vulgaire) run-of-the-mill (général).[43]
So far as external gifts were concerned, Peter was at a total loss.
His speech was anything but polished (he had a thick Italian accent);
physically, he was something of a runt; he had no business or admini-
strative sense; and he utterly lacked that all-important competitive

spirit. As for his interior gifts, they were certainly there; but these were of such a nature that others were not necessarily aware of them. And this was the hiddenness in which Peter, Thomas tells us, rejoiced. He loved this hiddenness, and did all he could to foster it.[44] But those who really knew Peter recognized the quality of his surpassing excellence. This was an excellence which made Peter superior to the great and mighty, even while his remarkable humility made him the equal of the weak and lowly; so that Peter was a man whom everyone could love.[45]

When Thomas draws things together by way of summing up the formative period of Peter's early life as a monk, he does so by weaving together strands from many different texts of Scripture-- usually not direct citations, but rather allusions:

> Not fairer than the sons of men was Peter [Ps 44:3], not robed in cloth of gold or many-colored garments [*ibid*., vv. 14-15]; neither was his confidence in horse or chariot [Ps 19:8]; he was not anxious and troubled about many things [Lk 10:41] in any busyness with things exterior; nor was he with the giants who groan beneath the waters (Jb 26:5); he pursued not great things far above him (Ps 130:1); but in all these things the Lord is not: not in the wind, as it is written; not in the earthquake, not in the fire--but in the murmur of a gentle breeze (3 Kgs 19: 11-12), and in the voice that came to Elijah and his fellow-prophet John: that voice which Peter, friend of the Bridegroom that he was, standing by heard, and heard often in his inner depths.[46]

And now there follows the first of several explicit comparisons of Peter with the great monk-bishop, Martin of Tours.

Jean Leclercq has written an extremely thoughtful article on St Martin in the monastic hagiography of the Middle Ages.[47] He demonstrates that, as we follow the chronological order of the texts about Martin from century to century, there is precious little evolution of thought. Martin is always first and foremost the great wonder-worker, the thaumaturgist bishop. Then we come to the Cistercian period, and with them Martin the wonder-worker yields place to Martin the simple, Martin the poor, Martin the obedient. One of Bernard's longest sermons, preached before an assembly of abbots,[48] is precisely on Martin as supremely imitable and as the personification of the gospel beatitudes. To describe Peter, then, Thomas of Reuil could find no model of monastic holiness better suited as a term of comparison than St Martin, pauper et modicus.

Peter was abbot successively of three different abbeys. First of Valroy, daughter-house of Igny (c. 1164-1169); then of Igny itself (1169-1179); and finally, in 1179, of Clairvaux. The single incident I wish to call attention to, during Peter's pre-Clairvaux period, actually touches more on Thomas' interpretation of an almost unperceived incident, than on the incident itself. It was the first anniversary of the death of a monk of Igny--a monk who had been an

exemplary religious, and whose terminal sickness had been a long,
painful purgatory dragged out over a two-year period. On the anniversary of his death, Peter was asked by the cantor to pronounce
the usual ritual absolution of the departed monk. "He needs it,"
Peter was heard to mumble by one of the seniors sitting close by.
How, Thomas asks, could that holy monk still need the prayers of
his brethren? His own reply bears on yet another aspect of simplicity, and is worth summarizing.

The need for further purification is based on the very nature
of God, the very nature of the Beatific Vision. No one can see God,
but only the pure of heart. But who can boast that his heart is
really all that pure? Our purification in the monastic life, then,
calls for a long ascesis directed towards the simplification of the
spiritual faculties and their activity, till the point is reached
that: 1, the *memoria* contains naught save God, who is the original
forma memoriae; 2, the *ratio* sees naught but God, who is the incor-
poreal light of reason; 3, the *voluntas* loves naught but God, who
is the burning "inciter" of the will, and man's supreme Good, that
is Itself blessed, and that makes man blessed.[49]

This metaphysical-theological approach to simplicity, based on
the nature of God and the nature of the soul, is bathed with Augustinian overtones.[50] It harmonizes, perfectly however, with Fr Louis'

sketch of St Bernard's teaching on interior simplicity;[51] and, surely, the basic idea could not find better expression than in Bernard's lapidary formula: <u>Simplex</u> <u>natura</u> [<u>Dei</u>] <u>simplicitatem</u> <u>cordis</u> <u>exquirit</u>.[52]

But before turning our attention to Peter at Clairvaux, it might be well to quote Thomas quoting a close companion of Peter. Gilbert had been Peter's prior at Clairvaux, before becoming abbot of Bohéries and, finally, in 1186, abbot of Foigny. Never, said Gilbert, had he seen anyone less affected for the worse by singularity than Peter. And Thomas adds his own clumsy comment that this was because Peter had such singular control over his singularity.[53] The context of this, of course, is St Bernard's well known diatribe in his enormously popular <u>Liber</u> <u>de</u> <u>gradibus</u> <u>humilitatis</u> <u>et</u> <u>superbiae</u>, where the Saint treats of the fifth degress of pride: singularity.[54] The ideal is simply to fade into the background, and it is in the light of this sort of thinking that we have to evaluate particular points of Cistercian legislation, such as the prohibition of praying prostrate at full length. "It is not our custom," n. 84 of the <u>Instituta</u> reads, for a monk or laybrother to prostrate full length during prayer, but rather to stand or kneel."[55] Numerous petty details of Cistercian customaries and General Chapter decisions could be understood in terms of a concerted effort to eliminate every

possible sign of individual personality. But it would doubtless
be better to read such texts against the background of a common
teaching on the common life, based on the degrees of humility
formulated in Chapter Seven of the Rule, and expounded in masterly
fashion by St Bernard. At any rate, the point Thomas is trying to
make is that, though Peter's spiritual gifts set him apart from
everyone, this extraordinary excellence of his resulted in no
apparent singularity. The only evident "singularities" were his
slow speech and generally non-descript appearance.

The account of Peter's years as abbot of Clairvaux begins with
a text of capital importance. The brethren are preparing for the
abbatial election. No one knows who is to be the next abbot. One
of the monks tells the prior, Gilbert, whom we have already met, that
he has had a puzzling dream.

> The message was brought us that Christ the Lord was coming
> to this house, We all went out to meet him at the monas-
> tery entrance. But what we saw was one who had no form
> or comeliness, short in stature, in a poor man's rags,
> contemptible in appearance, and yet, doubt there was none:
> this was the Lord Jesus Christ.[56]

Immediately Gilbert understands that Peter, who in a special
way is identified with Christ, the Suffering Servant of Chapter 53
of Isaiah, is to be the next abbot of Clairvaux.

> In the eyes of men, [Peter] seemed to be poor and humble
> [pauper et modicus--the classical description of St Martin],

the last of men, smitten, as it were by God (Is 53:4);
but all his glory was from within (Vg. Ps 44:14), where
the precious pearl shone radiant in his heart (Mt 13:
46), and where there was a place provided for the Lord,
a tabernacle for the God of Jacob (Ps 131:5); a tabernacle, I say, of faith, charity, and all the other
virtues, fashioned as with tapestries, silver, gold and
precious stones: well furnished, spacious, rich and
comely--but, viewed from without, covered with sack-
cloth. Within, his longing for the vision of God was
as an odor of fragrance sweet to the Lord; where reason
and the affections, in concord sweet and tuneful, gave
forth a honeyed melody to please the ears of God.
Fitting it was and right, then, that Christ should
appear clothed in the garb of poor Peter; fitting that
he who shall re-fashion the body of our lowliness,
conforming it to the body of his glory (Phm 3:21),
should, though God by nature, and equal to God,
empty himself, being made like unto Peter, and appear-
ing in his form (ibid., 2:6-7).[57]

The objection could be made at this point that we are no longer

dealing with the theme of ordinariness and simplicity, and the ob-

jection is a good one. But here my answer would be that Peter's

ordinariness is never far removed from a specific Christological

dimension; further, that this Christological dimension is coexten-

sive with all the humbler realities of the mystery of the Incarnate

Word: poverty, lowliness, the hidden, silent life, obedience, sim-

plicity. But, for all that, the inner content covered by the

visible forms of poverty and lowliness is compounded of all the

riches of the Spirit. The invasion of mysticism, so characteristic

of the thirteenth century is already with us in the highest possible degree, but its outward form is -- well, ordinary, simple, poor.

But to return to Peter's Clairvaux experience. It was rather difficult actually getting him there. He answered his summons by heading for the grange of some undesignated abbey of the Order. A search was made, and he was finally found--haying with the laybrothers in the field.[58]

Thomas gives us a fairly detailed account of Peter's subsequent summons to Verona. Pope Lucius III and his court were there. The Pope, old and decrepit, and soon to die, wanted Peter's help in setting his house in order. Thomas paints a moving scene of the poor man from Clairvaux, who from his poverty enriches the successor of Peter the Apostle, to whom kings come from afar, bringing tribute. Lucius is raised on the crests of the other mountains like a mountain of gold; yet, for God's sake, he makes himself subject to the humblest of men: and the humblest of men is Peter.[59]

Thomas, like many old men, is not precisely a model of chronological exactitude. He has Peter almost on his death-bed before he remembers to tell us how he lost his eye years ago, while abbot of Valroy. It was a loss borne without a murmur of complaint. Thomas, indeed, quotes Peter as remarking with relief, "Well, that is one enemy I have escaped from; I have more to fear from the eye that remains than from the eye I have lost." But Thomas gives this

remark a rather unusual twist. It is not, he explains, that Peter
ever had much difficulty on the score of unruly bodily senses.
Rather, this was the sort of remark he used to make for the sake
of others who had lost a limb or other bodily organ, and took the
loss rather badly. Once again, then, we have an example of Peter's
penchant for being pretty much like the average man in the pew.[60]
And yet another comparison with St Martin follows. Like the poor
man Martin, Peter enjoyed (fruebatur) God who was always present
as his constant help. The verb is carefully chosen; it belongs
to the vocabulary of contemplation. Thomas emphasizes what he intends to say by adding that, in Peter was fulfilled the text of
Scripture, "God's converse is with the simple."[61]

The next comparison with St Martin is the most charming of all,
though it is also the one with the least theological resonance. Peter
is mounted on his little horse scarce larger than Martin's donkey,
looking more like a poor peasant than the abbot of Clairvaux.[62]

But perhaps the most characteristic picture of Peter is given
us, not by Thomas, but by Conrad of Eberbach, whose years as a monk
of Clairvaux coincided in part with the years of Peter's abbacy
(1179-1186). Conrad devotes Chapters 32 and 33 of Distinctio II of
the Exordium magnum to Peter. He tells us that Peter left the tem-

poral administration of the house to the cellarers and other officials, so that he himself could be more free to give himself to God and to the pastoral care of the brethren. And so we find Peter as the man for others; Peter seated alone in the tiny room adjacent to the chapter room, in silence, with head bowed low. And what is Peter doing? He is simply there, wholly available to anyone who needs him, waiting to give his sons a father's encouragement and kindly word of advice in their struggles with temptation and trial.[63]

When Peter became abbot of Clairvaux, Bernard had been dead for more than a quarter-century, but his presence at Clairvaux remained a palpable reality. It was not easy to be abbot in Bernard's footsteps. In a passage of rare insight, however, Thomas does not hesitate to compare the two, and, in doing so, he expresses wonderfully well (I think) one of the most characteristic forms of holiness in twelfth-century Cistercian hagiography.

Bernard, Thomas says, in a litany of praise pieced together from many different biblical allusions,

> was supreme in the word of glory (Sir 47:9), a man of mighty counsel, the chariot of Israel and the guider thereof (4 K 13:14), a scribe instructed in the kingdom of heaven, bringing forth from his storeroom things new and old (Mt 13:52). In the Cistercian Order and in the Church of Christ, he brought forth much fruit in his time. He was a lamp,

> burning and shining (Jn 5:35), set on a lamp-stand,
> to give light to everyone in the house of God (Mt
> 5:15); a lamp of light resplendent, casting its
> rays far and wide on every side. But Peter...?
> Well, Peter was, in brief, like a burning coal
> covered with the ashes of his own poverty: not
> much light, but, for all that, plenty of heat.[64]

And this it seems to me, sums it up wonderfully well. For

Bernard and Peter, the inner content is the same, but the outward

form is different. And what is true of Peter is true, I suggest,

for most of the men and women to find their way into the pages of

the early Cistercian hagiographical writings. The outward form

their lives assume would be a bit like the sacramental species:

not much to look at, but beneath simple, commonplace appearances,

a reality of a transcendent order.

So many pages of that great collect of Cistercian *fioretti*,

the *Exordium* magnum, make this clear. The story of the laybrother

cowherd is typical. Our laybrother is an uncomplicated fellow (homo

purus), a man of great simplicity (mirae simplicitatis). Prompt,

devout obedience is his thing, though, admittedly, he has his eye

on the reward which will one day follow upon his years of long,

hard toil borne patiently. One night he has a dream. Jesus is

standing on the other side of the wagon, cow-goad in that tenderest

of hands (illa sua dulcissima manu tenentem aculeum), and bellowing

out at the cows along with our herdsman (boves secum minanetem).

That is all. But it suffices to fill our laybrother with a burning desire for Jesus, a longing to see face to face him who, he now realizes, is his "companion and fellow worker" (socialem collaboratorem) as he goes about his humdrum, quite ordinary chores. Not unexpectedly, Proverbs 3:32 is quoted as à propos: "The Lord walks with the meek, and his converse is with the simple."[65] The meaning is clear: the substance at the heart of the ordinary is companionship with the Lord.

Fastrad was abbot of Cambron, near Cambrai, when, in 1157, he was summoned to the abbatial election at Clairvaux. Fearing the worst, he headed in a different direction, and for some days hid away in the Carthusian monastery of Val-St-Pierre, near Laon. His days and nights of uninterrupted prayer were climaxed by a vision of our Lady, who held in her hands him who, though he is, King of Glory is yet her little one, Jesus. "Why so troubled?" she asks, and gives Fastrad the Child to hold. "Here, take my Son and keep him for me." The vision fades, and Fastrad understands.[66] The quite ordinary monks of Clairvaux are "sons of God and members of Christ." To be abbot of Clairvaux means to recognize in this rather remarkable assembly of all sorts of people the Body of Christ, and to strive to bring Christ in the community to full growth and maturity.

When William, the soul-weary abbot of the Benedictine monastery
of St-Thierry, was struggling with his yearning to turn Cistercian,
he kept something of a "spiritual journal"--meditations on his vocation, on the mystery of predestination, on his spiritual experience,
on his desire to lay down his abbatial charge. In the twelfth and
last of the original series of these meditations, he is on the brink
(I think) of actually going to the nearby Cistercian monastery of
Signy. What draws him there? Convinced of the slight quality of
his own love of God, he wants at least to be with those whose love
is deeper and more genuine than his own. He writes:

> O Father in heaven, these are the souls who love you.
> When I see such and do not find myself among them, I
> weary of my life. Their wisdom comes not from the
> spirit of this world, nor from the prudence of this
> present age. Being devoid of learning, they have
> entered into the power of the Lord, and, being poor
> in spirit, they are mindful only of your righteous-
> ness. Wherefore you have taught them, that in their
> life and conduct they may show forth your wondrous
> works. These are your simple servants, with whom
> you are wont to talk familiarly....
> Thus with your wisdom sweetly ordering all things
> for them they come by a short road and lightly laden
> to their appointed end, where chariots and horsemen
> fail....Your love, finding in them simple material on
> which to work, so forms them and conforms them to
> itself in both affection and effect, that, besides
> what is hidden within--namely, the glory and riches
> of a good conscience--the inner light is reflected in
> their outward appearance, and that not by deliberate
> effort but by a certain connaturality. And so much is
> this the case that the charm and simplicity of their

> expression and bearing provoke love for you....In
> such people nature indeed returns to the fountain
> whence it sprang....Their flesh that is sown in
> corruption begins even now to rise again in glory;
> so that heart and flesh together may rejoice in the
> living God....[67]

What William sees, then, is exactly what we find in so much of
the hagiographical literature of the first Cistercian century. This
is the simplicity of the poor of Yahweh, who are bearers of God's
revelation and who experience in the most direct manner possible the
divine realities which are the object of their simple faith. Being
simple and uncomplicated, they return to the simplicity of Adam in
Paradise ("nature returns to the fountain whence it sprang"), and,
already, they taste something of the blessedness of the Age to Come--
so much so that the fulness of the inward reality overflows even
into the outward appearance of their bodies, and there is some slight
hint of what the resurrection of the glorified body is to be like.

No, we do not have to wait till the thirteenth century to find
the invasion of the mystical biography. Just look a bit beneath
the humdrum ordinariness and simplicity of the Cistercian twelfth
century. The bread has already risen; the flower is in full bloom;
the tree already heavy with fruit.

Abbey of Gethsemani

NOTES

ABBREVIATIONS

The following are among the works most frequently cited in the
course of this study:

EM - Conrad of Eberbach, Exordium magnum Cisterciense sive Narratio
    de initio Cisterciensis Ordinis. Series Scriptorum S. Ordinis
    Cisterciensis, 2, ed. Bruno Griesser, O. Cist. (Rome: Editiones
    Cistercienses, 1961). Numbering of ed. in PL 185:995-1198
    somewhat different.

VA - Vita venerabilis Amedaei Altae Ripae, edited with commentary
    and notes by M.-A Dimier, O.C.S.O., "Vita venerabilis Amedaei
    Altae Ripae (t c. 1150), auctore monacho quodam Bonaevallensi
    synchrono et oculato," in Studia monastica 5 (1963) 265-304.

VP - Thomas of Reuil, Vita domni Petri abbatis Claravallis, in the
    Bollandists' Acta Sanctorum, Octobris, T. 13 (Paris: Victor
    Palmé, 1883) pp. 53-84. PL 209:1007-1036.

1. Thomas Merton, What Are These Wounds?: The Life of a Cistercian
    Mystic Saint Lutgarde of Aywières (Milwaukee: Bruce Publishing
    Co., 1950 [2nd printing]).

2. Simone Roisin, I.E.J., L'hagiographie cistercienne dans le dio-
    cèse de Liège au XIIIe siècle. Université de Louvain. Recueil

de Travaux d'Histoire de de Philologie. 3e Série, 27e Fascicule (Louvain: Bibliothèque de l'Université; Brussels: Editions Universitaires. Les Presses de Belgique, 1947)

3. Ibid., pp. 8-9.

4. Westmalle: Imprimerie Cistercienne, 1937.

5. Hagiologium cisterciense auctore P. Seraphino Lenssen O.C.S.O. monacho B.M. de Villa Regia prope Tilburg, in Hollandia. s.l. [Tilburg] 1948; Vol. II, 1949; Supplementum ad Hagiologium cisterciense, 1951.

6. Michel Aubrun, Vie de Saint Etienne d'Obazine. Faculté des Lettres et Sciences Humaines de l'Université de Clermont-Ferrand. Publications de l'Institut d'Etudes du Massif Central. Fascicule 6 (Clermont-Ferrand: Institut d'Etudes du Massif Central, 1970).

7. In Analecta Bollandiana 71 (1953) 21-52, with complements already printed earlier in Bruno Griesser, O. Cist., "Christian von l'Aumône: Eine neue vollständigere Handschrift seiner Vita," Cistercienser-Chronik 57 (1950) 12-32.

8. EM Dist. 4, c. 34, 269-70.

9. Bertram, art. "nḗpios, nēpiázō" in G. Kittel (ed.) Theological Dictionary of the New Testament 4, trans. and ed. G. W. Bromiley (Grand Rapids: Wm. B. Eerdmans Publishing Co., 1967) p. 912.

10. <u>Ibid</u>., p. 913.

11. <u>Ibid</u>., pp. 914-17.

12. <u>Ibid</u>., pp. 917-20.

12[a]. <u>Ibid</u>., pp. 920-21.

13. <u>Dictionnaire</u> <u>Latin-Francais</u> <u>des</u> <u>Auteurs</u> <u>chrétiens</u> (Turnhout: Editions Brepols S.A., 1954).

14. <u>Ibid</u>., p. 761.

15. R Ben. 71 (1961) 371-81.

16. The Cistercian Library, No. 3 (Trappist: Gethsemani Abbey, 1948).

17. London and New York: Sheed and Ward, 1955 (reprint).

18. The <u>Spirit</u> <u>of</u> <u>Simplicity</u>..., pp. 76-139. [To appear in <u>Thomas</u> <u>Merton</u> <u>on</u> <u>St</u> <u>Bernard</u>, CS 9 (1980) - ed.]

19. Mt 11:25.

20. See above, Abbreviations: VA

21. Aubrun, <u>Vie</u> <u>de</u> <u>Saint</u> <u>Etienne</u>, Prefatio, pp. 39/40.

22. <u>VA</u>, pp. 273-74.

22[a]. <u>VA</u>, pp. 278-80.

23. <u>Ibid</u>., p. 283.

24. <u>Ibid</u>., p. 284.

25. <u>Ibid</u>., pp. 285-86.

26. <u>Ibid</u>., pp. 286-87.

27. Fr Dimier uses this <u>Vita</u> as a witness to this deplorable quarrel, in his article "Un témoin tardif peu connu du conflit entre cisterciens et clunisiens," Studia Anselmiana 50 (1956) 81-94.

28. VA, p. 288.

29. See the article by Jean Leclercq, "Documents sure les fugitifs,"
    Studia Anselmiana 54 (1965) 87–145.

30. VA, p. 290-91.

31. Ibid., 292-94.

32. Ibid., p. 294.

33. Ibid., pp. 294-95.

34. Ibid., pp. 299-302.

35. Ibid., p. 302.

36. VP, n. 4, p. 69 AB.

37. Ibid., n. 3, p. 68 F.

38. Detailed discussion in the introduction to this edition, p. 54,
    n. 3.

39. Dialogi miraculorum, Dist. VI, c. 11.

40. Founded as Clairvaux's fourth daughter-house, 1126 (or perhaps
    1127).

41. VP, n. 5, p. 70 B.

42. As in the entry in Webster's Seventh New Collegiate Dictionary
    (Springfield, Massachusetts: G. and C. Merriam Co., 1967) pp.
    991-92.

43. Blaise, Dictionnaire, p. 848.

44. "...Super hac obscuritate gaudebat, et eam modis omnibus,
     salva solum conscientia, appetebat," VP, n. 6, p. 70 C.

45. Ibid., D.

46. Ibid., n. 12, p. 71 D.

47. "S. Martin dans l'hagiographie monastique du moyen âge," Studia
     Anselmiana 46 (1961) 175-87.

48. Op. S. Bern. 5:399-412; PL 183:489-500.

49. VP, n. 38, p. 76 BC.

50. See, for instance, De vera religione XXI, 41; XXII, 24-two
     Augustinian texts used by Dom Chautard, The Spirit of Sim-
     plicity, p. 6, note 4. Latin text in CC 32:212-13 and 202.

51. The Spirit of Simplicity, pp. 76-135.

52. Div 37:9; PL 183:643 C.

53. VP, n. 22, p. 73 C.

54. C. 14, n. 42; Op. S. Bern. 3:48-49; PL 182:965 AB-C.

55. Many editions; among them Instituta Generalis Capituli, p. 231,
     in H. Séjalon (ed.), Nomasticon Cisterciense (Solesmes: E
     Typographo Sancti Petri, 1892); Philip Guignard (ed.), Les
     monuments primitifs de la Règle cistercienne (Dijon: Impri-
     meri Darantière, 1878) p. 273; J.-M. Canievez (ed.), Statuta
     Capitulorum Generalium Ordinis Cisterciensis, (Louvain: Biblio-
     thèque de la Revue d'Histoire Ecclésiastique, 1933), I, 32.

56. <u>VP</u>, n. 43, p. 78 DE.

57. <u>Ibid</u>., n. 44, p. 78 EF.

58. <u>Ibid</u>., n. 45, pp. 78 F-79 A.

59. <u>Ibid</u>., nn. 48-51, p. 79 C-EF.

60. <u>Ibid</u>., nn. 53-54, p. 80, AB-C.

61. <u>Ibid</u>., n. 54, p. 80, C-D.

62. <u>Ibid</u>., n. 56, p. 80 E.

63. <u>EM</u>, Dist. II, c. 32, p. 142, lines 18-25.

64. <u>VP</u>, n. 61, p. 81 EF-F.

65. <u>EM</u>, Dist. IV, c. 18, pp. 243-44.

66. <u>Ibid</u>., Dist. I, c. 32, p. 90, lines 1-21.

67. <u>Meditations of Dom William Abbot of St Thierry</u>, Meditation 12:
    14-15, trans. Sr Penelope, CF 3:177-78.

CONTEMPLATION AND MYSTICAL EXPERIENCE

IN THE LIBELLUS DE CONTEMPLATIONE OF MASTER HILDEBRAND

DAVID N. BELL

THE DATE OF THE LIBELLUS

The brief manuscript of the _Libellus de Contemplatione_ was discovered in the library of the Cistercian monastery of Himmerod in
1718 by Martène and Durand on their notable "voyage littéraire."[1]
The opuscule was edited and published some fifteen years later, in
1733, in the ninth volume of the same writers' _Amplissima Collectio_,[2]
and then, finally, reproduced in the Migne Patrology with occasional
inaccuracies and a different paragraph enumeration.[3] The only study
of the work of which I am aware is Guy Oury's "Le 'Libellus de Contemplatione' de Maître Hildebrand" published in 1967,[4] but this communication, although of great value, has only a brief consideration of
Hildebrand's thought on contemplation itself, and the concomitant
mystical vision, and has not said all that needs to be said on
this important subject.

The editors of the _Patrologia Latina_ followed Fabricius in
attributing the _Libellus_ to Hildebrand the Young, an author of the
mid-twelfth century, whose commentary on Matthew still remains unedited,[5] but a brief examination of the work reveals immediately

that this attribution cannot be sustained. Hildebrand's use of the
Metaphysics of Aristotle[6] certainly implies the thirteenth century,[7]
and the subtle arguments of Guy Oury with regard to certain liturgical citations (we find in the treatise echoes of the Cistercian
office of Corpus Christi) would seem to indicate the later part of
that century.[8] If this is so, and it certainly appears to be so,
then Hildebrand's life and activity is to be seen firmly fixed in
the period of mature scholasticism; yet despite his use of Aristotle
and the scholastic divisions and sub-divisions which characterise
his analysis,[9] his work is redolent more of the monastic spirituality
of the twelfth century than the theological systematics of the
Schools. Only about a third of the work is concerned specifically
with methodical analysis and definition; the remainder consists
of prayers, passionate and perhaps a little florid, into which the
scholastic analysis smoothly merges. "The treatise owes much to the
formulas of scholasticism, but in its effusive style it remains
close to the Cistercian writers of the twelfth century."[10]

We cannot be absolutely certain that Hildebrand himself was a
monk of Himmerod, although, as Oury demonstrates, it seems eminently
likely.[11] I know of no other manuscript of the Libellus save that
at Himmerod, and the use of a Cistercian liturgy together (as we
shall see) with the strong influence of Bernard on the work would

certainly suggest a Cistercian provenance.

THE ACT OF CONTEMPLATION

Hildebrand divides the act of contemplation into three forms:

dispensativa, aestimativa, and speculativa, and describes them

thus:

> The "dispensative" form of contemplation is that in
> which a person who loves God "disposes" his exterior
> senses about the business of contemplation, and uses
> them well so as to be deserving of God. The "estima-
> tive" form is that in which the soul's faculties are
> separated from the body (though still attached to the
> bodily organs), and, being unclouded by any imagined
> forms, are raised to the knowledge and love of God...
> The "speculative" form is that in which a person
> aspires to see God in Himself, in His own Being (so
> far as it is permitted), and to be conjoined totally
> to Him (so far as it is possible). But these attain-
> ments are very rare, and are given only to the perfect.
> It pertains to Heaven rather than earth, and is possible
> only in true ecstasy.[12]

The first he calls motiva, in which God is found; the second cogni-

tiva, in which he is known (cognoscere); and the third affectiva,

in which he is seized or experienced (apprehendere).[13] Oury has

noted that the source of this terminology is Bernard's De consider-

atione V, ii, 4,[14] but he also observes that the wide usage of the

term contemplatio in the Libellus is not that of Bernard.[15] The

latter distinguishes consideratio from contemplatio, and is not

prepared to attribute the latter to active intellectual reflexion.[16]

Hildebrand, however, does not limit himself in this way, and follows rather the wider usage of the term contemplatio which we find in

both Hugh and Richard of St Victor,[17] and it is from the latter,

in fact, not from Bernard, that his specific definition of contem-

plation is taken. "Contemplation," says Hildebrand, "is the clear

gaze of the mind, fixed on the manifestation of wisdom in suspended

wonder."[18] There are, as Oury indicates, both similarities and

differences to be seen between this definition and that of the

Carthusian Guigo II in his Scala Claustralium: "Contemplation is

the ascent of the mind to God and its suspension in him, tasting

there the joys of eternal sweetness."[19] But the actual source

is Richard's Benjamin Major,[20] and the quotation is a useful illus-

tration not only of the influence of the great Victorine himself,[21]

but of the equally important fact that in discussing the nature and

development of later medieval spirituality, one cannot speak of the

schools of Cîteaux and St Victor (or of others, for that matter) in

isolation. Bernard himself was in communication with Hugh of St

Victor,[22] and the latter certainly had an important influence on

Aelred of Rievaulx,[23] Isaac of Stella,[24] and the later Cistercian,

Garnier of Rochefort.[25] The Planctus Mariae of Ogier of Locedio was

clearly inspired by Godfrey of St Victor,[26] and, as we have seen,

Hildebrand quotes Richard. It may be that this is an obvious point,

but it is one, I feel, which is too easily overlooked.

Of the three modes of contemplation, Hildebrand informs us
that he will deal primarily with the second, for the first is
simply a necessary basis for any sort of contemplation at all,
and the third is altogether too rare,[27] and it is this intention
of Hildebrand which really lies at the back of Oury's designation
of his spirituality as "somewhat intellectualist."[28] That is to
say, although it is perfectly clear that the highest form of contemplation, contemplatio speculativa, is "affective-experiential",[29]
the rarity of the experience means that we must spend most of our
time in this world in pursuit of the "estimative" form which is
indeed "cognitive,"[30] and which involves the use of the "apprehensive and motive powers of the rational soul."[31] I would prefer,
therefore, to amend slightly the comment of Oury which, if taken
in isolation, could be a little misleading, and say that Hildebrand's
spirituality may be "intellectual" de facto, but is affective-
experiential de jure. Fortunately, however, Hildebrand does not
abide by his decision, and in fact spends some considerable time
discussing the highest and most comprehensive form of mystical
experience, and it is to a discussion of this that we may now
finally turn.

THE SOUL IN CONTEMPLATION

In order to experience the joy of contemplation on this earth, the soul (which Hildebrand conceives in basically Augustinian

terms[32]) must be transformed. More precisely, the <u>intellectus</u> must

become "deiform," the <u>voluntas</u> "boniform," and the <u>animus</u> (by which

Hildebrand appears to mean the <u>mens</u>[33]), "luciform," and our author

explains what he means thus:

> I call the intellect conformed to God when it is not
> obscured by any cloud of the things of the senses; I
> call the will conformed to good when it does not de-
> light in any mutable good; and I call the soul con-
> formed to light when it is neither disquieted nor
> disturbed by any evil which might occur.[34]

He then goes on to inform us that these ideas may be found in the

<u>Hierarchies</u> and <u>Divine Names</u> of pseudo-Dionysius, and this is at

least partially true. <u>Deiformis</u> does indeed correspond to the

<u>theoeidēs</u> of the Areopagite; <u>boniformis</u> to the term <u>agathoeidēs</u>;

and <u>luciformis</u> to his <u>phōtoeidēs</u>, and Hildebrand's source for the

translated terms is almost certainly that version of pseudo-Dionysius,

produced in about 1167 by John Saracenus.[35] But although our author

is prepared to use Dionysian terms, the ideas expressed with these

terms are not themselves Dionysian. The typical characteristics of

Dionysian mysticism--the "dazzling darkness", the hyper-attributes

and the tendency to anti-intellectualism which we witness clearly,

for example, in Thomas Gallus[36]--are absent in Hildebrand, and his

consideration of the highest mystical experience has more in common

with Augustine than with pseudo-Dionysius. Augustine's <u>Confessions</u>,
indeed, have left an obvious and deep impression on the <u>Libellus</u>,
an impression which is revealed not only by the style of the prayers
in the work, but also by direct quotation of the Augustinian text.
The account of mystical rapture, for example, which we find in section 12 of the work is taken almost directly from the tenth book of
the <u>Confessions</u>.[37]

Contemplation, for Hildebrand, is a one-pointed suspending of
the soul in God, when naught but God is known, naught but God desired, and naught but God tasted and experienced.[38]   And although it
is not the Beatific Vision itself, it is yet a true foretaste of
that sublime experience.[39]   As Hildebrand puts it, it is a full
knowledge of God's grace, although not yet a full knowledge of His
glory,[40] but until this final consummation is attained, the soul is
restless and forlorn. "You have made us for yourself," says Hildebrand, once again quoting Augustine, "and our heart is restless until
it finds its rest in you."[41]   Only God can provide the true satisfaction of the soul.[42]

The most comprehensive vision of God possible for us on this
earth, therefore, is far from the glory of the post-mortal vision,
but it is nevertheless a very remarkable experience, and Hildebrand's

description of it is equally remarkable[43]:

> The highest form of vision...is when we are permitted by
> you to see in you whatsoever is from you. The light which
> shines in you will illumine for me all that you are, and
> all that is from you....For in your light we shall see
> light. In your light, O Son of God, we shall see the
> light of God the Father, and see too the light of God the
> Holy Spirit. Yet we shall not see three lights of God,
> but...in three separate Persons, we shall see the one
> inseparable light, which is God. And we, who are dei-
> formly illumined by your light, shall see not only you,
> the divine uncreated light, but we shall also see--now
> and then, and as much as the light of your face is upon
> us, and as far as you shall decree--the shining created
> lights before the Lord.[44]

What we appear to have here is a vision not only of the oneness

and threeness of the Trinity, but also of the whole created order,

though whether the latter is understood as being in its archetypal

form or in its physical manifestation is not altogether clear. If

the latter possibility should be the case, then we may perhaps see

here the influence of the vision of Benedict, related by Gregory the

Great[45] and transmitted through Bernard.[46] If, on the other hand,

his conception is that of the archetypal world, then it is to Platonic

thought that we must look for its ultimate source, and--more especially--

to Middle Platonic rather than Neo-Platonic speculation.[47] The dis-

tinction which concerns us here (and our discussion in this brief

account is necessarily general) is that in Neo-Platonic thought,

the world of the Forms, the multiplicity-in-unity of Nous, is trans-

cended by the absolute unity of the Supernal One; whereas for Albin-
ian Middle Platonism at least, the First Principle is also the First
Nous, and thus comprises, at this highest level of all, unity and
multiplicity at the same time.[48] Here we have the conception of
the Ideas as the thoughts of God, and since God's thoughts are ever
with Him, so the highest vision of God is a vision of God and His
thoughts/Ideas at the same instant.[49] In the Neo-Platonic system
on the other hand, the supreme vision must transcend all multiplicity,
and it was this latter approach which, with the tremendous force of
Augustine's authority behind it, was to dominate the mystical theology
of the Middle Ages.[50] It is admirably clear in the thought of
Achard of St Victor, and only slightly less so in Hugh of St Victor,
Garnier of Rochefort (following him), Alan of Lille, and others.[51]
But this dominating Neo-Platonic-Augustinian conception is not that
of Hildebrand. His view clearly tends more to the ideas of Middle
Platonism, for there can surely be no doubt that for him the
vision of God is the vision of unity, trinity, and multiplicity all
at the same time. It is a remarkable and rare description in the
spirituality of the Middle Ages.

What then is the direct source of Hildebrand's description? As
in the case of his discussion of the transformation of the soul in
contemplation, we must turn once again to the Dionysian tradition,
and, in particular, to Hugh of St Victor's fascinating commentary on
pseudo-Dionysius' remarks on divine illumination to be found in the

early part of the <u>Celestial</u> <u>Hierarchies</u>.[52] Hildebrand does not, of
course, reproduce this lengthy text in its entirety, but I think
there can be little doubt that it lies behind his thinking, and in
looking to Hugh for his inspiration in this matter, Hildebrand
succeeds in producing an interesting and important amalgam of Victorine, Bernardine, Augustinian, and pseudo-Dionysian ideas.

The <u>Libellus</u>, it seems to me, is thus more important than
either its brevity or its comparative obscurity would indicate.
Apart from the remarkable description of the highest contemplative
experience, it is an excellent example of the survival of pre-
scholastic, monastic spirituality in the age of the Schools, and
an equally excellent example of the way in which this older tradition could be "translated" into contemporary terminology. For
wherever Hildebrand's head might have been, his heart was still
entrenched in the twelfth century. Yet it cannot be denied that
the brevity of the work is annoying. It presents us, we might
say, simply with a foretaste of what Hildebrand could do, and it
may be regretted that we know of no other text from the hand of its
author. Hildebrand would appear to have been both a fervent and
original thinker, and certainly deserves to be raised from his
present obscurity to occupy a proper and apportioned position in the
history of Cistercian spirituality.

Memorial University of Newfoundland

NOTES

1. See E. Martène and V. Durand, Voyage littéraire de deux religieux bénédictins... (Paris, 1724) II, 275-78.

2. Veterum Scriptorum et Monumentorum...Amplissima Collectio
   (Paris, 1733) IX, cols. 1237-50.

3. PL 181: 1691-704. Since the Migne edition is more easily available, we shall use the paragraph and column enumeration of the
   PL text.

4. In Revue d'ascétique et de mystique 43 (1967) 267-76 (we shall
   hereafter cite this article as "Libellus"). A brief summary by
   Oury of his article appears in the Dictionnaire de Spiritualité,
   VII (Paris, 1971) cols. 504-505, s.v. Hildebrand (hereafter cited
   as "Hildebrand"). Both of these studies contain summaries of
   the Libellus, and we shall not therefore present a further summary here. In any case, the brevity of the work enables one to
   read it in its entirety with ease.

5. See J.A. Fabricius, Bibliotheca Latina Mediae et Infimae Aetatis
   (Florence, 1858) III, 241. His comments are reproduced in PL
   181: 1691-92.

6. Libellus 1693A-B: "Desire is a certain movement of the rational
   soul...which is produced by the object desired. As the Philosopher says: 'That which is desired moves the desire.'" See Oury,

"Libellus," p. 268. Comparè <u>Metaphysics</u> Lambda 7 1072a26-
29; Theta 5 1048a10-15.

7. The twelfth-century <u>Metaphysica</u> <u>Vetustissima</u> went only as far
   as Bekker 1007a32. After that, we are in the thirteenth century.

8. See Oury, "Libellus," pp. 268-69.

9. Hildebrand's basic scheme is three stages of contemplation with
   each stage being further divided into three. It is the same
   principle as appears so very clearly (and tiresomely) in Thomas
   the Cistercian's (Thomas of Perseigne's) late twelfth-century <u>Com-</u>
   <u>mentarium</u> <u>in</u> <u>Cantica</u> <u>Canticorum</u>; PL 206: 21-862. Hildebrand,
   however, does not quite complete his scheme. See Oury,
   "Libellus," p. 270.

10. Oury, "Hildebrand," col. 505.

11. See Oury, "Libellus," pp. 269-70.

12. <u>Libellus</u> 1696D. There are further definitions of the last two
    varieties in <u>ibid</u>. 1697A-B.

13. See <u>ibid</u>. 1697A-B.

14. In PL 182: 789D-90A.

15. See Oury, "Libellus," pp. 271-72, with a translation of Bernard's
    text.

16. See Bernard, Csi 11, ii, 5; PL 182: 745B; Op. S. Bern. 3:414.

Contemplatio is "when the mind understands something intui-
tively, truly, and certainly, or when it apprehends the
truth beyond any doubt. But consideration is thought searching
intently for truth, or the straining of the mind in the quest
for truth." Hugh of St Victor also makes the distinction, but
does not abide by it: "There are two forms of contemplation:
the first, that of beginners, involves the consideration of
created things; the second and higher form, that of those who
are perfect, is the contemplation of the Creator." In Eccles-
iasten, Hom. I PL 175: 117B. Compare also Richard of St.
Victor's conception of circumspectio in his Adnotitia mystica
in Psalmum 30; PL 196: 274B and ff.

17. For Hugh, see Roger Baron's account in his Science et sagesse
chez Hugues de Saint-Victor (Paris, 1957) pp. 192-93, n. 101
(with all necessary references). For Richard, see especially
his own account in Benjamin Major I, 6; PL 196: 70B-72C (which,
in turn, is inspired by Hugh's De Sacramentis I, iii, 30; PL 176:
231C-32B. Compare also R. Javelet, "Thomas Gallus et Richard
de Saint-Victor mystiques" I, RTAM 29 (1962) 214.

18. Libellus 1698B. Compare also note 38 below.

19. Guigo, Scala Claustralium i; PL 184: 476B. See Oury, "Libellus,"

p. 274, n. 18.

20. <u>Benjamin</u> <u>Major</u> I, iv; PL 196: 67D: "Contemplation is the
    free and clear gaze of the mind, fixed on the manifestation
    of wisdom in suspended wonder." See further R. Javelet,
    "Thomas Gallus...," pp. 210-11, n. 16; p. 225, n. 57.

21. There is a brief but useful discussion of this matter in Clare
    Kirchberger's introduction to her translation of Richard:
    <u>Richard</u> <u>of</u> <u>Saint-Victor</u>: <u>Selected</u> <u>Writings</u> <u>on</u> <u>Contemplation</u>
    (London, 1957) pp. 57-74.

22. See, for example, <u>Epistola</u> <u>77</u> <u>ad</u> <u>Hugonem</u> <u>de</u> <u>Sancto-Victore</u>,
    <u>de</u> <u>baptismo</u>...; PL 182: 1031-46. Roger Baron's otherwise
    useful study, "L'influence de Hugues de Saint-Victor" in RTAM
    22 (1955) 56-71, has hardly anything to say of Hugh's influence
    on Cîteaux.

23. See, for example, A. Squire, "Aelred of Rievaulx and Hugh of St
    Victor," RTAM 28 (1961) 161-64.

24. For examples, see B. McGinn, <u>The</u> <u>Golden</u> <u>Chain</u>: <u>A</u> <u>Study</u> <u>in</u> <u>the</u>
    <u>Theological</u> <u>Anthropology</u> <u>of</u> <u>Isaac</u> <u>of</u> <u>Stella</u> (Washington, 1972)
    Index, s.v. Hugh of St Victor.

25. Garnier, in <u>Sermon</u> <u>23</u>; PL 205: 730A, quotes Hugh's <u>Commentariorum</u>
    <u>in</u> <u>Hierarchiam</u> <u>coelestem</u> <u>sancti</u> <u>Dionysii</u> <u>Areopagitae</u> I, i; PL 175:

927B-28A. And there are other examples of dependence in Garnier.

26. For the evidence, see H. Barré, "Le Planctus Mariae attribué à
S. Bernard," RAM 28 (1952) 245-66.

27. See Libellus 1696D-97B.

28. Oury, "Hildebrand," col. 505. Compare his "Libellus," pp. 274-
75.

29. See Libellus 1697A-B, cited at note 13 above. Contemplatio
speculativa, says our author, is affectiva, and the verbs used
of it are gustare and apprehendere. Gustare appears again in
ibid. 1697D; sapere in 1698A; 1694C speaks of the Deitatis...
sapor melifluus; and so on. Compare Thomas of Perseigne,
Commentarium in Cantica Canticorum IV, 1; PL 206: 207D-209A.

30. As Hildebrand says in Libellus 1697A-B: "...Secunda cognitiva
[est],...secunda adorat,...secunda cognoscit." In actual fact,
one cannot altogether separate "affective" and "cognitive" states
in medieval spirituality, but we cannot discuss that matter here.
For an excellent introduction, see R. Javelet, "Intelligence
et amour chez les auteurs spirituels du XIIme siècle," RAM 37
(1961) 273-90, 429-50. It is interesting to note that Hildebrand himself, in his account of "estimative" contemplation,
speaks of it as raising the soul "in Dei agnitionem et dilec-
tionem" (Libellus 1696D).

31. *Libellus* 1697B: estimative contemplation consists in"...
the exercise of the apprehensive and motive powers of the
rational soul--that is, of reason, will, free choice, and the
rest--as they are apportioned and fixed to the bodily organs."
Hildebrand's source for this terminology is ultimately John
of Damascus (see *Libellus* 1697C), *De fide* orthodoxa II, xxii,
PG 94: 941C. The precise terminology here reflects John of
Rupella rather than Burgundio of Pisa (see O. Lottin, *Psych-
ologie* *et* *morale* *aux* XIIe *et* XIIIe *siècles* [Gembloux, 1957]
I, 397-98, 401), but we cannot discuss the question in detail
here.

32. What we have, in fact, is an Augustinian analysis expressed in
terminology which stems from John of Damascus. See Oury,
"Libellus," pp. 272, 273, 275, and "Hildebrand," col. 505.
I agree with Oury's conclusions here, although I have minor
disagreements on certain specific matters.

33. Oury, "Libellus," p. 272 suggests that by *animus* Hildebrand
means free-will, and on p. 273 says that *animus* should certainly be identified with the Augustinian *memoria*. I would
prefer simply to take the term in contrast to *anima*, seeing
the latter as the generic term for soul, and the former as
referring more specifically to its higher rational part, the

<u>nous</u> or <u>mens</u>. This distinction has the authority of Augustine behind it (see <u>De civitate Dei</u> VII, xxiii, 1; PL 41: 212), and appears elsewhere in medieval theology (see especially William of St Thierry, <u>Epistola ad Fratres de Monte Dei</u> II, ii, 4; PL 184: 340B-C. The <u>animus</u>/<u>mens</u> then "contains" both <u>memoria</u> and free-will.

34. <u>Libellus</u> 1697D. See also 1700B (quoted at note 44), and 1703B.

35. For <u>agathoeidēs</u>, see <u>De divinis nominibus</u> IV, 2; PG 3: 696B; IV, 18, PG 3: 716A; and elsewhere. <u>De coelesti hierarchia</u> VII, 4; PG 3: 212B; XV, 9; PG 3: 340A. For <u>phōtoeidēs</u>, see <u>ibid</u>. II, 3; PG 3: 141B. Theoeidēs (<u>deiformis</u>) is fairly common, see <u>ibid</u>. VII, 4; PG 3: 212C, and a number of other places. Only the versions of Saracenus and Robert Grosseteste (c. 1235) use the terms <u>boniformis</u> and <u>luciformis</u> with regularity, and of these two translations, that of Saracenus was unquestionably the more influential. Either, however, could (in theory) have been a possible source for Hildebrand's terminology. Eriugena certainly renders <u>phōtoeidēs</u> as <u>luciformis</u> (see, for example, PL 122: 1044B), and hence too Hugh of St Victor (see PL 175: 960C, 990C), but does not use <u>boniformis</u> at all. I think there can be little doubt that Saracenus is

our source.

36. See R. Javelet, "Thomas Gallus...," *passim*.

37. <u>Libellus</u> 1702C: "...I seem sometimes to be admitted to a
     certain rare affection, changed into I know not what sweet-
     ness. And if it were perfected in me, it would be something
     unknown to me, something which this life shall never be."
     This is dependent on <u>Confessiones</u> X, xl, 65, PL 32: 807.

38. <u>Libellus</u> 1698A: "When, therefore, true contemplation is borne
     up into God, it knows and understands him alone, it desires
     and wishes for him alone, it tastes and savors him alone."

39. See especially <u>ibid</u>. 1696A (cited in note 40 below), and
     compare also 1702D (but this latter becomes involved with
     the tricky area of "eucharistic mysticism," and that is an-
     other story.)

40. <u>Ibid</u>. 1696A: "For there is in this life a certain full
     possession of your grace, but it shall surely be followed
     by a full experience of your glory."

41. <u>Ibid</u>. 1693C quoting <u>Confessiones</u> I, i, 1; PL 32: 661.

42. See especially <u>Libellus</u> 1694A, B, 1696A, B.

43. The last part of this paper, dealing with Hildebrand's account
     of the mystical vision, is basically a summary of certain
     parts of my much longer and much more detailed study, "The

Vision of the World and of the Archetypes in the Latin Spirituality of the Middle Ages." This may be found in AHDL 44 (1977)
7-31, and, with the reader's permission, I shall refer to it for
all details.

44. Libellus 1700A-B. The Martène/Durand edition (Amp. Coll. IX,
col. 1245E) ends: "...before you, the Lord."

45. See Gregory, Dialogues II, 35, PL 66: 198B-200B.

46. See Bernard, Div IX, 1; PL 183: 565D-66A; Op. S. Bern. 6/1:
118-19. For a fuller account, see my "Vision..." part 1. It
is remotely possible that we may detect some influence from
Boethius, De consolatione philosophiae II, pr. vii (whom
Hildebrand cites in Libellus 1696C), but not, I think, very
likely. See P. Courcelle, La Consolation de Philosophie dans
la tradition littéraire (Paris, 1967) p. 355 ff.

47. There is, in fact, a certain amount of overlap between these
two possibilities. Courcelle, for example, has shown that
Gregory the Great's account and analysis of Benedict's vision
has been influenced by Macrobius. See Courcelle, op. cit.,
pp. 366-70 (with all references).

48. We cannot actually make a hard and fast distinction between
Neo- and Middle Platonism, for there can be no doubt that a
number of important Middle Platonists (for example, Celsus,

Origen, Philo, pseudo-Archytas, and others) were well aware
of the idea of a <u>Nous</u>-transcending First Principle. In the
case of Albinus, however, the contrast between Middle and
Neo-Platonism is somewhat clearer. For all details, see the
excellent study by John Whittaker, "EPEKEINA NOU KAI OUSIAS,"
<u>Vigiliae Christianae</u> 23 (1969) 91-104, and my "Vision...,"
part III.

49. For the conception of the Ideas as God's thoughts, see A.
Rich, "The Platonic Ideas as the Thoughts of God," <u>Mnemosyne</u>
Series IV, vol. 7 (1954) 123-33. See also my "Vision...,"
part III.

50. For a discussion of this matter, and an account of the importance of Augustine, Eriugena and the School of Chartres
in the transmission of Platonic thought, see my "Vision...,"
part. IV.

51. For all references and details, see <u>ibid</u>., part II.

52. See Hugh, <u>Commentariorum in Hierarchiam Coelestem Sancti
Dionysii Areopagitae</u> II, i; PL 175: 935C-56C (especially
936C, 938B, 939D-40A, 942A, 945C-D, 955A-B.

THE LITERARY GENRE OF BERNARD OF CLAIRVAUX'S

SERMONES SUPER CANTICA CANTICORUM

EMERO STIEGMAN

St Bernard's Sermones super cantica canticorum (1135-1153),
once the most treasured book of medieval spirituality, has, of
course, lost its vogue. It is a difficult work; some say it is dangerous. The Reformation tradition, in largest part, does not accept
its systematic asceticism. It belongs to a type of writing which a
Catholic like Professor Robert Bultot of Louvain, among others,
would place under a cloud of doubtful Christian orthodoxy. What
authors like Bernard say of man's relationship to the world, believes
Bultot, is erroneous.[1] The Sermones is the paradigm of this medieval
spiritual writing, a literature which a not inconsiderable number of
theologians consider irreconcilable with disciplined theology.[2]

I repeat these views while not sharing them because scholars
like Bultot do us the service of providing a forthright assertion
open to rebuttal, in contrast to the vastly more common and less
courageous tack of those who speak about the literature that concerns us in the manner of the ageless proverb, "It is monastic; it
is not to be taken seriously." What we intend to take seriously

here is not theological controversy so much as literary method. An awareness, however, of the theological implications of understanding or failing to understand what is finally a cultural phenomenon will properly and inevitably dramatize the interpretative effort.

The view of Bultot is rejected by Reginald Grégoire, who replies that monastic spiritual writers like Bernard are misunderstood because readers fail to recognize the literary genre in which they write Their work is experiental rather than doctrinal and normative.[3] This suggestion, that the spiritual authors should be understood within the context of a special genre, though it has been neither accepted by the antagonists addressed nor indeed developed by its own proponants, seems promising; for literary genre should indeed be the fusion point of what hermeneutical method comes increasingly to recognize as two coordinate approaches to interpretation, philology and history.

The difficulty lies in the fact that genre, or generic criticism, is a notoriously under-developed heuristic tool. Philology and aesthetics have been rather generally thought of as the sole determinants. "The artistic conventions in which a work participates," we are told, "shape its character."[4] But, we are becoming increasingly aware that an existential understanding of language, as one finds in Heidegger--or, as a more proximate example to the theologian, in John

Macquarrie's methodological appropriations of Heidegger[5] --enlivens

our historical sense. For this reason one may suspect that generic

criticism has more to offer the trans-cultural interpreter engaged

in the fundamental business of determining an author's intention

than it has to offer the literary critic,whose concern is aesthetic

evaluation. What must be added to traditional concern with artistic

conventions is full consciousness of the discourse situation, where

language is seen not merely as the representation of an object and

the expression of an author, but also as communication with an audi-

ence. The subtle presence and complex dynamics of the audience with-

in the text demands an awareness of conventions other than the lit-

erary-aesthetic. Determining the genre of Bernard's Sermones then,

will mean delineating the interface of the artistic and social imper-

atives to which this work responds.

Something of this was attended to by Landgraf, already before

the resurgence of Bernardine studies. He spoke of one of the genres

of Early Scholasticism as the sermon collection.[6] It is necessary

to add as qualifications of this genre, or further determinations of

it, all that has since been learned about the distinctiveness of

twelfth-century monastic theology in relation to the less discrim-

inating category "Early Scholasticism." The Sermones is more than a

collection; it is a sermon-series--an integral book rather than an aggregation. Unlike the logical sequential divisions of a Scholas-

tic treatise, or of the linear biblical commentary, each of the

eighty-six sermons stands as an autonomous unit; yet, the whole

exists in each of the parts. We know this in large part from Jean

Leclercq, who has gathered so much data about the Sermones and has

made so many astute observations on it that one cannot discuss it

without careful schooling in his works.[7]

The sermon-series, resembling in some measure St Gregory the

Great's Moralia in Job and In Ezechielem Prophetam, became the fav-

orite form of what Leclercq calls the "school of St Bernard."[8]

All the evidence suggests that a sermon-series was the liter-

ary work of the scriptorium rather than the pulpit. Such sermons

were not delivered. In Bernard's case this is certainly so.[9] Yet,

he affects total spontaneity and artlessness, to the point of explic-

itly calling attention time and again to the guilelessness of his lit-

erary manner. How can one submit such irrepressible eructations, he

asks, to rules or to the laws of composition (67.4)?[10] It is cer-

tain, nevertheless, that he applies much art in the concealment of

his art. The spontaneity which he describes is proper to an experi-

ence--God speaks to us through the heart in its excessus (its over-

flow), and His word should not be censured (1.4)--but the experience

is transposed into language. The writing, as all good writing,

mirrors the spontaneity of the experience in proportion to the suc-
cess of the artistic calculations and contrivances.

Bernard confessed in a letter how laboriously he composed his
writings.[11]   The richest stylistically and the most carefully or-
namented is the Sermones.[12]   That he is intrigued by the creative
involvement of literary composition quite beyond the demands of
ordinary communication was demonstrated by Deroy, who discovered
several cryptograms in the saint's writing--a complex example among
them in sermon 74.[13]   "All the opulence that Bernard criticized in
the plastic arts," commented Thomas Merton, "here runs riot in his
prose."[14]   Clearly, the work is literary. Bernard's insistence upon
spontaneity should be understood to regard the superiority of integral religious experience over merely rational objectification.

This assertion, I believe, is not merely a way of absolving the
author from a contradiction; it is a thesis regarding his central
meaning.

It is helpful to think of the spontaneity which the abbot affects in terms of an even more immediate literary objective--the
representation of live speech. The Sermones is an idealization of
oral sermons, and, as such, is a work of creative imagination. Something of its oral quality may derive from the relation of twelfth-
century literary Latin to the spoken Latin of the day, though the

present state of medieval Latin scholarship allows for little more
than conjecture.[15]   Certainly, the sermons will be affected by the
oral quality of the homiletic tradition of the Fathers.[16]   From the
moment, however, that it is recognized that the author intends an
imaginative portrayal of true sermon conditions, this creative intent becomes the sufficient explanation of the live-speech characteristics of the literary text, with both the speech patterns of the
day and those of the homiletic tradition understood as informing the
imagination.

That the text mimics an oral presentation cannot be doubted.
One finds not only syntactical characteristics of spoken language--
for example, coordinate rather than subordinate structures--but a
resourceful recreation of the homiletic setting. The abbot makes
the imaginative presence of an audience vivid by addressing himself
to specific parts of it--the novices, the senior members, some with
whom he is dissatisfied, and some who sleep during the sermon (for
example, 60.6; 63.6; 84.4). He speaks familiarly about himself--
his illness, his return from a journey, his forgetfulness, his
doubt about interpreting the text, his need for prayers, his contemplative experiences (24.2; 25.1; 38.5; 42.11; 44.8; 77.8). He
alludes to community routines and events--work to be done, guests
to be received, the office to be chanted, the monks who were absent

from the last sermon, the necessity of stopping at an incomplete
unit because he has been already too long, etc. (1.12; 47.8; 52.7;
63.7; 85.1; etc.). He imagines a time interval between one sermon
and the next, with the necessity of reviewing, summarizing, or re-
establishing the sequence (38.5; 39.1; 42.11; 63.7). The most obvious effect of this imaginative dimension of the work is that an
element of drama is introduced: the frequent reference to the audience renders the situation dialogical, constantly oriented to the
struggle of persuasion. A sermon becomes, not merely a reading, but
an event; the word remains "an event in sound."[17]

    It is unlikely that a reader of the Sermones will not be con-
scious of the identity of Bernard's audience. The abbot of Clairvaux addresses his community. His constant and explicit insertion
of his audience into the text renders one hermeneutical principle
obvious to his reader: the work has an institutional character; it
derives from the community for whom the writer speaks.[18] The abbot
represents the mind of his institute--not primarily as one who
stands above his audience in talent, knowledge, and sanctity, but as
one who echoes the thought and tradition of his audience--as one
with them. His thought is an "echo with something added."[19] There
must be, naturally, evidence that the community has recognized the
writer in question as its spokesman. In the case of St Bernard this

is abundantly clear. He was the head of the Cistercian "school" of
spirituality,[20] "Magister noster, ille interpres Spiritus Sancti."[21]
A proper translation of this expression would be, "our professor is
Bernard, for in him the Holy Spirit is interpreted." Bernard's most
esteemed text was the Sermones.[22] This work, then, speaks not only
to the Cistercians, but speaks in their name--in the name of twelfth-
century monasticism at the height of its fervor.

The imaginative dialog the author carries on with his audience--
something in its style--suggests one example of how the work speaks
for its audience. Let us pick up the thread of spontaneity again.
We notice a remark like ni fallor (24.2): "Last time we were saying,
if I remember correctly, that, etc." It is, of course, pure contriv-
ance--all histrionic. It communicates the attitude of a speaker who
refuses to preoccupy himself with minutiae of formal organization.
The attitude fits the author's admiration for the irrepressible
simplicity and personal expressiveness of the bride's language--
her insignis verborum incuria (79.1). Observe how certain units
within the sermons are referred to as excursus (80.9) or digressio
(82.1). Contrary to a critical commonplace, the association of these
"digressions" with the central topic is not a loose one, and they
might easily be provided with the structural apparatus that would
demonstrate their unity in the sermon. But for this creative

craftsman, such formal unity seems not to serve the chosen end.

Part of this attitude is a kind of familiarity, not inconsistent
with the crystaline wit of the author's perfect epithets and precise rhetorical parallels and antitheses.[23]

An occasional humorous remark highlights this familiarity. And
there is gentle banter: the preacher turns to one side of the abbey
church, for example, and says, "Do you see these novices? They
have dressed themselves up in an ascetical face and a fine composition of the whole body. I must say, what's on the face is pleasant
enough" (63.6).[24]   And, he goes on to speak of the necessity of per-
severance. (The abbot who wrote this way was known to his comtem-
poraries as a person of overwhelming charm).[25]   This contrived
casualness, disregard for structural neatness, and familiar relationship to the audience suggest a simplicity of manner highly prized
by those for whom the author wrote. Perhaps neither simplicity nor
familiarity nor any one word captures all of this. In the negative,
however, we can be more exact: the monks of Bernard's day reacted
against the formal trappings of superior intellect, precisely struc-
tured processes of mind, and an arrogance that seemed to come with
the learning that inflates. With great resourcefulness Bernard
created in the Sermones the model of a contrasting manner.

Clearly then, to say that the author of the Sermones super

cantica canticorum writes a literary sermon-series, is to call attention to more than homiletic rhetoric. Literary here means in-
vention of a very high order; viewed extrinsically, it points to the
manner in which mastery of a set of artistic conventions creates a
language artifact bearing the faithful impress of a concrete discourse situation. The creative imagination has conceived the form
a sermon takes in a specific setting and has realized an idealization
of that form.

Consider one significant implication. We are saying that the
ostensible fact-content of the work belongs to the order of creative
fiction, that it is faithful not to truth as fact but to truth as
the humanly viable ideal. It must, then, present an abbot who is
eminently but plausibly a vehicle of the Word to his monks--one
who, for example, in the tradition of the original commentary of
Origen, experiences visitations of the Bridegroom. It must, then,
present a community of monks, whose receptive faces ask all the
right questions, who are eager (were there only time enough, as
among the Black Monks) to sit through a two-hour sermon, who nevertheless do fall asleep; who know the Eastern Fathers currently under
study by their abbot, but who (out of inherited bias) will mumble in
rebellion when Origen is directly quoted. We may say of the Sermones
what has been said of imaginative fiction: "Everything in the story

is true except the whole of it."   It is not a factual sermon.   The

whole of it is, of course--as all authentic poetry--true-er than

history.

Literary, in the meanings which we have accumulated, becomes,

therefore, an essential note in a genre designation of this work.

There are other notes, which I shall here have to treat more sum-

marily. The Sermones is, for example, biblical and liturgical.

The work is biblical in the obvious sense that it comments on

a book of the Bible, though it is not a commentary in the Scholastic

manner.   Beyond this the language of Bernard is biblical in its

imitation of Hebraic concreteness, in its identification with the

objectives of the sacred writers, and in its use of their very

words.   Here one must accept the author in an institutional dim-

ension: he speaks of the Bible to his monks as he and they know it

in their milieu. It is not a book they read only: it is what they

hear in choir, in the refectory, in the cloister, and in chapter.

It is at the center of their community life.

Most often the Bible was heard in a liturgical setting. The

sermons themselves are presented as part of the monastic liturgy and

they relate to the Bible within this context. As such, the sermons

have a ritual character. The doxologies which conclude most of them

are an index of this. Several crucial observations about the work

are suggested simply in this relationship to the liturgy: the sermons are not dominantly instructional; they are experiential rather
than speculative; their asceticism is oriented to contemplation.
These traits are proper to a sermon which is, as the monastic sermon, not a proclamation of the Kerygma--for, this will have occurred
already in the liturgy--but a reflection upon the sacred text, a
human dialog, the complement in which the heart accepts the word,
an awakening of desire for union with the Word.

Although there are no artistic conventions to signal it, does
it not seem necessary to include this circumstantial element in a
genre designation? Not explicitly, perhaps, for a genre title must
not be made into a catalog of type characteristics, but as subsumed
in a larger category. Already it has been possible to observe a
common strand running through all the characteristics discussed so
far. The sermon-series of which the <u>Sermones</u> is an example is
written by monks; it is literary according to traditions obtaining
among monks; in both its biblical and its liturgical character it
is monastic--particularly as a certain use of the Bible and conduct
of the liturgy are proper to the early Cistercians. The genre title
I would suggest, therefore, is monastic literary sermon-series.

However, until we entertain the question whether the author's
intended readers were monks exclusively--perhaps we have not yet

fixed the extention of the designation "monastic." In the matter
of the work's asceticism, for example, it is not indifferent to ask:
does St Bernard propose his attitudes of renunciation to the Christian as such, or only to the monk?

Many parts of the text make a monastic audience seem unarguable.
For example, the very opening remark of the book is, "To you, my
brothers, one must speak of other things than to those in the world,
or at least speak differently"--Vobis, fratres, alia quam aliis de
saeculo, aut certe aliter dicenda sunt (1.1). Late in the work he
says the Bridegroom cannot accept the gifts of some of those addressed; he is speaking, he says, "about every monastic observance,"
de omni observantia monachi (71.14).

Such internal evidence is even more striking on the preacher's
side of the communication. The dramatic situation imaginatively
created by the author gives us two dramatis personae: the author
writes to his problematic reader in the role of, or through the mask
of, an abbot preaching to his monks. The abbot, even as his community, is a literary persona. The fact that the author is an abbot
in real life and truly addresses monks may give added authority to
his words, but what we must take explicit notice of here is that he
chooses to employ a literary form which will dramatize, or render
imaginatively present, his abbatial function. What is imaginatively

created in the Sermones is not only the presence of a congregation
but also the preacher's juridical relatinnship to it.

Let us note in passing some implications of this fact for the
interpreter: the speaker of the Sermones, unlike a Scholastic
magister submitting a treatise to the analytic consideration of his
peers or of his pupils, stands on an altogether special kind of
authority. The abbot is bound to preach to his community (57.5;
74.5; 82.1). God communicates Himself to the monks in the overflow
of the abbot's contemplation. Prudence would seem at times to suggest, thinks the abbot, that he reserve some of his thoughts for a
later occasion; but, in sermon 82, it occurs to him that these
thoughts are not his. Once, he says, when he had decided to save
something in this way, a voice told him he would receive no further
inspiration until he passed on to his monks what was being given
him only for their sake (82.1). Now, if we move from this comment
to the reflection that the author who writes this composes it in
all deliberation as part of a fictive situation, and that he certainly will add to, or omit from, his composition what literary art
dictates, then we understand it as the development of a theme: it
is a way of saying that the abbot's sermon is of a sacramental nature, that God speaks to the monks in the words of their spiritual
father. The author tries to make this spiritual reality more easily

credible by heavily playing down the fact that the hearer receives
the word through the literary judgment of the speaker. He removes
all claim to personal genius (10.1). Secondary causes, he seems
to think, can obscure the Primary Cause.

We will remember too that the monastic sermon, as all preaching,
was popularizing--the way medieval religious poetry or medieval
church sculpture was. It presented a typological understanding of
human life and history--a radically eschatological one, therefore.[30]
The eternal Bridegroom visited the community in the overflow of the
abbot's prayer (26.6).

If Bernard could write this way, it can only be because his
institute thought this way. He is formed by it, and it will accept
from him only an expression of its own ethos.[31] His authority is
juridical, but in institutional understanding it is the authority
among monks of him who is more completely a monk. If he interprets
to them, therefore, his own experience, it is merely according to a
virtual commission he receives from the community to do so. The
abbot persona device allows the author to keep these convictions
continuously in the foreground.

In the terms of our argument, we may ask whether all this does
not sweep away the problem of identifying St Bernard's intended
readers. I do not believe so. From the moment we establish that
the discourse situation is a fiction, it becomes impossible to deter-

mine the author's intention in this regard from internal evidence. As in the drama, we are working within a closed system. To know the preacher's hearers is not necessarily to know the writer's readers.

History does provide some external evidence: (1) Bernard published only those sermons intended for monks, and the Sermones was published.[32] (2) The manuscript tradition shows that of the 922 known manuscripts only fifty are from Cathedral libraries, the rest from monasteries.[33] But, even this does not establish that monks were thought of as an exclusive readership. If such external evidence and a study of the discourse situation are both inconclusive, we are left with a theoretical issue: how and to what extent may monastic ascetical attitudes apply to the Christian life in a different milieu? From the text of the Sermones and the life of Bernard, interesting material on the question may be deduced.[34] Yet, what we have here considered helps us to see that this is not a question the author puts to himself in his work. Therefore, though the question must be asked by every nonmonastic reader, it does not determine the work's literary genre. If, in default of a rich lay spirituality, we urge our question upon the monk, he will give us what, on the one hand, we may consider no answer at all, and what, on the other hand may be the central insight of monasticism itself:

consult your experience.³⁵   This is, in any case, what the abbot

of the Sermones incessantly repeats to his community (for example,

1.9, 3.1, 41.3, 44.4, 67.8, 69.8, 84.7).   In place of an appeal

to universal and demonstrable norms, St. Bernard prefers to intro-

duce his counsels with a simple condition, "If you consult your

own experience" (1.9), Si vestram experientiam advertatis.

We must, in the end, become modest about the demands we may

make upon generic criticism.   The discourse situation of the

Sermones involves an abbot and his monks.   But, to have pointed to

this obvious fact, and thereby to have called attention to a

wealth of implications governed by the relationship of abbot and

monks, is not to have cracked some code by which we may read the

further relationship of monks to the Church at large.   The lay

Christian must still read as he can that sign in the world, the

monk.

Nevertheless, good hermeneutical method seems to dictate that

the interpreter become aware of artistic form and historical set-

ting to the point of establishing genre where this is feasible.

A genre is a literary institution, one which mirrors a social

institution.   To say that is to go beyond indulging the philosophic

penchant for precise categorization and the literary penchant for

nice labeling.   In the case of the Sermones, it is to say that the very form of a monastic literary sermon-series is the true <u>speculum</u> <u>monachorum</u>, an image of the monastic life. Here we may observe the monk about his chief business, listening in communicative silence, in the context of the <u>opus Dei</u>, to the word of God--not as read or copied, nor even as merely preached, but as heard in the response of the brethern, the paradigm of which is the <u>excessus</u> or, more broadly, the experience of the abbot. Here we see a scene of heaven, where the interruption to struggle gives struggle its meaning, and the only adequate song is the Song of Songs, a proleptically eternal, lyrical Eucharist. This image, which is the <u>Sermones</u>, is the imprint of St. Bernard and his community.

How, then, can so sublime a work, and all the literature of its type, leave Bultot in doubt of its Christian orthodoxy? The point of the question should be reversed: if a large number of lay readers interpret the <u>Sermones</u> outside its proper genre (the suspicion seems legitimate), why do not they, even as Bultot, conclude that such work misconceives man's relation to the world? The asceticism appropriate to a monastic setting certainly cannot be urged upon the lay Christian. In defense of monastic literature present-day monks respond that the question is not one of orthodoxies. The monk deals in the given, in his personal experience. He need not be lectured on the dialectic of experience and meaning.

He believes our own awareness of this phenomenon will grow if we
read Bernard's <u>Sermones</u> in its proper genre.

In order that we may do this, it seems useful to point out
how our interpretation may be aided by a wedding of artistic and
social conventions--that is, by employing philology and history in
their proper existential relationship. If the genre we have tried
to establish is a literary institution, a reader must recognize
its numerous "institutional imperatives"[36] in order to receive it
as did the social institution which it represented and to which it
was addressed.

St. Mary's University, Halifax

NOTES

1. Robert Bultot, <u>Le</u> <u>XI</u>e <u>siècle</u>: <u>Pierre</u> <u>Damien</u> (<u>Christianisme</u> <u>et</u>
   <u>valeurs</u> <u>humains</u>: <u>La</u> <u>Doctrine</u> <u>du</u> mépris <u>du</u> <u>monde</u> <u>en</u> occident <u>de</u>
   <u>S</u>. <u>Ambroise</u> <u>à</u> <u>Innocent</u> <u>III</u>; Louvain, 1963) p. 12.

2. See Robert Bultot, "Spirituels et théologiens devant l'homme et
   le monde," <u>Revue</u> <u>Thomiste</u> 64 (1964) 517-48, <u>passim</u>. Pierre
   Daubercies, <u>La</u> <u>condition</u> <u>charnelle</u>: <u>Recherches</u> <u>positives</u> <u>pour</u>
   <u>la</u> <u>théologie</u> déune réalité <u>terrestre</u> (<u>Morale</u> <u>Chrétienne</u> 482;
   Tournai, 1959) pp. 15-68; "La théologie de la condition char-
   nelle chez les maitres du haut moyen âge, <u>Recherches</u> <u>de</u> <u>Théolo</u>-
   <u>gie</u> <u>Ancienne</u> <u>et</u> <u>Médiévalle</u> 30 (1963) 5-54. Yves Congar, <u>Lay</u>
   <u>People</u> <u>in</u> <u>the</u> <u>Church</u>: <u>A</u> <u>Study</u> <u>for</u> <u>a</u> <u>Theology</u> <u>of</u> <u>the</u> <u>Laity</u>
   (Westminster, Maryland, 1965) p. 407, notes in the spiritual
   authors "a prejudice against the body, or just against the
   physical world altogether." Marie-Dominique Chenu, <u>L'Evangile</u>
   <u>dans</u> <u>le</u> <u>temps</u>, II, <u>La</u> <u>Parole</u> <u>de</u> <u>Dieu</u> (Paris, 2 vols., 1964)
   esp. pp. 49, 448. The resistance to St Bernard is highly quali-
   fied in the writings of Congar and Chenu.

3. See Reginald Gregoire, "Terrena despicere et amare caelestia:
   Note à propos d'une thèse récente," Studia monastica 7 (1965)
   195-200.

4. René Wellek and Austin Warren, <u>Theory</u> <u>of</u> <u>Literature</u> (3rd ed.,
   New York, 1956) p. 226. A similar emphasis is found in P.

Vincent, O.P., La Théorie des Genres Littéraires (Paris, 1934).
The facile dismissal of the genre problem, such as one finds in
the Encyclopedia of Poetry and Poetics (ed. Alex Preminger;
Princeton, 1965) s.v. genre, does not address itself to our
problem. Literary critics seek means of aesthetic appreciation
and evaluation; the trans-cultural interpreter has other needs.

5. See John Macquarrie, God-Talk: An Examination of the Language
and Logic of Theology (New York, 1967). Donald F. Dreisbach,
"Paul Tillich's Hermeneutic," Journal of the American Academy
of Religion 43 (1975) 84-94. Note also René Wellek, Concepts
of Criticism (New Haven, 1963) p. 362, on the influence of
Heidegger upon literary criticism.

6. Arthur Michael Landgraf, Einführung in die Geschichte der
theologischen Literatur des Frühscholastik (Regensburg, 1948)
pp. 47-48.

7. See, above all, Jean Leclercq, Recuil d'études sur S. Bernard
et ses écrits (Rome, 3 vols., 1962-1969). Volume 1 is concerned with the Sermones. An excellent introduction is Jean Leclercq, "Un Guide de la lecture pour St. Bernard," La Vie
Spirituelle 102 (1960) 440-47; "Saint Bernard and the Monastic
Theology of the Twelfth Century," Cistercian Studies 1 (1961)
1-18; The Love of Learning and the Desire for God: A Study of
Monastic Culture (trans, Catherine Misrahi; New York, 1961),

esp. pp. 187–232 on monastic literary genres, and the Leclercq
bibliography up to 1960 at pp. 339–54.

8. First, there are the continuations of the Sermones by Gilbert
of Hoyland, PL 184:11–252; Geoffroy of Auxerre, whose work is
unedited (see Leclercq, "Les Ecrits de Geoffroy d'Auxerre,"
Recueil d'études, 1:27–46; at pp. 30–33); and John of Ford, also
unedited; see anonymous article, "Les Sermons inédits de Jean
de Ford sur le Cantique des cantiques," Coll. 5 (1938) 250–61.
There is the outstanding commentary on the Song by Gilbert of
Stanford, which is edited in extracts by Leclercq in Analecta
Monastica, first series (Rome, 1948) pp. 205–230. Other imita-
tions of Bernard are given in "Ecrits monastiques sur la Bible,"
Mediaeval Studies 15 (1953) 98–100, see "La littérature pro-
voquée par les sermons sur les cantiques," Recueil d'études,
1:175–90.

9. Jean Leclercq, "Les Sermons sur les Cantiques, ont-ils été
prononcés?" Recueil d'études, 1:212.

10. See Op. S. Bern., vols. 1 and 2. Parenthetical references in
the text are to the Sermones, according to sermon and numbered
paragraph, thus: (67.4).

11. Ep. 89, 1; PL 182.

12. Christine Mohrmann, "Observations sur la langue et le style de
Saint Bernard," in Op. S. Bern., 2:xxv.

13. J. P. Th. Deroy, Bernardus en Origenes (Harlem, 1963) pp. 149-
     54; cited by Leclercq, "Sur le caractere littéraire des sermons
     de S. Bernard," Recueil d'études, 3:163-212, at p. 193.

14. The Last of the Fathers: Saint Bernard of Clairvaux and the
     Encyclical Letter Doctor Mellifluus (New York, 1954) p. 65.

15. V. Paladini and M. de Marco, Lingua e letteratura mediolatina
     (Bologna, 1970) pp. 3-6, for comments and a bibliography on
     the question.

16. Christine Mohrmann, "The Style of Saint Bernard," Cistercian
     Studies 2 (1962) 1-19, trans, from "Le Style de Saint Bernard,"
     S. Bernardo (Milan, 1954); see p. 5. Miss Mohrmann seems to
     think that to explain oral characteristics one must choose be-
     tween the homiletic tradition and the spoken Latin of the times.

17. Walter J. Ong, The Presence of the Word: Some Prolegomena for
     Cultural and Religious History (New Haven, 1967) p. ix.

18. For a convincing case study of the inter-action of writer and
     community, see Charles H. Lohr, "Oral Techniques in the Gospel
     of Matthew," Catholic Biblical Quarterly 23 (1961) 403-435.
     It becomes clear in the author's study that Matthew's organiza-
     tion of the sayings of Jesus reflects the traditional expecta-
     tions of the early Christian community.

19. Ong, The Presence of the Word, p. 221.

20. Leclercq, Recueil d'études, 1:133.

21. Guerric of Igny, Sermo in Nat. Apost. Petri et Pauli, 3, 1; PL 185:183.

22. Leclercq, Recueil d'études, I, 177.

23. Such examples as the following occur on virtually every page: The kiss of the Bridegroom is melius impressum quam expressum (9.3); God uses bodies, but indulgentia est non indigentia (5.9); His litteralis lusus....Quid enim serium habet haec litterae series?" (61.2).

Regarding familiarity in Bernard's style, see Leclercq, Recueil d'études, 3:163-71, where the author discusses two styles found in Bernard's sermons. The Sermones and the liturgical sermons are in a grander style; the sermons De diversis in a familiar style. The present writer, nevertheless, finds much significance in those elements of familiarity in the Sermones which co-exist with its grandeur.

24. "Videtis istos novitios? Induerunt sibi faciem disciplinatem et bonam totius corporis compositionem. Placent, fateor, quae in facie sunt" (63.6).

25. Watkin Williams, Saint Bernard of Clairvaux (Westminster, Maryland, 1952) pp. 9-10.

26. Wilson Follett, The Modern Novel (New York, 1918) p. 29; quoted in Wellek and Warren, p. 213.

27. Leclercq, The Love of Learning, pp. 263-70.

28. In a large literature on this subject, see Jean Leclercq, "Vocabulaire biblique," Recueil d'études, 3:229-37; "De quelques procédés du style biblique de S. Bernard," Ibid., pp. 249-66.

29. Corneille Halflants, "Le Cantique des cantiques de Saint Bernard," Coll. 15 (1953) 250-94, at p. 292.

30. Erich Auerbach, "Typological Symbolism in Medieval Literature," Gesammelte Aufsätze zur romanischen Philologie (Bern, 1967) pp. 110-11.

31. Gilbert of Hoyland, one of the "school" of St. Bernard, reminds his monks of their relationship to his work: "From you I received my commission, from you the matter of my sermon" (A vobis accepi mandatum, a vobis materiam." Sermo, PL 184C, 288B).

32. Jean Leclercq, "Saint Bernard et ses secretaires," Recueil d'études, I, 193-212, esp. p. 8.

33. Leclercq, in ASOC 9, fasc. 1 and 2 (1953) 12, 21-28, 39, with map of the spread of Bernardine manuscripts, after p. 247.

34. In 66.10, for example, Bernard continues the practice of medieval spiritual writers of allowing the older conception of marriage as one of three "orders" to become the least of three "degrees." DeLubac laments the practice in Exégèse

médiévale, 2:573, but erroneously exempts Bernard from it.
The married state is considered in 66.10 to be for those who
are not strong enough to practice the counsels. One may de-
duce, therefore, the conclusion that monastic asceticism would
be urged upon the laity in accordance with their strength.
For Bernard's pessimism regarding sexuality, see 61.2, 81.11,
and 82.2.

35. Hans Urs von Balthasar, Herrlichkeit (Einsiedeln, 1961) I,
275, believes Bernard saw in the oft-repeated statement "He
is wise who experiences [tastes] all things as they truly
are"--Est enim sapiens cui quaecumque sapiunt prout sunt
(Div, 19, 1)--the foundation of Christian spirituality.

36. This is the phrase of N. H. Pearson, "Literary Forms and Types,"
English Institute Annual, 1940 (New York, 1941) pp. 61-72, at
p. 70; quoted in Wellek and Warren, p. 226.

BERNARD VS. ABELARD: AN ECCLESIOLOGICAL CONFLICT*

THOMAS J. RENNA

The Bernard-Abelard confrontation at the synod of Sens in 1140 has been traditionally interpreted as the clearest proof that the two protagonists were separated by basic differences. This dissimilarity has been seen as a contest of faith versus reason,[1] authority versus reason,[2] monastic versus scholastic theology,[3] rural aristocracy versus bourgeoisie,[4] Burgundian versus Briton "races."[5] But since 1932[6] the tendency in serious scholarship[7] has been to stress the similarties in their theologies and methodologies.[8] These recent studies have clarified the theological and methodological presuppositions which influenced their casts of mind.

But to explain Bernard's and Abelard's mental dispositions is not to explain the conflict itself. Clearly they both believed that their struggle involved more than just abstract ideals. Bernard's propensity for rhetoric notwithstanding, he was surely correct in assuming that their feud transcended personality differences.[9] Only lately have historians examined Bernard's monastic theology in the broader context of his idea of the universal church.[10] Abelard is finally gaining some recognition as a monastic reformer.[11]

What is currently needed is an approach which will at the same time, (1) account for the Bernard-Abelard dispute, and (2) evaluate the conflict in the contexts of monastic history and of early twelfth-century ecclesiastical politics. The conflict could be treated more thoroughly as a reflection of the tensions within ecclesiastical structures. This paper proposes an ecclesiological model which may serve to integrate the diverse approaches of modern Bernardian and Abelardian historians.

SIMILARITIES

The concept of the church shared by Bernard and Abelard was typical of monastic reformers at the time. Both monks saw the church primarily as a mystery. The church is the means by which the Holy Spirit directs the ongoing work of salvation in the world.

Recent studies have emphasized the spiritualist thrust of Bernard's ecclesiology [12] --a welcome corrective to the more usual stress on his role as a monastic organizer and defender of ecclesiastical authority. All of Bernard's conceptionalizations of the church-- especially the idea that the church is a hierarchy of orders modeled after the heavenly hierarchy--have been shown to be tentative and subordinate to his idea of the church as the Bride of Christ. Thus it is impossible to isolate any one of Bernard's many descriptions

of the church; all descriptions are for Bernard analogies which at
best approximate the reality of the Bride. Bernard's <u>ecclesia</u> is
not a rigid structure with each "order" fixed for all time; it is
a subtle balance between the real, interior "church of love" and
its visible, organizational counterpart.

The key to Bernard's ecclesiology is the monastic community.
The monks occupy a unique place in the church universal. Indeed,
the monks in a sense give the church its meaning. They give "spiritual juices" to the other members of the christian community.[13]
True monks are the spouses--Bernard employs "spouse" both as the
soul and as the church [14] --who are closest to God. They are the
descendants of the angels, the predestined elect who unite heaven
and earth. [15] Hence they are the only members of the church who
have their origin directly in heaven. Since they are united to God
in charity the monks perform the function of interceding for the
rest of mankind.[16] Their love-relationship with God is intensely
personalist. The entire church universal is, as it were, an extended monastic community. The true spouses provide the Bride's
"friends"--the prelates, who watch over the church--with spiritual
guidance. In their governance of the terrestrial church bishops
and popes should attempt to emulate monastic virtue.

One of Bernard's favorite typologies is the Noah-Daniel-Job triad.[17] Noah is the prelate, Daniel the contemplative monk, Job the married layman. Bernard's treatment of Noah reveals his high esteem for the active life and the episcopal office. His idea of the earthly church is not so otherworldly that he deems the hierarchical church accidental or secondary. He insists on the need to maintain an orderly church, the instrument of God's providence and his plan of salvation. While the contemplative life is certainly superior *per se* to the active, the two states of life are twin manifestations of the church's leadership, and are dependent on each other.

But the line between the active and contemplative states is not as unbending as it first seems, for Bernard does not object in principle to transfers from one state to another. Bernard's chief criterion is always: does the impulse to change states come from God or from self?[18] Ordinarily the temptation to switch should be considered as self seeking and should accordingly be overcome. But God does, on occasion, will the crossover from one state of life to another. Thus Bernard's notion of a tripartite church is not tied to legal distinctions, but rather is founded on an arrangement of "callings" or vocations.[19] When giving advice to monks or prelates who want to alter their state Bernard rarely dictates a solution. More often, he acts as a sort of spiritual director who assists the subject in perceiving God's will. Bernard seems convinced that such "extraordinary" spiritual guides are needed to ensure that monks and prelates are performing their proper tasks.

Abelard's ecclesiology has received scant notice from modern historians. It seems to be assumed that the maverick Abelard wore his monastic habit as casually as did a later monk, Erasmus. Abelard's modern admirers have concentrated on his place in philosophical, theological, and educational history; Bernard's students generally perceive Abelard in the context of the Sens synod. Nonspecialists rely on the Historia calamitatum for their image of Abelard.

Compared to the works of Bernard, those of Abelard contain little on the life of the church. Yet his remarks do point to a coherent pattern which is similar to Bernard's. Abelard's concept of the church is likewise mystical and monastic.[20] The Bride is served by activist prelates and contemplative monks. Abelard's blasts against the worldly lives of bishops could be interchanged with Bernard's.[21] The contemplative life is so far removed (and superior in dignity) from the active life that monks and prelates should keep apart.[22] The monk is characterized by his solitude, poverty, chastity, prayer, obedience, abstinence. The prelate should devote his entire energy to the spiritual well-being of his flock. Abelard has a strongly spiritualist--almost neodonatist-- concept of ecclesiastical office. While not completely denying the sacredness of the episcopal office per se, Abelard vehemently insists on the necessity of virtue in the officeholder. Although Abelard's notions of the monk and prelate are the same as Bernard's, it must be admitted that Abelard's thought on the "objective" basis of the episcopal office is less developed.[23]

Abelard's diatribes against worldly monks, prelates, and canons regular converge on a single point: the monk should be totally detached from the world. The monastic and prelatal vocations are distinct; any attempt to blend the two states would dilute the purity of the monastic ideal. It should be noted that Abelard's writings do not reflect Bernard's grand vision of the church universal. Not active in church politics as was Bernard, the scholar of Pallet makes little effort to elaborate on the proper role of bishops and popes in the church. Bernard's more constructive remarks on the function of the secular clergy gives his idea of the church more balance. While Bernard places the prelate in the highest rank of the visible church,[24] Abelard tends to stress the intrinsic inferiority of the prelate in the "interior" church. Yet despite this

occasional shift of emphasis, Bernard and Abelard come to the same
general conclusion regarding the proper roles of monk and prelate
within the ecclesia. The ecclesiologies of the two abbots are join-
ed by their belief in the prophetic mission of the monk.

DIFFERENCES

At the center of the opposition between Bernard and Abelard is
the latter's introduction of a new kind of church guide, the dialectician. Abelard is less interested in dialectics qua dialectics
than he is in dialecticians. He singles out dialecticians as the
Christians best able to refute heretics, demonstrate the intelli-
gibility of Revelation to Jews and philosophers, prepare students
for theology, explain the faith, aid in the interpretation of Scripture, strengthen the church's authorities (including ecclesiastical).[25]
Dialecticians serve to make prelates more effective pastors and
defenders of the faith; as the prelates' "assistants," they provide
the episcopacy with the tools necessary for the understanding of
Scripture and the Fathers. A better grasp of Revelation will
induce the prelate to live like Christ and preach the true gospel
to his flock. Without the benefit of dialecticians the prelate is
reduced to repeating theological formulae.

Abelard's dialecticians are indispensible for the church. They
make up a select group which has a dual origin in heaven (as does

Bernard's Cistercian order). First, the true dialecticians have

been prefigured throughout human history. They are the messianic
26
fulfillment of the Old Testament prophets, the great pagan phil-
27 28 29
osophers, John the Baptist, the Apostles, and the Fathers,
30
especially St Jerome. Abelard justifies the dialecticians as

the end product of a long process of gradual revelations. It should

be stressed that Abelard invoked the ancient philosophers not pri-

marily to demonstrate the potential of unaided reason, as is often

said, but rather to illustrate their spiritual mission. The orig-

inal philosophers revealed something of the nature of God to their
31
contemporaries. Their successors, the Christian dialecticians,

reveal more of God to a world better equiped (through grace) to

receive him. What counts for Abelard is the universal social fun-

ction performed by the pagan philosophers and their continuators,

the Christian philosophers.

Second, as a corollary, dialecticians receive a special kind of
32
knowledge--logic--which enables them to carry on their saving work.

Dialectics is the highest kind of divine Wisdom, which is Christ

himself. Indeed, logic comes from Logos. True Christian philoso-

phers are consequently closely united with Christ in charity. These
33
philosophers receive their special knowledge by diving illumination

which not only imparts dialectical knowledge to the recipient, but

also enables him to live a life of the highest virtue. Knowledge
of logic cannot be attained by one's personal effort; it is a free
gift of God.

Thus Abelard elevates two groups to the highest rank in the
interior church: true monks and true dialecticians. Abelard's dilemma was to find a way to combine these apparent opposites. In part,
this intellectual problem grew out of his personal situation.[34] He
was accused of being less a monk for his logic and his wanderings.
Abelard attempted to prove to himself and to the world that he was
both a true dialectician (who had the gift of dialectical knowledge,
and who employed dialectics for its intended end) and a true monk
(who lived the gospel in total detachment from worldly concerns).
While Abelard shared many attitudes with Bernard and other monastic
reformers of the early twelfth century, the former did not consider
dialectics foreign to monks, at least certain kinds of monks. The
refrain among contemporary reformers was that learning and dialectics were superfluous, even dangerous, in the true schola Christi.[35]
Abelard agreed that the monk's task was to weep.

Abelard resolved the dilemma by making the monk-dialectician
a prophet. The monk-dialectician is descended from the Hebrew
prophet and the philosopher-prophet of the pagan world. As prophets these two forerunners revealed something of divine doctrine.

Their claim to prophecy is clearly displayed in their styles of
life.[36] Their monastic witness was God's way of manifesting Himself in each historical era. Hence Abelard focuses on the "monastic" characteristics of the Old Testament prophets--especially
Elias, "our leader"[37] --and Socrates and the other philosophers.
God gave Socrates a special grace to live a quasi-monastic life.[38]
Abelard goes to great lengths to describe the virtue of the philosophers: charity, solitude, abstinence, poverty, integrity. Abelard's point is not merely that virtue is necessary as a prerequis-
ite for true knowledge, but that the philosopher was a proto-monk,
a typus of the Christian-monk-philosopher; the ancient philosopher
was primarily a teacher of ethics by his word and example.[39] Philosophers taught the wisdom of Christ as much by their personal witness as by their arguments. Abelard is less concerned with Plato
as a venerable authority or as a pagan whose "natural" reason ap-
proached the Trinity, than he is with Plato the ascetic who prepared
the world for the advent of the true monks of Christ. Thus Plato is
seen as a part of a grand providential scheme of salvation. The new
prophet, who brings the Wisdom of Christ to his church, is the fulfillment of the Old Testament and ancient philosophy. The most
"complete" widsom is found in the true monk who is also a dialectician.

Abelard makes John the Baptist--the precursor of Christ--the immediate forerunner of Christian monks.   John is the monks' model who is distinguished for his solitude.[40]   It may seem strange that Abbot Abelard in a sermon to his cenobitic monks chooses the fierce Baptist as the symbolic ideal to be imitated. But the choice is consistent with Abelard's concept of the monk as the Christian most totally detached from the world. (This standard explains Abelard's attack on the canons regular who profess to be monks while at the same time caring for souls in the world.) Moreover, the choice conforms nicely with Abelard's own unsettled life. Abelard could argue that his own misunderstood, itinerant life--which seemed foreign to the Benedictine Rule--matches that of the persecuted desert prophet who found no rest.[41]

While John the Baptist prefigured the new prophet, St. Jerome was that prophet. Abelard frequently quotes Jerome to support his arguments for detached monks and teaching dialecticians.[42]   Erasmus would later see in Jerome the prototype of the activist Christian humanist; Abelard implies that by being a monk-dialectician he is simply carrying on the tradition of Jerome and the fathers.

It might be added that Abelard's praise of both the solitary and the communal life follows no discernible pattern. Despite his strong support of the eremetical alternative, Abelard's representa-

tion of the pagan philosophers and his advice to monks and nuns[43]
reflect his belief in the common life and the observance of the
Rule. Yet he studiously avoids a direct comparison of the cenobitic
with his preferred anchorite.[44] The resulting ambivalence can perhaps be resolved only if it is assumed that he believed a few monks
are in some way both communal and eremetical. His own life vacil-
lated between the two modes of life.

Abelard saw himself as living proof of the vitality and use-
fulness of the monk-dialectician in the church. It would seem
that Abelard's emphasis on the solitude of the true monk would
have little meaning for an itinerant professor who inhabited cathedral schools.[45] Abelard implies that his norm for monks applied
to monks ordinarily, but that the norms sometimes did not apply,
that is, not in the case of a prophet. It was consistent, from
this perspective, for Abelard to criticize monks (and bishops) who
violated his standard while he himself sometimes bypassed that
standard. Although there is no evidence that Abelard ever ceased
to view himself as an abbot and a monk faithful to the Rule, he
also defined himself as a solitary bound by a higher law, the law
of prophetic witness.[46] As a prophet he need not belong to any
conventional monastic community.

It must be emphasized that Abelard did not consider all dialecticians monks, nor did he believe all monks should be dialecticians. True dialecticians were, to be sure, the perfection of the
wisdom of Elias and Plato; the highest wisdom was attained by the
ascetic monk who was also a philosopher. But Abelard never developed a synthesis of the roles of dialectician and ascetic. His
ideal of the prophetic monk-dialectician constituted only a sub-
division within his general category of dialectician. He was the
fulfillment of a threefold prophetic tradition: Hebrew, philosopher, Christian monk.[47]

If Abelard's solution to the role of the dialectician seems
contrived, it is partly because the dialectician was ecclesiolog-
ically ambiguous in the early twelfth century. At the time many
theologians worked out typologies which corresponded to the church's
states of life.[48] Although the dialecticians had a solid enough
place in the schools, they seemed for many an anomaly; they were
church members without, as yet, a niche. After justifying the
practice of the dialectical method Abelard had to justify the dialectician as a bona fide member of Christian society. This he did
chiefly by arguments from final causality: the dialecticians' service to the church. Also, he felt compelled to link conceptually
the dialectician to the monk, the most perfect member of the eccles-

ia. The conservative Abelard fell back upon a monastic ideal.
This was done partly for rhetorical reasons (to answer his critics),
partly out of a sincere belief in the new evangelical spirit. It
must have appeared self-evident to Abelard that the dialectical and
monastic "life" could be combined since he himself exemplified both.
Abelard never said that dialecticians comprised a separate "state
of life" (Noah, Daniel, or Job) in the church. Rather, he assumed
that dialecticians would remain somewhat undefined in the ecclesiastical hierarchy; they were sort of "outsiders" who would restore
the relative equilibrium between the interior and exterior church.
Moreover, there were a few monk-dialecticians--like himself--with-
in this group who a fortiori could not be classified according to a
conventional typology.

Thus Abelard felt a need to protect "his" dialecticians from
detractors. He assailed pseudo-dialecticians less for overstepping
the bounds of reason than for presuming to be members of the elect;
they did not have the natural gift for logic, the knowledge of the
true end of dialectics, or the necessary virtue. He attacked anti-
dialecticians for obstructing the application of dialectics to
statements about divine mysteries. Lacking the grace needed to
comprehend logic, the anti-dialecticians undermined the faith they
claimed to uphold, for they--in their lives as monks and pastors--

merely parroted doctrines they did not understand. Abelard accused
his enemies not only of being envious of his intellectual prowess,
but also of being jealous of his leadership role in the Paris schools.

For Bernard such a notion of the dialectician's role was pre-
posterous. Dialectics could add little if anything to a monk's
spiritual progress; indeed, it could be perilous. [49] A dialectician
who claimed to be a monk and a prophet would upset the normal func-
tioning of the episcopacy by interferring in the prelates' responsibility to preach and teach. Such a monster would lead the unwary into
heresy and usurp the place of true monks. Thus the monk-dialectician
would undermine the legitimate functions of monastic and episcopal
authority.

But while Bernard remained convinced of the prophetic mission of
his Cistercians, he was uncertain about his own vocation. The monastic ideal he describes in his treatises, sermons, and letters
frequently bears few resemblances to the career of the abbot who
cajoled princes, lectured bishops, arbitrated disputes, ended schisms,
preached crusades, converted heretics. No one was more aware of the
distance between the life he preached and the life he led than Bernard himself. Even his admirers were embarrassed and hard put to
explain away his extramonastic activity. [50]

Prior to 1130 Bernard seems to have experienced no contradiction

in his actions. Most of his outside-the-monastery deeds were related to the survival and expansion of his order. But once the
papal schism began, Bernard shifts his emphasis to the church
universal.[51] He explains his activity during and after the schism
not in terms of directly or indirectly defending Cistercian
communities, but rather in terms of protecting the entire ecclesia.[52] No longer does Bernard have the responsibility only to
pray for the church;[53] he is now compelled to engage in actions nor-
mally forbidden a monk. Bernard's letters reveal a painful uncertainty about the propriety of his interventions; he repeatedly reminds his readers that the hierarchy summoned him to take the init-
iative.[54] He insists that he finds such worldly distractions distasteful and that he prefers to be in the monastery. Bernard asks
for compassion for his "grief" at being in "exile" in the world.[55]
His life does not correspond to any classification within his own
typology of states of life. Hence Bernard laments his "monstrous
life." "I am a sort of modern chimera, neither cleric nor layman."[56] While admitting that ordinarily only prelates should teach
the gospel and correct the rebellious, his love for the Bride of
Christ obliges him to abandon temporarily the contemplative life.

Bernard counsels his Cistercians to follow the Rule and remain
secluded. But in an emergency--when the faith and the church are

endangered--certain monks should descend from Jerusalem to rescue

the church by direct action. Although he never exhorts his own

monks to imitate their abbot's behavior in this respect, Bernard

does assume that a monk can most clearly perceive God's will. A

monk can at times counsel prelates or even act when the hierarchy

moves too slowly. Following his extensive involvement in the
57

papal schism, the abbot of Clairvaux may have felt a greater need

to clarify to himself and others the ecclesiological basis of his

own peculiar role in the life of the church.

Bernard's idea of the monastic life, then, is twofold. First,

he saw his Cistercians--along with other contemplative orders--as

the summit of the spiritual church; their purity and charity pro-

vide guidance for the visible church. Second, God occasionally

sends a monk--not necessarily a Cistercian--into the corrupt world

to redirect it back to himself. The church's prelates can and

acter of Innocent and his electors conforms with his spiritual con-

The hierarchy should involve the prophetic arm of the church for

the duration of the emergency. During this exceptional activity

such a monk is not bound by the usual strictness of the Rule.

Bernard's notion of the special prophetic mission of a few monks

must have seemed vindicated following his victory over Anacletus in

1137--just two years before his conflict with Abelard.

Bernard did not invoke the names Anacletus and Arnold of Brescia during the clash with Abelard solely for reasons of expediency. To be sure, the name of Anacletus reminded Innocent of his debt to Bernard; Anacletus and Arnold were for the curia synonymous with rebellion and anarchy. But, more to the point, Bernard's use of Anacletus and Arnold was consistent with his idea of church authority. Bernard favored Innocent during the schism primarily because of the Frangipani candidate's association with the reform party. The struggle on behalf of Innocent was also the struggle to assist the reform movement, especially in Rome.[59] Bernard's stress on the good character of Innocent and his electors conforms with his spiritual concept of ecclesiastical office. Bernard's conviction that he knows which candidate is God's choice rests ultimately on his awareness of his own prophetic powers.

Thus Bernard's identification of Abelard with the Pierleoni was no mere rhetorical pose. Abelard is for Bernard another Anacletus who seeks to destroy the church's authority by diminishing the influence of true prophets. When Bernard refers to Abelard's influence in the curia he is not referring primarily to doctrinal matters;[60] rather, Bernard fears that Abelard and his disciples will seize control of the curia and expel the reform party from Rome. Bernard's concern is that Abelard and his dialecticians will turn

the church's authority upside down by frustrating the spiritual
witness of Cistercians and certain prophetic monks and by usurping
the authority of the episcopacy and the papacy.

Bernard compares Abelard to Arnold in order to depict the evils
of schism.[61]   Claiming his authority directly from God, Arnold
preaches without episcopal permission. By implication Abelard pre-
sumes to circumvent the church hierarchy and to teach without auth-
orization. Only prelates have the simple faithful entrusted to
them; Abelard assumes the responsibility to care for the flocks.

No doubt Bernard believed Abelard a heretic. But Bernard's
charges sometimes seem conventional; they are not always based on
a close acquaintance with Abelard's writings.[62]   Bernard is more
concerned with the results of Abelard's heresy: Abelard the teacher leads the faithful astray. Moreover, Bernard seems to assume
that Abelard must be a heretic because, (a) he arrogates episcopal
authority to himself, and (b) he leads an immoral life.

First, the magisterium has not authorized Abelard to teach and
explain the divine mysteries. Bernard is not opposed to the examination of the mysteries by reason; he objects that someone like
Abelard is doing the examining. Secular clerics may legitimately
employ dialectics to strengthen their faith and to make them more
effective pastors and administrators. But only a true monk can

enter most fully into the mysteries by means of prayer. Bernard

fears that dialecticians will set themselves up as the ultimate

interpreters of Revelation. The teaching function of the prelates

and the "teaching" function (giving witness to the perfect life) of

the monks would diminish.

Second, Abelard's mode of life clearly disqualifies him from

teaching and from prophecy. Bernard implies that Abelard teaches

"novelties" because he seeks self glorification.[63] Abelard's pride

prevents him from perceiving truth. A true prophet would be con-

cerned for the salvation of others. Abelard fails moreover the

three tests of prophecy. First, Abelard's doctrines are in error.

His misuse of dialectics leads him into unorthodoxy. Second, Abbot

Abelard does not act like a monk.[64] He consorts with women and

boys. He knows nothing of the fruits of contemplation. Clearly

he lacks the grace possessed by true prophetic monks, who act out

of love of God not self. Abelard wanders about in search of fame;

he does not follow the Rule. Third, Abelard does not fit one of

the usual states of life: Noah, Daniel, Job. Abelard is a "monk

without a rule, a prelate without responsibility, an abbot without

discipline."[65] Abelard is neither a pastor of souls (authority for

which must derive from the hierarchy) nor an ascetic monk united

with the Bridegroom. He does not belong to one of the ministering

orders such as the canons regular. Abelard's life makes no sense.
He occupies no known position in the ecclesia. While secular clerics could profitably use dialectics as a tool, there could be no
separate state of "dialecticians" with a unique function in the
church. Abelard's behavior causes confusion and disunity in the
church.[66] Since Abelard is neither a Daniel nor a Noah, he must be
either antichrist or a prophet. But Abelard's pretensions to prophecy and the monastic vocation have to be rejected because his intentions and his lifestyle are perverse.[67] Finally, Bernard used
the same standard of prophecy which he applied to the would-be
prophet Raoul.[68]

Bernard seems to assume Abelard's motives are selfish; it was
inevitable Abelard should stray into false doctrine and dubious
methods of inquiry. This norm of judgment may be analogous to
Bernard's belief that Innocent II's good character helped to prove
he was true pope. In sum, Bernard objects to Abelard's implicit
claim to a singular leadership calling in the church.

ECCLESIOLOGICAL RESOLUTION

Abelard and Bernard made the monastic community the spiritual
pivot of the ecclesia. The visible societal church was in constant
need of rejuvenation from the "interior" church. In particular, a

select group of holy monks ideally provided the Christian testimony which would unite the Bride with her Spouse. These ascetic souls would also furnish the prelacy with the torch of example; monastic virtue would permeate Christian society at every level. Only after these monks made their perfect commitment to Christ would the necessary adjustments be made in the church's external structure. Typical of early twelfth-century evangelists, Bernard and Abelard preached the conversion of individuals, not the overhaul of institutions.

But Bernard and Abelard differed as to which group should exercise this prophetic function. For Bernard, this honored place was reserved for the new ascetic monks in general, his Cistercians in particular; for Abelard, this elite was the ascetic dialecticians.[69] It is curious but understandable that leaders within the same movement often show more hostility toward each other than toward enemies of their common cause. In his letters relating to the Sens synod Bernard focuses on the differences separating them; he glosses over their very real likenesses. He feared Abelard because he saw in the latter a spiritual kinsman, a mirror image of himself. It was only during the events subsequent to the letter from William of St Thierry concerning Abelard that Bernard came to a full awareness of the dialecticians' claims. Prior to 1130 Ber-

nard's opposition to the misuse of dialectics was commonplace for
a monastic reformer; during the dispute with Abelard Bernard came
to view the dialecticians as a threat to his personal leadership--
within his order and within the church universal--and a threat to
his Cistercians. The dialecticians appeared to want to usurp the
place of the Cistercians in the church. Hence Bernard in his letters virtually ignores Abelard's position as monk and reformer;
instead he concentrates on Abelard's non-monastic traits: his
dialectics, his violations of the Rule, his sinful life (especially
his pride), his contempt for ecclesiastical authority, his doctrine. [70]

While Abelard was sympathetic to Cistercian ideals he ridiculed
monks who engaged in affairs outside the monastery. He came to
consider Bernard--an abbot of enormous influence following the end
of the papal schism--a personal enemy only during the events of
1139-1140. Bernard appeared a dangerous opponent of dialectics.
Hence while dialecticians could exist in principle alongside Cistercians and other ascetic orders, Abelard saw Bernard as a com-
petitor and false monk who attacked dialectics under the guise of
restoring true monasticism.

For Bernard and Abelard their respective notions of prophetic
leadership in the church may have been only implicit before their

confrontation in 1139. Before that year they probably enjoyed a
correct relationship.[71] It was only after the outbreak of open
conflict that each was compelled to clarify his own position to himself and to others. The intensity of the struggle was due not only
to an abstract ideal concerning prophetic groups in the ecclesia,
but also to personal competition. They each feared the loss of
their leadership within their respective movements. They imagined
they were rivals for the highest rank in the charismatic hierarchy.
It would be unfair, however, to attribute to this personal power
struggle the chief reason for their antagonism. For in their minds
the survival of the entire church was at issue. For them, three
goals became intertwined: the protection of personal power, main-
tenance of the elite group involved, and defense of the Bride herself.

CONCLUSION

The conflict between Bernard and Abelard arose mainly from
their idea of church authority. They agreed that a vanguard within
the church was required to exemplify the Christian life and to but-
tress the organizational church. But while they shared the notion
that a charismatic elite should provide spiritual leadership within
Christian society, they each had a different group in mind. As
participants in the prophetic tradition they felt compelled on occasion to act decisively in defense of their respective monastic
groups as well as the church universal.

The ecclesiological thought of Abelard and Bernard is still
imperfectly understood. As critical texts of their works continue
to appear, the points of contact in their ideas of the church could
be determined more precisely. Such analyses could help clarify
church politics in France and Italy from 1120 to 1140.

The conflict between Abelard and Bernard demonstrates how much
of the Gregorian program had become axiomatic for early twelfth-
century Europe. Abelard and Bernard, two of the church's most
severe critics, accepted many Gregorian principles: juridical
separation of the clergy, increased jurisdictional rights of the
papacy, refinement and extension of canon law, exceptional virtue
for popes and prelates, [72] decreased influence of monks in church

administration. To be sure, Bernard impugned unwarranted exemptions
and too many appeals to the curia; Abelard's attitude toward episcopal office was hardly legalistic. But the principal complaints
of Abelard and Bernard were leveled at the worldly lives of monks
and prelates--not at real or imagined defects in the church's
institutional frame. The two conservative abbots were classic
moralists heralding a wayward flock back to the true way. As reformers, their basic tool was radical biblical criticism, a criticism founded in the evangelical monastic community. Since they
were both sensitive to the workings of the "spiritual" church, they
were disposed to remain content within the existing societal structure. Indeed, their wish to interiorize the church frequently
blinded them to the realities of ecclesiastical politics and church-
state relations.

Herein lies the tragedy of the Abelard-Bernard controversy. By
setting their educational and monastic movements against each other
they ultimately assisted what they dreaded most: the tendency to
centralize the church around the papacy with the aid of law, leg-
ates, and armed force. Unlike the extreme Gregorians, Abelard and
Bernard had hoped for a church united in love and led by ascetic
charismatics, the Cistercians for Bernard and the dialecticians for
Abelard. Instead, they weakened the place of prophetic teachers
who could act as a brake on the temporal preoccupations of eccles-

iastical administrators.

NOTES

*This article is a revision of a paper read at the Ohio Conference on Medieval Studies, John Carroll University, 19 October 1974.

I wish to thank the National Endowment for the Humanities, the American Philosophical Society, and Saginaw Valley College for providing me with grants which aided me in the research for this article.

1. This view was popularized by Rémusat and Cousin in the nineteenth century.

2. See J. Cottinaux, "La Conception de la théologie chez Abélard," Revue d'histoire ecclésiastique, 28 (1932) 247-95, 533-51, 788-828. But Cottinaux also argues that Abelard upheld both authority and reason; the conflict with Bernard arose out of Abelard's method.

3. The clearest exposition of this approach is the classic work by J. Leclercq, The Love of Learning and the Desire for God (New York, 1961).

4. See N. Siderova, "Abélard et son époque," Journal of World History, 4 (1958) 541-52; 6 (1960) 175-82. Siderova is not convincing.

5. See P. Lasserre, Un conflit religieux au XIIe siècle: Abélard contre Saint Bernard (Paris, 1930).

6. In that year Cottinaux and J. Sikes (Peter Abailard) published their seminal works.

7. Most popular books on Abelard and especially Bernard still build

their narratives on the faith-reason fiction. See, for example,

A. Luddy, The Case of Peter Abelard (Dublin, 1947); D. Meadows,

A Saint and a Half: A New Interpretation of Abelard and St

Bernard of Clairvaux (New York, 1963).

8. Recent works: R. Weingart, The Logic of Divine Love (Oxford, 1970

p. 173, passim (J. Leclercq agrees with Weingart that the difference

between Abelard and Bernard was one of emphasis not substance:

Medium Aevum, 41 [1941] 59-61); C. Morris, The Discovery of the

Individual 1050-1200 (London, 1972) p. 74f.; P. Zerbi, "Panem

nostrum supersubstantialem: Abelardo polemista ed esegeta nell'Ep.X

Contributi dell'Istituto di storia medioevale, II, Raccolta di studi

in onore Sergi Mochi Onory (Milan, 1972) pp. 624-38, and "'In clunia

vestra sibi perpetuam mansionem elegit' (Petri Venerabilis Ep. 98),"

Storiografia e storia: Studi in onore di Eugenio Duprè Theseider

(Rome, 1974) pp. 627-44; C. Waddell, "La Carta 10 de Pedro Abelardo

y la reforma liturgica cisterciense," Cistercium, 25 (1973) 56-66;

J. R. Sommerfeldt, "Abelard and Bernard of Clairvaux," Papers of

the Michigan Academy of Science, Arts, and Letters, 46 (1961)

493-501; J. Jolivet, "Sur quelques critiques de la théologie

d'Abélard," Archives d'histoire doctrinale et littéraire du môyen

âge, 38 (1963) 7-51; C. S. Jaeger, "The Dispute between Bernard

and Abelard: Some Aesthetic Considerations" (unpublished); E. Littl

"Bernard and Abelard at the Council of Sens 1140," Bernard of

Clairvaux (Washington, D.C., 1973) pp. 55-71, and "Abelard's

First Theology" (unpublished). I am grateful to Professors

Zerbi, Jaeger, and Little for allowing me to see copies of

their articles. In the tradition of Geyer and Grabmann, im-

portant research continues on Abelard's linguistic-logical

methods; see J. Jolivet, <u>Arts</u> <u>du</u> <u>langage</u> <u>et</u> <u>théologie</u> <u>chez</u>

<u>Abélard</u> (Paris, 1969).

9. A. Borst argues that the conflict grew out of a series of mis-

understandings ("Abälard und Bernhard," <u>Historsche Zeitschrift</u>,

186 [1958] 496-526). See also A. V. Murray, <u>Abelard</u> <u>and</u> <u>St</u>

<u>Bernard</u> (Manchester, 1967)--to be used with caution.

10. See J. Leclercq, "St Bernard of Clairvaux and the Contemplative

Community," <u>Cistercian</u> <u>Studies</u>, 7 (1972) 97-142, and "S. Bernard

et la théologie monastique du XIIe siècle," <u>S. Bernard Théologien</u>

(ASOC, 9 [1953]) 7-23; P. Deseille, "Théologie de la vie monastique

selon S. Bernard," <u>Théologie</u> <u>de</u> <u>la</u> <u>vie</u> <u>monastique</u> (Paris, 1961)

pp. 503-525; Y. Congar, "L'ecclésiologie de S. Bernard," <u>Saint</u>

<u>Bernard Théologien</u> (ASOC, 9 [1953]) pp. 136-90.

11. See J. Leclercq, "'Ad ipsam sophiam Christum' Le Témoignage monas-

tique," <u>Revue</u> <u>d'ascetique</u> <u>et</u> <u>de</u> <u>mystique</u>, 46 (1970) 161-82, and

"Notes Abélardiennes," <u>Société</u> <u>internationale</u> <u>pour</u> <u>l'étude</u> <u>de</u> <u>la</u>

<u>philosophie</u> <u>médiévale</u>, 8-9 (1966-1967) pp. 59-62; J. Miethke,

"Abaelards Stellung zur Kirchenreform: Eine biographische Studie,"

<u>Francia</u>, I (1972) 158-92. I wish to thank Professor Miethke for

making available to me a copy of his important article.

12. See Congar and Deseille articles (above, n. 10); J. Leclercq,
    "Saint Bernard on the Church," Downside Review, 85 (1967) 274-94;
    T. Extejt, "St Bernard and the Foundations of Church Authority,"
    Resonance, 6 (1971) 94-103.

13. Text in H. Rochais and I. Binont, "La Collection de textes divers
    du ms. Lincoln 201," Sacris erudiri, 15 (1964) 15-219 at pp. 86-88

14. Bernard uses both senses in his sermons on the Song of Songs.

15. SC 27, 46, 62, 68; Op. S. Bern., I, II.

16. SC 46, 76; Div 4, 93.

17. Div 35; Nat 1, 4; Palm 1; Apo 3:5. See J. R. Sommerfeldt, "The
    Social Theory of Bernard of Clairvaux," Studies Presented to
    Jeremiah F. O'Sullivan (Spencer, Massachusetts, 1971) pp. 35-48.

18. This norm is particularly evident when Bernard justifies advance-
    ment within the monastic state, from a less strict rule to a more
    strict one. See Epp 3, 32-34, 65-68, 253, 382, in PL 182. It
    must be admitted, however, that Bernard is sometimes quick to im-
    pute selfish motives to non-Cistercian abbots who desire to recove
    their lost monks Finally, God may elevate monks to the episcopal
    calling (Epp 8, 144).

19. Bernard did not of course want to reduce the church to a voluntary
    society in which the change of state would be based solely on an
    individual's subjective disposition. Bernard operated within the

church's canonico-juridical structure. He refers to papal authority
when forbidding monks to join the crusade (Ep 396 in B. James'
translation of the letters; Chicago 1953). He cites the Rule--a
monastery may receive monks from an unknown monastery--in defending
his receptance of monks (Epp 67, 68 in PL 182). He forbids a
bishop to become a monk unless he has committed a grave crime or
has permission from the pope (Ep 319 in PL 182).

20. See Ep 4 (ed. J. Muckle; Mediaeval Studies, 15 [1953] 82-94);
     Ep 6 (Muckle; Mediaeval Studies, 17 [1955] 253-81); Ep 7 (ed. T.
     McLaughlin; Mediaeval Studies, 18 [1956] 241-92); Epp 9, 12, 13;
     Sermones 30, 33; Hymn to the Paraclete (Cousin, Opera, I). Note
     that letters 4, 6, 7 are listed as 5, 7, 8 in PL 178. There are
     passages in the Historia calamitatum which resemble the idea of
     the monk--and the monk's role in the church--outlined in Sermo
     33; see especially, J. Monfrin (ed.), Historia calamitatum
     (Paris, 1959) pp. 77-79, 92-94 (Abelard describes his students as
     quasi-monks).

21. Sermo 33 (Cousin, I, 583-90); Ethics (ed. D. Luscombe; Oxford,
     1971) pp. 112-26. Abelard's idea of the church, however, is not
     so spiritualist that he rejects the juridical side of the church.
     In Sermo 23 Abelard discusses the powers Christ gave to Peter.

22. Sermo 33:581 and passim; Ep 7 (McLaughlin, 247-48).

23. Important monographs have recently been written on various aspects
    of Abelard's theology. It remains for historians to draw out the
    ecclesiological implications of Abelard's theology of the Atone-
    ment, Redemption, penance and other sacraments, sin, faith. A
    comprehensive synthesis of his theology from the perspective
    of his idea of the church would be a valuable contribution to our
    understanding of Abelard and his time.

24. SC 46, 76; Div 35; Nat 1 and 4. See B. Jacqueline, Papauté et
    épiscopat selon saint Bernard de Clairvaux (Saint-Lô, 1963) pp.
    104-114.

25. Theologia Christiana (ed. E. Buytaert; Opera Theologica, XII;
    Turnholt, 1969) Bks. II, III, IV; Theologia 'Summi Boni' (ed. H.
    Ostlender; BGPTM; ed. M. Grabmann, 35, 2/3, 1939), Bks. I, II;
    Theologia 'Scholarium' (PL 178), II; Dialectica (ed. L. Rijk;
    Assen, 1956) IV, 469-71; Ep 13. See Weingart, Divine Love, pp.
    17-31.

26. Abelard argues that the dialectician is distinguished by his
    wisdom. God imparted a special wisdom--partial understanding
    of the Trinity--to the Jews through the prophets (Theologia
    Christiana, I, 8-53; II, 15 and passim). This section on Old
    Testament prophets is immediately linked to the wisdom given to
    the ancient philosophers. See also Historia calamitatem, 77-79;
    Sermo 33:576.

27. Christian philosophers are the perfection of the pagan philoso-
    phers: this is the theme of Theologia Christiana, II.

28. The Baptist is the model of Christian "wisdom" (Sermo 33:569-
    70, passim). Here Abelard fuses his ideas of the monk and the
    Christian philosopher.

29. Sermo 33:569, 576; Theologia Christiana, II, 49; Ep 6, 260f.
    Abelard associates "philosophers" (those who truly love Christ)
    with monks. In considering the early church a quasi-monastic
    community Abelard was in conformity with the opinion of other
    monastic reformers of his time.

30. Theologia Christiana, II, 5, 8, passim; Sermo 33:569, 573, passim;
    Historia calamitatem, 76-79, 92-94; Ep 7:247, 249, 250, passim;
    Jerome is the model for nuns and monks. See also Problemata
    Heloissae XIV (Cousin, I, 258-64).

31. Theologia Christiana, I, 7, 54, etc. The pagan philosophers were
    part of God's plan of progressive Revelation.

32. Ep 13; Dialectica, IV, 469-71; Theologia Christiana, III, 30;
    Sermo 33:576; Historia calamitatem, 69, 77. See M. M. McLaughlin,
    "Abelard's Conceptions of the Liberal Arts and Philosophy,"
    Actes: IVe Congrès international de philosophie médiévale
    (Paris, Montral, 1969) pp. 523-30; Leclercq, "Ad ipsam Sophiam,"
    (above, n. 11), 165-67.

33. In <u>Theologia Christiana</u>, Bks. I-III, Abelard never states explic-
    itly that the dialectical knowledge of the pre-Christian philoso-
    phers was "natural," while the logic of the Christian philosophers
    was "supernatural." The gift of knowledge to the ancients was
    "divine," but it did not involve Christian grace. Abelard re-
    fuses to distinguish clearly between natural and supernatural
    knowledge because he does not want to make pagan dialectics and
    dialecticians seem any less "divine." See Weingart, <u>Divine Love</u>,
    p. 14.

34. Perhaps it is artificial for the historian to distinguish between
    Abelard's dilemma as a personal crisis and as an intellectual
    problem, since the two were probably never disjoined in his mind.
    Abelard was trying to justify not only his own behavior, but also
    the entire dialectical push in the schools. For Abelard's attempt
    to synthesize the vocations of philosopher, teacher, and monastic
    reformer, see M. M. McLaughlin, "Abelard as Autobiographer: The
    Motives and Meaning of his 'Story of Calamities,'" <u>Speculum</u>, 42
    (1967) 463-88.

35. See P. Delhaye, "L'Organization scolaire au XIIe siècle,"
    <u>Traditio</u>, 5 (1947) 211-68 at pp. 225-28; Bernard, Epp 89, 106,
    108, 385, 397, 412; Abelard, 7:283.

36. Theologia Christiana, I-II; Historia calamitatem, 77; Dialectica,
    IV, 469-71; Sermo 33:567-70, 576-78; Ep 6:275-76; Ep 7:247-48, 285-
    87.

37. Sermo 33:569; Ep 7:270. The "monks" of the Old Testament were
    "sons of the prophets"; Historia calamitatem, 77-79, 92-94; Ep 7:
    247-48, 286; Ep 12 (Cousin, I, 689-90).

38. Theologia Christiana, II, 31-37. The idea that the philosopher
    performed a special intercessory function in society was apparently
    widespread after the twelfth century. The averroist Jean Vate
    warns princes not to interfere with the speculation of philoso-
    phers; princes should summon these naturalist seers for advice
    (BN Lat. 16089, f. 75v).

39. Sermo 33; Historia Calamitatem, 77; Ep 7:247.

40. Abelard wrote this sermon (33) while abbot at St Gildas (1127-1135).
    See Van den Eynde, "Le recueil des sermons de Pierre Abélard,"
    Antonianum, 37 (1962) 17-54 at pp. 48-51. While Abelard in Sermo
    33 talks about the monk's intercessory function in the church,
    this function is secondary to the monk's primary task of living
    near to God; see n. 57 below. Bishops act to save others; monks,
    to save themselves (Sermo 33:584). Yet monks do inspire others
    to virtue just by being. Other Christians will seek out monks
    in the desert. Abelard warns his monks not to seek to do good

outside the monastery. Monks gain "merit" neither by service nor by simply belonging to the monastic state, but rather by personal virtue (in solitude). John the Baptist is a "philosopher" who seeks "wisdom" in the desert (Ep 12:689); see also Ep 13:695-99, and Hymnarius Paraclitensis (ed. G. Dreves; Paris, 1891) pp. 205, 206, 229, 231, 238-43.

41. In his Historia Abelard parallels his life to the persecuted Jesus. See D. Frank, "Abelard as Imitator of Christ," Viator, I (1970) 107-113.

42. Theologia Christiana, II, 5, 8, passim; Sermo 33:569, 573, passim; Historia calamitatem, 76-79, 92-94, 108; Ep 7:247, 249-50. Abelard cites Jerome in support of his contention that his "monastic" students at the Paraclete were living in imitation of the ascetic "philosophers of old"; in the passage Jerome designates Plato as the ideal hermit (p. 93). This quotation from Jerome is the longest single quotation in the Historia. See Miethke, "Abaelards Stellung," pp. 165, 178.

43. Abelard's idea of the religious life is virtually the same in his sermons to his monks, his advice for nuns (with allowances for "feminine weakness"), and his self evaluation in the Historia.

44. Despite his emphasis on solitude in Sermo 33, Abelard does condemn

obedientaries (p. 573; see also Ep 7:250). In the Historia

he distinguishes, in passing, between the "common life of the

apostles" and the "earlier life of solitude of John the Baptist"

(p. 77). Solitude characterized the lives of ancient philosophers

(Theologia Christiana, II, 60, passim) and Old Testament prophets

(Sermo 33:569, passim); but Abelard also alludes to the philoso-

phers' lives as similar to the primitive Christians (Theologia

Christiana, II, 45). Nuns should live in solitude (Ep 7:247, etc.).

Abelard lauds his students at the Paraclete for their solitude

(Historia calamitatem, 94). Abelard stresses poverty, continence,

and solitude--not community.

45. Abbot Abelard castigates monks (Sermo 33:579ff.) and abbots (Ep

7:283-84) who leave their monasteries. He says a monk should

not preach (Ep 7:283); he admits to preaching himself (Historia

calamitatem, 101). While Abelard insists that a monk should not

change states of life, he bewails his own change of state (Historia

calamitatem, 99). He criticizes William of Champeaux for switching

states and for continuing to teach while a monk (Historia calamita-

tem, 65).

46. Abelard saw himself as the descendant of the great philosopher-

prophets and Hebrew prophets discussed in Theologia Christiana,

II, III (see above, nn. 36, 37). He stresses the necessity of
both kinds of prophets in God's economy of salvation. A few vi-
dentes "after the manner of the prophets" (Ep 7:286) have the
gift to understand Scripture; these few are morally bound to
assist others in this understanding. Abelard's ideal monk is
a prophet (see Leclercq, "Ad ipsam...," pp. 166-69). Abelard's
choice image of John the Baptist in Sermo 33 (see also Ep 7:247)
is the onager, the wild ass in Job (39:5-8) which roamed the
"higher" pasture. Abelard uses the image to describe the monk's
liberty from the temporal and the sensual. Perhaps Abelard saw
himself as an onager, a free spirit unbounded by the restraints
of the usual states of life. It may be significant that Abelard
never portrays the Baptist, the alleged founder of monasticism,
as part of a community, except in the broad sense of belonging to
a prophetic tradition.

as, (a) the monk who separates himself from the Christian community
at large, and/or (b) the monk who is distinguished from other monks
--either in the same community or in other communities--by reason
of his exceptional virtue.

47. I have not analyzed the Dialogus inter philosophum Iudaeum et
Christianum from this perspective. Such a task might be relevant
to the present study, especially in light of the recent suggestion

that the Dialogus was written before Sens; E. Buytaert, "Abelard's

Collationes," Antonianum, 44 (1969) 18-39.

48. See Y. Congar, "Les Laïcs et l'ecclésiologie des 'ordines'

chez les théologiens des XIe et XIIe siècles," I Laici nella

Societas Christiana dei secoli XI e XII (Milan, 1965) pp. 83-118;

J. Châtillon, "Une ecclésiologie médiévale: L'idée de l'église

dans la théologie de l'école de St Victor au XIIe siècle,"

Irenikon, 22 (1949) 115-38, 395-411; B. Rosenwein and L. Little,

"Social Meaning in the Monastic and Mendicant Spiritualities,"

Past and Present, 63 (May 1974) 10, n. 21.

49. See G. Paré et al., La Renaissance du XIIe siècle (Paris, Ottawa,

1933) p. 43ff.; J. R. Sommerfeldt, "Bernard of Clairvaux and

Scholasticism," Papers of the Michigan Academy of Arts, Science,

and Letters, 40 (1963) 265-77.

50. See G. Webb and A. Walker (trans.), St Bernard of Clairvaux

[Vita Prima Bernardi] (Westminster, Maryland, 1960), Chaps. 15,

23. The authors forgive Bernard for "overstepping his limits"

in view of Bernard's pure intentions and the good results which

followed from his actions.

51. I base this hypothesis largely on Bernard's letters

dealing with the papal schism and the Abelard controversy. An

analysis of the forthcoming critical edition of the letters will

be needed before any firm conclusions can be drawn regarding
the evolution of Bernard's self-definition.

52. Epp 12, 48, 70, 89, 125, 256, 139, 143, 144, 145, 166, 185-89,
201 (ed. C. Talbot), 230, 236, 241, 291, 306, 327, 330, 333.
See SC 50, 51, 60, 62, 64.

53. Ep 52.

54. Epp 48, 70, 143, 144, 187, 189, 201 (ed. Talbot), 291.

55. Epp 12, 144

56. Ep 250.

57. Monks play a role in determining who is true pope (Ep 126). While
the topic in the present study is Bernard's ecclesiology, I do not
wish to overplay the "service" aspect of his monastic ideal. The
intercessory role of monks was for Bernard secondary to their
"being" as a school of holiness. See Deseille, n. 10 above.

58. Bernard is unclear as to when the prophet can act on his own initia-
tive and when he requires the "summons" from the hierarchy. Frequently Bernard acts on his own authority. Indeed, he exhorts
prelates to fulfill their duties. See Epp 12, 78, 126, 128, 129,
158, 166, 185 (Bernard writes "uninvited"), 187, 188 (after telling
his bishops he is their "child," he instructs them in their respon-
sibilities), 201, 223 (corrects Jocelin after denying the right
to do so), 224, 230 (after directing his "teachers," Bernard

disclaims his right to so teach), 236, 255, 306 (Bernard could resort to "force"), 330, 332, 333, 365. In his letters to Innocent II and his *De consideratione* Bernard takes for granted that he can ascertain proper papal behavior, the nature of heresy, the punishment for heresy, and those who are heretics; he usually assumes that his recipients will act upon his directives. Bernard offers no specific rules for extraordinary intervention in church and secular affairs; he seems to weigh each case separately. More often than not, he refers to some sort of mandate from the church hierarchy.

59. See H. Klewitz, "Das Ende des Reformpapsttums," *Deutsches Archiv für Geschichte des Mittelalters*, 3 (1939) 371-412; F. Schmale, *Studien zum Schisma des Jahres 1130* (Köln, 1961); S. Chodorow, *Christian Political Theory and Church Politics in the Mid-Twelfth Century* (Berkeley, 1972) pp. 24, 47; J. Leclercq, "S. Bernard parmi nous," *Collectanea Cisterciensia*, 36:1 (1974) 3-23 at p. 9, and "Notes Abélardiennes," p. 62; H. White, "The Gregorian Ideal and St Bernard of Clairvaux," *Journal of the History of Ideas*, 21 (1960) 321-48, and *The Conflict of Papal Leadership Ideals from Gregory VII to Bernard of Clairvaux* (Diss. Michigan, 1956). White's thesis has been often challenged; the latest criticism is J. Sommerfeldt, "Charismatic and Gregorian Leadership in the Thought of Bernard

of Clairvaux," Bernard of Clairvaux [Jean Leclercq Festschrift] (Washington, D.C., 1973) pp. 73-90. I support White's contention that Bernard's idea of office was charismatic and anti-Gregorian --in the sense that Bernard opposed curial centralization and the more constitutionalist and judicial notions of the hierarchy at the time (see Leclercq article above, n. 12). While Bernard's cast of mind was far from legalistic, some scholars (for example, B. Jacqueline) have traced some of Bernard's canonist sources. Although White is basically correct he defines "Gregorian" too narrowly, and he fails to recognize the nuances in Bernard's principles for the monks' intervention in ecclesiastical politics.

60. Ep 189.

61. Epp 189, 195, 196.

62. See J. Leclercq, "Les Lettres de Guillaume de St.Thierry à St Bernard," Revue Bénédictine, 79 (1969) 375-91; J. Chatillon, "L'influence de S. Bernard sur la pensée scholastique au XIIe et au XIIIe siècle," S. Bernard Théologien, pp. 268-288 at p. 284f; E. Little, The 'Heresies' of Peter Abelard (Diss. Montréal, 1969). I thank Professor Little for allowing me to read his dissertation.

63. Epp 188, 189, 190, 192, 193, 330, 331, 332.

64. Epp 193, 331, 332.

65. Ep 332.

66. Bernard refers to Abelard's schismatic tendencies (Epp 188, 189, 192, 193, 330, 331, 332, 334. Peacemaking is another test of prophecy. In De conversione Bernard alludes to false mediators (Abelard?) who usurp the name of peacemaker (Op. S. Bern., IV, 109-110, 114-15). Bernard implies that only those peacemakers who have been truly converted have a claim to prophecy. Bernard, a frequent mediator in ecclesiastical and secular politics, saw his interposition in the papal schism as directed towards the restoration of peace and unity in the church (for example, Ep 126).

67. William of St Thierry likewise attacks Abelard for not "living" the life of a theologian. See T. M. Tomasic, "William of Saint-Thierry Against Peter Abelard: A Dispute on the Meaning of Being a Person," *Anaclecta Cisterciensia*, 28 (1972) 3-76.

68. Ep 365. See SC 65 and 66.

69. While Abelard certainly held to a prophetic mission for ascetic monks and nuns, he singled out the dialecticians (especially those who were monks) as most perfectly suited for this prophetic role.

70. Abelard may have considered Bernard hypocritical in accusing him of instability and rootlessness. Long before 1139 Abelard had censured monks who were active in the world.

71. The arguments in favor of Bernard as one of the "new apostles"
     in Abelard's Historia (p. 97) are not convincing. The latest
     dissent from the traditional view is E. Little, "Relations
     between St Bernard and Abelard, prior to 1139," unpublished
     paper given at the Cistercian Studies Conference, Dallas, 1972.
     The older case for pre-1139 conflicts between Abelard and Bernard
     rests largely on this passage in the Historia. In two forth-
     coming articles J. F. Benton questions the authenticity of the
     Historia. I am indebted to Professor Little and Professor
     Benton for kindly showing me advance versions of their articles.

72. While many historians emphasize the legal and jurisdictional
     dimensions of early twelfth-century "Gregorians," Gregory VII
     himself saw the necessity for office holders to manifest excep-
     tional virtue. The Gregorian reform remained multifaceted even
     after Pope Calixtus II. Finally, both Abelard and Bernard dis-
     played no interest in the anti-imperial stance of many curial
     Gregorians.

NUNS IN THE AUDIENCE OF GILBERT OF HOYLAND (d. 1172)

LAWRENCE C. BRACELAND, S.J.

Gilbert continued Bernard's Sermons on the Canticle, according to the Chronicler of Clairvaux, "in Bernard's style and manner."[1] His Sermons generally were published immediately following Bernard's, and thanks to the many manuscripts and to print,[2] wherever Bernard went, Gilbert followed. His Sermons shared Bernard's honor and concealed his own identity in Bernard's shadow. Yet if Gilbert in any way seemed to be another Bernard, in many ways he was other than Bernard.

Mabillon's preface to Gilbert's Sermons on the Canticle suggests that Gilbert was Abbot of a double monastery: "_Duplex_ _videtur_ _fuisse_ _illud_ _monasterium_, _virorum_ _ac_ _virginum_."[3] The suggestion that Swineshead, although originally a Savigniac Monastery, was a double monastery under the Cistercian, Gilbert of Hoyland, still seems to give some historians apoplexy. Mabillon supports his suggestion with two arguments. First, in Aelred's second sermon on Isaiah, (the third in Migne), a holy Father Gilbert is highly praised and a nun in a monastery under him is credited with visions. The same information is communicated in the recent Cistercian Atlas of Van Der Meer.[4] Aelred's tribute however, seems to do honor to Gilbert of Sempringham and the nun he mentions seems to be a Gilbertine at Watton, the only Gilbertine monastery near Rievaulx.[5] Mabillon's second argument, is that two sermons of Gilbert of Hoyland, are addressed to these same nuns. So we are left with two sermons 17 and 18, addressed to nuns, if not to Cistercian nuns.

In the Victoria History of the Counties of England, 1906, the problem recurs: "Some of the sermons which form the commentary (of Gilbert) were obviously addressed to Cistercian nuns; perhaps in some of the Lincolnshire houses."[6] Jean Leclercq, in 1952, translated this note into French in an article which calls attention to "the first redaction of the printed edition" of Gilbert, and John Morson, in 1956, says that "Gilbert of Hoiland was abbot of a monastery at Swineshead, Lincolnshire, which with Savigny had passed to the Cistercians, and superior of an adjoining convent of nuns."[7] Edmund Mikkers, in 1963, indicated that some of Gilbert's Sermons seem to have been intended not for monks but for nuns: 16, 17, 18, and perhaps 40 and 45,6, (which may mean sermon 45, par. 6, or sermons 45 and 46).[8] Jean Vuong-dinh-Lam, says that Gilbert was responsible also for nuns, to whom he addressed a number of sermons: 16, 17, 18, 19.[9] The text of Gilbert seems to indicate clearly enough that six sermons, 16–21, were intended for nuns, but not exclusively; Gilbert may have been using a literary device.

Only one of Gilbert's Sermons shows the plural of address throughout, Sermon 41, which includes his eulogy of Aelred on receiving news of the latter's death.[10] Thirteen sermons show the

singular of address throughout, to which may be added another four
with one or two words, or one or two sentences, easily detachable.[11]
The remaining thirty sermons have singulars and plurals of address.
Sermons addressed to an individual, seem to be meant for the "fidelis
anima" or "humana anima" or for the individual as "sponsa," feminine
or masculine. Many of the plurals of address are meant for "fratres,"
which need not exclude the ladies. If sermons 16-21 prove to have
been addressed to nuns, "anima fidelis" and "fratres" would also be
in Gilbert's thoughts. Look for a moment at Sermon 15, which precedes our series.[11a] After the text, three sentences follow in the
plural, and the rest of the Sermon is in the singular of address.
Change the one plural word "fratres" and you could use this sermon
for nuns; the "bonus qui" and "felix qui" could be left as the generalizations they are; "bonus" closely follows Gilbert, and "felix"
closely anticipates Paul. The text is as appropriate for nuns as
for monks: "Who is she who ascends through the desert, like a column of smoke from spices of myrrh and incense and all the powders
of the perfumer?" Indeed the ladies would be no less interested in
these cosmetics. Appropriate for Everysoul, for Everyself, are Gilbert's reflections about Christ as the forge, the fertile field, the
wind, the cloud and the fire. He explains for all: "In myrrh, you
have the virtue of continence; in incense devotion to prayer, in
the powders of the perfumer, amid a wealth of virtues, the humility

of a contrite heart." Would that every sermon were as easily convertible from monks to nuns!

Sermons 16-21 form a recognizable series. Gilbert discusses
the Canticle, Sg 3:6-11, a natural unit in the Vulgate edition, sung
by the Chorus. Sermon 16 is one of the richest in scriptural references and in theological teaching.[12] Gilbert speaks of Christ as
our Solomon, our Peacemaker, our Border, our Guard. He uses the
second person singular of address throughout, so that "our Solomon,"
for example, means Gilbert's and his reader's Peacemaker. If this
sermon be considered as given to nuns, then par. 5, becomes an apostrophe to any preacher and good advice to nuns in the silent pews:
"If you are a man (vir) of the Gospel, let yours be wholly the language of the Gospel." Gilbert then deftly handles the word of God
as a sword, and Roger Sherman Loomis credits this passage with in-
fluencing the author of Queste del Saint Graal, in the symbolism of
the word as a sword ready at one's side.[13] Gilbert ends par. 6,
with a return to the bride:

> One who is a bride does not seek the task of argument and
> refutation but rather the freedom to embrace. Let others
> take their places around the bed; it is yours to enjoy the
> embraces long desired.

After a comparison of the bride's little bed with other beds in
Scripture, in par. 8, Gilbert has a moving passage on the sick bed

of a Cistercian, spiritually dead, and brought back to life by Christ
in the lap of the widow, the Cistercian Order, that Cistercian theory
and practice may be an example to others: "Even now, good Jesus, if
a son of our mother be dead, I mean a son of this holy community,[14]
this widow with whom so to speak you lodge, do you restore him to
life."[15] In his final paragraph, Gilbert returns to the bride, who
leaves her little bed in search of her Bridegroom: "Hasten, daughter,
hasten consecrated virgin, hasten to enter into his retreat."[16] So
the references to Esther, to the valiant woman, to Mary the Mother
of the Lord, to the widow visited by Elijah, followed by the delicate touchstone to test men of the Gospel by their use of the word
as a sword and the role of women in restoring the spiritually sick
and dead, conclude with the last words addressed to the consecrated
virgin.

To confirm our suspicions about S16, Gilbert begins S17 as follows: "You heard, holy virgins, brides of Christ, you heard in yesterday's sermon, about 'the little bed of your Solomon.'" Further
references within S17 to "Solomon the Peacemaker," and to the "good
tidings," confirm Gilbert's statement, that S16 was given to the
same audience of nuns. After addressing the nuns in the plural, in
the second half of par. 1, he speaks more intimately to each in the
singular: "Listen daughter . . . holy soul; <u>Audi filia</u> . . . <u>sancta</u>
<u>anima</u>." In par. 2, however, we become aware that there are young

ladies present, "<u>adulescentuale</u>," for whom also the Canticle was
written: "let the young girls be fed; sinite <u>adolescentulae</u> <u>pas-</u>
<u>cantur</u>." Then in a passage on the carriage of Solomon, Gilbert
pictures a nun, again singular, as a carriage for the Lord; the
young girls may have had their own views of some portly or pompous
carriage of the Lord!

> Paul wishes Christ to be borne by you, but proudly, not
>
> with ennui, not with complaint, nor with indignation and
>
> a wavering resolution. Paul wants him borne, not dragged.
>
> For to one who drags him, Christ is burdensome; a burden
>
> is chastity, a burden is humiliation, **obedience** is heavy,
>
> poverty is squalid. You are a misshapen porter, if such is
>
> your deportment.[17]

After a transitional plural between par. 2 and 3, Gilbert returns
to the individual, who has been planted like a cedar ("<u>plantatus</u>
<u>es</u>," twice), thinking of Paul as a pillar breathing the good fra-
grance of truth without corruption. In par. 5, he speaks of the
fragrance of virginity, where his singulars again become feminine
and in mid-paragraph **feminine plural**.[18]

> These words seem to belong especially to the Mother of the
>
> Lord. She was really the frankincense of Lebanon and Le-
>
> banon uncut. She filled her dwelling-place with fragrance,
>
> holy virgins, a heavenly dwelling-place, an angelic dwelling-

place, when she filled you with examples of a virginal way

of life and inspired you with the love of perpetual chastity.

He continues in the feminine singular in par. 6, with the exception

of one sentence in the masculine, where either the statement is ge-

neric or where to an audience of nuns he suggests that only men have

lapses:

From a sudden fall, immediately corrected, no odor is no-

ticeable; malodor comes rather from a fault in which one

persists. Ex subito quidem lapsu, sed statim correcto,

nullus est odor aestimandus; magis vero ex eo in quo quis

est sedulus vitio.

Either I have misread the passage, or Gilbert wryly suggests that

only a man persists in vice. He ends par. 6, with a tribute to

Mary:

But Mary the Mother of the Lord does not so much procure

as breathe forth ointments, for she gave birth to Christ

himself, who is anointed with the oil of gladness.[19]

In par. 7, he returns to each of the nuns, feminine singular, as the

participles show: sollicita, suffulta, subnixa, and finally ends in

the plural, par. 8:

To you, Lord, I commend this Lebanon, this noble Lebanon,

this choir of virgins, this assembly of holy women. Guard

it, that it may not be cut down and may remain uncut. Let

integrity be **reserved** for it and the purity of its chastity
for Lebanon means purity. Let purity of intention be preserved that all may be holy in body and spirit. Safeguard
this Lebanon, for you have consecrated its wood as material
for your carriage.[20]

The next four sermons should be considered in pairs, for S18
without the usual concluding prayer runs on into S19 as S20 without the usual concluding prayer runs on into S21. Gilbert begins
S18:

In the wood of Lebanon was expressed for you (vobis)
freedom from corruption in the flesh and the splendor
of purity.

He continues in the feminine singular, with the participles "con-
tenta . . . instructa," and ends the first paragraph:

You, holy virgins, always sing his praises, Seven times,
of course, sing his praise according to the canonical
hours, but at all times sing and chant in your hearts.[21]

The sermon is filled with color: the white wood of Lebanon, the
silver pillars which remind Gilbert of silver trumpets for praise
with no leaden metal of criticism, the gold canopy where the Lord
may rest his head and the purple steps of the ascent of the royal
road of Christ's passion. From the plurals of par. 2, he proceeds
with feminine singulars in par. 3. The one masculine "qui" and

the one plural "accipite" may be taken as generalizations, or as mis-
prints for "<u>quae</u>" and "<u>accipe</u> <u>tu</u>."

Do you also, O virgin, bear the image of your Bridegroom

for this purpose, that you may have a learned tongue, a

gentle tongue, not erroneous, not wandering, not prone to

idle talk, but one which speaks judiciously, proffers a

word of comfort, a tongue which is a pillar and prop,

"for building up of the faith,"[22] whether your own or that

of another.

After the purification of Lebanon, the silver trumpets and pillars
of the word, comes the golden couch of contemplation on the look-
out:

In your turn retrace these stages of progress, if you

(<u>tu</u> <u>quae</u>, feminine) aspire to the grace of contempla-

tion . . . Do you see, Lord Jesus, how many golden

couches you have yere? Never does the head of your

Majesty recline more gladly than on the golden bosom

of virginity. Look upon these virginal breasts,

breasts reserved for you. Upon these frequently you

recline and rest and sleep at midday, in the golden

calm of your splendor. Not here do foxes have their

dens; not here do birds of heaven build their nests. . .[23]

But do you, O bride of Christ, tread the purple steps

with feet snow-white! Noble is the path which your Beloved
trod before you. For how beautiful are the purple steps,
which Christ with sacred tread sealed before you with his
holy feet, snow-white feet to which no dust adhered![24]
How beautiful are the steps which he marked with footprints
of his Blood! Passionately retrace these footsteps; slip
from your feet the shoes of the flesh;[25] holy indeed is
the ascent you prepare for yourself. Climb these steps
barefoot and unshod. This purple was dyed not by shell-
fish but by Christ's Blood.

S18 ends without the usual prayer and leads directly into S19 on
"the center inlaid with gold," charity which drives out fear.

The link between S18 and S19 suggests that both were given to
the same audience of nuns. What is the evidence from the text?
Gilbert begins S19:

1. You wish to hear something new, but I have no news
except that love should renew you. This commandment is
the news I give you;[26] nothing is better known to you,
yet nothing is newer. You are not unskilled and untried
in this craft (_inexercitatae_, feminine). This is your
particular duty. For you have been consecrated especially
for the commerce of love (_consecratae_, feminine). . . .
2. "Strive then for the better gifts,"[27] daughters of

Jerusalem, but especially that you may love . . . Love
boils over, does not contain itself, overflows itself,
rivals immensity, while it knows not how to set a limit
to its affection. It is oil which cannot stop its flow,
until no other containers are available, except that not
even then can it be checked.[28] Love shows a characteristic
of new wine, which by fermenting as it is born and by
wantonness as it ages, bubbles up and overflows, unable to
contain itself; love always seethes and ferments with fresh
affection. In its infirmity, love does not excuse but
accuses itself. Nothing is enough for love, nothing less
than love itself.

After a beautiful passage where my brother Jonathan becomes my
Brother Jesus, Gilbert returns to the plural in the transition from
par. 2 to 3:

"He does not blush to call us brothers."[29] If he does
not blush, why should you not say confidently: "My brother
Jonathan," or if you prefer to use his familiar name: My
brother Jesus, you are lovable and very handsome, "You are
lovable beyond the love of women!" Your desires for Christ,
holy women, burn with a restless and passionate affection,
but he is much more lovable than he is loved by you.[30]

In par. 4 and 5, Gilbert addresses an individual throughout, where two indications of gender occur: in par. 4, speaking of the oil in

neighboring vessels, he says:

> They will be yours surely, if you rejoice in the common
>
> good. Erunt autem, si communi fueris bono laetatus.

and at the end of par. 5, where he comments:

> Do not look back on torments, O virgin (virgo), when such
>
> great charms are set before you in the Bridegroom. Fear
>
> should retire, where so many signs of love catch the eye.
>
> Charity disdains all traffic with fear; charity cannot be
>
> coerced, just as it cannot be constrained.

One is tempted to emend "laetatus" to "laetata" to agree with "virgo."

One other word, in par. 7, does not seem to require such emendation;

it is not a word of address and the masculine is explained by the

generalization:

> But this holds true (that eternal punishment must be feared)
>
> as long as human affairs hang in the balance, as long as
>
> praise is not assured to man (homo) in his own lifetime.
>
> But when after his lifetime, a man is introduced to truth
>
> (introductus), thereafter fear of this kind will cease,
>
> giving place to a third fear, which, though it succeeds the
>
> first two, is never superseded, since it endures for ever
>
> and ever.

Having completed his discussion of the third fear which is reverence, in par. 8, Gilbert returns to the plural:

> This third fear, daughters of Jerusalem, you must capture.
> Beware of the first, which charity sends packing: "He in-
> laid the center with charity." In mentioning the center he
> intends the whole to be understood. Let charity inlay, let
> charity clothe the center of your heart. This is your wed-
> ding dress and this your dowry. If this is demanded of a
> wedding guest, how much more will it be expected of a bride. . .

And Gilbert concludes S19 with the words:

> "Strive then for the better gifts,"[31] daughters of Jeru-
> salem. But especially that you may have charity and have
> it more abundantly,[32] pass wholly into the affection of
> love, for wholly lovable is our Beloved, Jesus Christ,
> who lives and reigns for ever and ever. Amen.

The scriptural texts for Sermons 20-21, are part of a unit in the
Vulgate, sung by the Chorus, and the two sermons are interconnected
in the same way as Sermons 18-19. As in the previous Sermons 16-19,
there is no mention of "<u>fratres</u>" which will recur only in S22, a
word which of course need not exclude the feminine. What can be
learned from the text of Sermons 20-21?

In S20, after citing the text: "Go forth and behold King Solomon in the diadem with which his Mother crowned him,"[41] Gilbert
begins:

You have heard whither the daughters of Sion have been
invited, but you have not yet heard whence they are
bidden go forth.

Admitting his disagreement with the opinion of some learned and eloquent man he has heard, Gilbert explains:[34]

To me however, the daughters to whom these words of ex-
hortation are addressed, seem to be too well placed.
Where is that, you ask (quaeris). Upon the golden couch,
the subject of yesterday's sermon.

Now yesterday's sermon the nuns certainly heard. Were they deprived
of today's sermon?

The argument is complex. After the plural of address in the
first sentence, Gilbert addresses one individual throughout the
first two paragraphs. The two examples of the masculine, "Happy the
man who in descending, is welcomed on this level and who in ascend-
ing, begins on this level; Felix qui hoc gradu cum descendit, excipi-
tur; et cum ascendit, incipit;" and "Happy the man who has shed
tears enough in the little bed of his heart, who has lamented enough;
Felix qui satis lavit lectulum cordis, qui sufficienter ploravit;"
both seem explicable as generalizations: "Happy the one who. . ."

In par. 3, after repeating the text and making a generalization
in the masculine plural, Gilbert seems to be addressing nuns directly and cloistered men indirectly:

3. "Go forth, daughters of Sion, and behold King Solomon."
They are indeed held worthy of this joyful vision, who have
cloistered themselves under a penitential rule and confined
themselves by the observance of discipline, whose soul refuses to be consoled. (Illi ... digni ... qui ... quorum ...).
Would you learn (Vis nosse) how good seclusion is? "A garden enclosed, a fountain sealed."[35] "Arise, hasten, my love
and come."[36] Do you see now (Vides jam) how he invites and
calls his love, because she knows how to cloister herself?
But if you have been daughters cloistered, refuse to come
forth until Christ invites you; Quod si conclusae estis,
nolite egredi, donec Christus vos invitet. Dinah came forth,
not escorted; ...

Yes, the "daughters enclosed" refer directly to nuns and indirectly
to monks who are prefigured in the text, and the example of Dinah
is followed by the examples of Lazarus, Noe and Abraham. Gilbert
continues:

You also, daughters of Sion, come forth, invited (invitatae)
to the grace of a happier vision.

Gilbert continues with a generalization in the masculine singular:

Imprisoned and woefully imprisoned is he who neither endeavors
nor deserves to come forth to this blessed vision. Imprisonment is the lot of a serf; coming forth is the lot of the free.

<u>Conclusus</u> <u>est</u>, <u>et</u> <u>conclusus</u> <u>misere</u>, <u>qui</u> <u>beatam</u> <u>ad</u> <u>hanc</u>
<u>visionem</u> <u>egredi</u> <u>nec</u> <u>nititur</u> <u>nec</u> <u>meretur</u>. <u>Servilis</u> <u>con</u>-
<u>clusio</u>, <u>egressio</u> <u>libera</u>.

The next three paragraphs do not seem to present a problem in
verbs of address: <u>vis</u> ... <u>vultis</u> ... <u>videtis</u> ... <u>definies</u>, in par.
4; <u>nolite</u> ... <u>vultis</u>, in par. 5; an apostrophe to the Synagogue in
par. 6, <u>videte</u> ... <u>vultis</u> <u>vos</u>, <u>Sion</u> <u>et</u> <u>Synagogae</u> <u>filiae</u> ... <u>videte</u>
... <u>videte</u> ... <u>videte</u> ... <u>videte</u>. In par 7, "<u>Ipsi</u> <u>potius</u> <u>videre</u> <u>de</u>-
<u>lectemur</u>," the masculine does not present a difficulty, for "<u>Ipsi</u>"
includes Gilbert. Gilbert quotes Paul and Christ (through Isaiah)
to show that the hosts of believers are the ornament, or rather the
crown, of Christ in the Church. He proceeds in the masculine to include all the hosts of believers but not to exclude the nuns, apparently in his audience.

I see that your interest is at last aroused; you are already
referring to yourselves the interpretation of this word. In
the right to a crown, you already see your own prerogative,
because you are drawn by the profession of a purer life,
schooled in its practice, unflagging in enthusiasm for it and
exultant in its peace; <u>qui</u> <u>purioris</u> <u>estis</u> <u>vitae</u> <u>et</u> <u>profes</u>-
<u>sione</u> <u>astricti</u>, <u>et</u> <u>exercitatio</u> <u>instructi</u>, <u>et</u> <u>indefessi</u> <u>studio</u>,
<u>et</u> <u>otio</u> <u>festivi</u>. Rightly are they considered entitled to the
diadem, who are no longer called to arms but celebrate a

triumph, whose joust is no longer against flesh and blood,
who no longer eye the head of a serpent but adorn the head
of Christ (quos ... quibus ... qui).[37] You are Christ's
crown and joy and therefore, as you have begun, so stand
firm, most dearly beloved (charissimi), "so stand firm
in the Lord," or rather so encircle the Lord.[38] ... "Consider your own calling;"[39] consider to what service you have
been elevated (assumpti).

Gilbert ends par. 7, with an address in the singular, noli, and
continues in par. 8, with the singular, vis ... habes. Having discussed the shape of the crown, he proceeds to its material. Again
notice the masculine plural: "About its material, why do you ask?
For you know personally that a lofty position scorns fragile and
cheap material; De materia quid quaeritis? Ipsi enim scitis quod
fragilem et obscuram materiam dedignatur locus sublimis. He speaks
of the crown of brethren which surrounded Jesus, the crown of
twelve stars, the twelve apostles, and concludes with a striking
passage on espousals and divinisation.[40]

But one (crown or diadem) is pre-eminent, that with which
he was crowned on his wedding day,[41] on the day on which he
espoused the Church in the person of his disciples. He espoused her in faith, he espoused her by setting in their
hearts an earnest and a pledge and the firstfruits of the

Spirit.[42] An espousal is likewise called a sharing in the
Spirit, when anyone clings to God and there exist not two
"but one spirit."[43] In Paul's words, the Bridegroom also is
a man who left father and mother to cling to his wife, and
they became two in one flesh.[44] O blessed exchange! You
were made with the bride in one flesh, and she was made with
the bridegroom in one spirit. O beatum commercium! facta es
cum sponsa in carne una, et ipsa cum sponso in uno spiritu.
The last sentence has been translated as literally as possible; the
subject of "facta es" seems to be the faithful soul in the flesh, for
the next paragraph begins with an address to that soul, "fidelis
anima." Gilbert continues in paragraph 9:

9. How you ought to have rejoiced over such a wedding, faithful soul! How you ought to have rejoiced and kept high holi-
day![45] Dress, dress in the robes of your glory, holy city,[46]
bride of the Lamb; rejoice and be glad, Sion united to Christ.
How will you not rejoice when he himself rejoices?

The last two very moving paragraphs are full of apostrophes to
Christ and to the human soul, "anima humana," masculine and feminine.
The sermon ends without the usual prayer and flows easily into S21.

Gilbert addresses one individual throughout S21, until the last
third of the final paragraph, par. 6: "putas" in par. 2, "vis" and
"adde" in par. 4. The one plural in par. 5, here seems out of place

and perhaps should read "vide tu" in the light of the singulars which
follow in par. 6, "vide ... scis ... vide." The one masculine of address, par. 6: "si istud scis, beatus es si sequaris," can be explained as a generalization, or may be a quotation. Some striking
passages in a striking sermon seem especially appropriate to an audience of nuns. The Angels, daughters of the heavenly Sion, descend
to view the revolution of the Incarnation.

The Lord "will bring about" something new upon earth:
"a woman will encompass a man."[47] Who is this man?
"Behold a man," says Zechariah, "whose name is the Day-
Star."[48] The Day-Star, the splendor of eternal light,
is encompassed in the womb of a woman, yes in a virginal womb, and clothed in flesh. This is that revolution,
which by the very excess of its novelty would have im-
peded belief, if faith had not previously been fostered
by unprecedented signs.

Later Gilbert continues with the ministry of the Angels, daughters
of the heavenly Sion.

But at the end of the ages, his coming forth is from
the womb of the woman who encompassed him. Therefore
the daughters of the heavenly Sion come forth, to mar-
vel at the realization of what they always marvelled
at in anticipation.[49]

Shortly after, Gilbert continues:

> "A woman will encompass a man," as a crown encompasses
> the head. For "the head of the Church is Christ."[50]
> He is radiant indeed in the brilliance of God's glory
> and is the impress of the Father's substance;[51] but
> with the added dye, as it were, and inlaid coloring of
> our nature, while he dims his own light, he increases
> the delight, not only of those, who otherwise could not
> bear his light but also of the Angels, on whom his
> splendor shines in its purity.

Another striking passage occurs before his conclusion:

> The angelic spirits were introduced into the nectar-
> sweet cellar of eternal Majesty, or rather they were
> stored there from the first moment of their creation.
> Now at last at the end of the ages, this cellar of ours
> upon earth ferments with must of a new kind. O plenti-
> ful stores, stores spilling over and bubbling out from
> cask to cask![52] Come forth, daughters of Sion, from
> the cellar of nectar-pure wine to this must, which wis-
> dom has blended in a new mixing bowl.[53]

The Father gives and the Mother crowns the Bridegroom, with a circle,
a crown, a diadem:

> The Father gives and the mother crowns. She herself

crowns, because she believes, because she encompasses,
because she crowns as a mother. The Church, good
Jesus, adorns you with herself, with clothes for your
body, shoes for your feet,[54] and a crown for your
head. Her shoeing is for the journey, her crowning
for journey's end. Here is a surprising metamorphosis,
for after any accumulated dust has been shaken off, shoes
are transformed into a crown!

A final passage illustrates Gilbert's striking thought and concludes
S21.

In effect, either the Church or an individual soul, but
one and the same, is all three: crown and heart and bride;
a crown upon his head, a bride from his side, the heart
in his **breast**; the crown on top, the bride at his right
hand, the heart within him. What here is not arranged to
perfection? What is not in readiness for a wedding feast?
Go hence, "daughters of Sion, and behold," that you may
pass into the affection of his heart, into the grace of the
bride, into the beauty of his diadem. Do not take pride in
an empty name. Be what you are said to be, daughters of
contemplation. Let your practice be a witness to your title.
For the day of your betrothal is a feast day, one worthy to
welcome God, and it reaches from our day to one more festive

still, a wedding day, a day on which no writ of divorce is
given, no separation takes place, a day on which the Bridegroom does not depart on the longest journey, nor even on
the shortest, but on which the Bridegroom Christ Jesus remains evermore at home, for he lives and reigns with God the
Father and the Holy Spirit, for ever and ever. Amen.[55]

Following the suggestion of Edmund Mikkers, one must examine
Sermons 40, 45, and 46. In S40 Gilbert addresses "fratres" in par.
1 and 5; writes "tu . . . qui" (masculine) in par. 1, and "unusquisque" (masculine) in par. 7, and "Tu, fidelis anima," in par. 9.
Though at first blush the printed text favors the masculine (fratres
... tu qui ... unusquisque), the text needs but few changes for an
address to nuns and the matter seems most appropriate. The Sermon
was meant for the Feast of St. Lawrence, August 10, probably 1166,
and is one of the richest. In the final paragraph, "Run, O bride ...
and you, faithful soul," "Curre, sponsa ... et tu, fidelis anima,"
send us back to "the little fig tree" of par. 2-3, which first produced fruits of virginity and after a lapse produced fruits of repentance. The passage shows the delicate heart of Gilbert and the greater
heart of the Bridegroom. Throughout Gilbert speaks in language which
telescopes "the little fig tree" (feminine) and the cloistered soul,
not necessarily feminine. "For my part," says Gilbert, "I know a fig
tree, Novi ego ficulneam, which bore morning fruit from its first

childhood," and he traces the lapse of a soul from virginal graces

through the grace of contrition to the graces of penitence.[56]

We may wonder about the identity of this soul who after a fall returns

to produce fruits of repentance. We do not know whether this little

fig tree was a cloistered man or woman, just a soul restored to life

like Lazarus, but still a contemporary of Aelred's nun of Watton.[57]

   In S45, Gilbert addresses one individual, except for one sen-

tence to "fratres" in both par. 1 and 3. Dom Mikkers may be think-

ing of the last sentences of par. 6, as directed especially to nuns.[58]

   Happy the day on which, divested and relieved of this cloak

   (of office), I shall invite you, daughters of Jerusalem,

   with more open-hearted affection, to share my joy!

However, in par. 3 of the same sermon, Gilbert addressing the brethren,

"fratres," defines the "daughters of Jerusalem" as faithful souls:

   Then the daughters of Jerusalem will begin to commend you to

   your Beloved; then heavenly spirits and spiritual souls,

   sharing your joy will proclaim that you languish with love.

   Tunc te incipient filiae Jerusalem commendare dilecto:

   tunc coelestes spiritus et animae spirituales congratu-

   lantes languorem nuntiabunt amoris.

Again in par. 4, even more clearly the "daughters of Jerusalem" are

"faithful souls."

   And lest anything be wanting to her crown, she (the bride)

is helped by the commendation of the daughters of Jerusalem, that is of faithful souls. Et ne quid desit ad
cumulum, filiarum Jerusalem, fidelium scilicet animarum,
commendatione adjuvatur.

Gilbert's "faithful soul" includes nuns and monks, Everysoul or
Everyself; it would be a simple matter to change "fratres" or even
to leave it unchanged in the wider sense of "brethren," for an address to nuns, as I suspect Gilbert did, though the text is not con-
clusive.

In S46, Gilbert addresses one individual but with plurals in the
last sentence of par. 1, "fratres," the first of par. 2, which has
both "fratribus" and "tu qui," masculine, the third sentence of par.
3, "recogitate," with a masculine singular in par. 4, "Tunc quidem
languet amans, quia spiritus vehemens pertransit in illo," probably
a masculine for a generalization, and finally in the last sentence
of par. 5, "fratres." The conclusions in par. 13 above, are again
applicable here.

Gilbert, then, was using the Canticle as an interesting peda-
gogical tool for teaching Everysoul or Everyself how to progress in
virtue and Christian perfection. The material in the making or already made, he used in addresses to both nuns and monks. Most of
the sermons address one individual. Sermons 16-21 give evidence
that they were addressed to nuns, though with slight variations they

were suitable for monks.   Sermon 15, analyzed in par. 3 above, could
easily be added to this series, if one word, fratres, were changed
or understood in the wider sense of "Brethren."   The sermons indeed
were intended for anima fidelis, Everysoul, including nuns and
monks; it is misleading to ask whether they were intended for monks
or for nuns, when they seem to have been intended for both.

The nuns we meet, with their adolescentulae, seem interested in
a man of the Gospel who can wield the sword of the word deftly and
who can show the Cistercian way to every pilgrim soul, whether that
soul be Cistercian or not.   Gilbert may disappoint the historian,
but not the historian of salvation.   For an appreciation one might
look less to the inestimable Dom David Knowles than to Dr. Little-
dale.   The former dismisses the sermons as "a cold and correct
exercise, lacking entirely the mystical insight and the doctrinal
value of Bernard's Sermons,"[59] but the latter says the sermons of
Gilbert "approach more nearly than any others to the beauty and fervour" of St. Bernard's style.[60]   Perhaps the passages in a new English
translation may give the reader an opportunity for independent judgement.   Gilbert need not be compared with Bernard.   He might thrive
on his own.

St. Paul's College,
University of Manitoba

NOTES

1. Edm. Mikkers, "De Vita et Operibus Gilberti de Hoylandia," Cîteaux 14 (1963) 34, and nn. 3-5; hereafter Mikkers.

2. Mikkers, 269-72.

3. Migne, PL 184, Preface.

4. Ibid., Preface. Mabillon refers to Aelred's Sermon III on Isaiah in PL 195:370D-371D. Frédéric van der Meer, Atlas de l'Ordre Cistercien, (Amsterdam: Elsevier, 1965) p. 298, under Swineshead, adds "OCm, tout près, couvent mentionné par s. Aelred (in c. xiiie s. Isaiae)"; Mabillon's reason with a misprint.

5. Aelred Squire, Aelred of Rievaulx, (London: SPCK, 1969) pp. 139-40. Hereafter, Squires.

6. The Victoria History of the Counties of England, ed. Wm. Page, A History of Lincolnshire, II:145, note 17.

7. Jean Leclercq, "Les Ecrits de Geoffroy d'Auxerre," Revue Bénédictine 62 (1952) p. 290 and n. 4; John Morson, "The English Cistercians and the Bestiary," Bulletin of John Rylands Library 39 (1956) p. 151.

8. Mikkers, 39.

9. Jean Vuong-Dinh-Lam, "Gilbert of Hoyland," Dictionnaire de Spiritualité 6 (1967) 372. Hereafter DSp.

10. F. M. Powicke, in The Life of Aelred of Rievaulx by Walter

Daniel, (London: Nelson, 1950) p. xxxix, comments: "Gilbert of Hoiland and Jocelin of Furness give the salient traits of Ailred's character more clearly than Walter Daniel does." Hereafter, Powicke.

11. SS 1, 3, 5, 8, 9, 10, 11, 12, 13, 14, 15 (except first few sentences of par. 1) 16, 24 (except first word of par. 1) 25 ("fratres" once in par. 4) 26, 29, 48 ("videte" once in par. 1).

11a. Cistercian Fathers Series 14, pp. 178-79.

12. M.-André Fracheboud, "Divinisation: IV. Moyen Age. Auteurs Monastiques du 12e Siècle. 2. Cisterciens," DSp 3 (1957) cc. 1407-8 cites or refers to par. 1, 2, 5, 8, 9, of this S.

13. Tt 1:9. Roger Sherman Loomis, The Grail, from Celtic Myth to Christian Symbol, (New York: Columbia U.P., 1963) p. 189, in showing the influence of G. on the "Queste del Saint Graal," quotes three sentences of S16:5 and continues: "Thus the symbolism of the sword was fixed by St. Paul, and the obligation of the Christian to hang it by his side was proclaimed by Abbot Gilbert." See Jean-de-la-Croix Bouton, Fiches Cisterciennes, Histoire de l'Ordre de Cîteaux, pp. 225-8.

14. "Conventus hujus sancti."

15. Cistercian Fathers Series 20 p. 213 (hereafter CF).

16. CF 20, p. 214.

17. CF 20, p. 219-20.

18. CF 20, p. 222.

19. Ps 44:8; CF 20, p. 224.

20. CF 20, p. 225.

21. Eph 5:19; RB 16:1-3; CF 20, p. 228.

22. Eph 4:29; CF 20, p. 229-30.

23. Lc 9.58 CF 20, p. 332. For the fox in the Bestiary, see T. H. White, The Bestiary, (New York: Putnam, 1956) pp. 53-4; see also John Morson, "The English Cistercians and the Bestiary," Bulletin of John Rylands Library, 39 (1956) pp. 146-170. Hereafter White and Morson.

24. Lk 10:11.

25. Ex 3:5; CF 20, p. 232-33.

26. Jo 13:34; CF 20, p. 237.

27. 1 Co 12:31; CF 20, p. 238.

28. 2 K 4:6; CF 20, p. 239-40.

29. Heb 2:12.

30. 2 S 1:26; CF 20, p. 240.

31. 1 Co 12:31.

32. 2 Co 2:4; CF 20, p. 247.

33. Sg 3:11.

34. Possibly Gilbert refers to Bernard of Clairvaux, whom in S22:1 Gilbert calls "eruditus et eloquens," not unlike the preacher

here who is "disertus et eruditus." Cornelius à Lapide, Com-
mentaria in Scripturam Sacram, (Paris: Vivès, reprint of 1860)
8:27, quotes a written comment of Bernard on the verse Gilbert
is discussing, which would fit Gilbert's description without
being the words Gilbert heard and quoted. Gilbert quotes:
"Male locatae videntur quae jubentur egredi." Bernard wrote:
"Egredimini de sensu carnis ad intellectum mentis, de servitute
carnalis concupiscentiae ad libertatem spiritualis intelligentiae.
Egredimini de terra vestra et de cognatione vestra et de domo
patris vestri . . ." (Ep 2:2; SBOp 4:302).

35. Sg 4:12. See Jean-de-la-Croix Bouton, Histoire de l'Ordre de
Cîteaux, p. 239, who thinks this passage is addressed to nuns.

36. Sg 2:10.

37. Eph 6:12, Nb 21:7.

38. Ph 4:1.

39. 1 Co 1:26. Bouton, pp. 239-40.

40. Fracheboud (see note 12 above), referring to this and other
passages, comments: "les expressions qui decrivent la consom-
mation de l'âme ressemblent absolument à celles de Bernard."

41. Sg: 3:11.

42. 2 Co 1:22; Rm 8:23.

43. 1 Co 6:17.

44. Eph 5:31-32.

45. Reading exclamation marks for question marks.

46. Is 52:1.

47. Jr 31.22; CF 20, p. 264.

48. Zc 6:12.

49. CF 20, p. 265.

50. Eph 5:23.

51. Heb 1:3.

52. Ps 143:13.

53. Pr 9:5; CF 20, pp. 266-67.

54. Eph 6:15; CF 20, pp. 269-70.

55. Bernard frequently refers to the Angels in his SC (5, 7, 19, 27, 30, 31, 39, 41, and so on); see E. Boissard, "La doctrine des anges chez S. Bernard," S. Bernard Théologien, ASOC (1953) pp. 214-263 and "S. Bernard et le Pseudo-Aréopagite," RTAM 26 (1959) 214-263; see also Joseph Durr, "Anges," in DSp 1 (1935) cc. 580-635; and Jean Chatillon, "Cor et cordis affectus," DSp 2 (1953) c. 2294.

56. CF 26, pp. 479-81.

57. Aelred of Rievaulx relates the story, reprinted in Migne, PL 195:789-95. See Powicke, lxxxi-lxxxii, and Squire, pp. 117-8; the latter sets the date at about 1160.

58. CF 26, p. 545.

59. Dom David Knowles, The Monastic Order in England (Cambridge,

1949) p. 295.

60. Cited in <u>Victoria</u> <u>County</u> <u>History</u>, II, p. 145, n. 16; see note 6
    above.

WILLIAM OF SAINT-THIERRY: AN ARCHETYPAL DISTINCTION

BETWEEN "SELF" AND <u>PERSONA</u>

THOMAS MICHAEL TOMASIC

The attention so earnestly paid by medieval thinkers to the
mystery of the Trinity has, as a matter of historical fact, advanced
the question of the person, its structure and role, to a rather prominent position in Western philosophy. Every philosophically-inclined
medieval thinker of note has had his <u>De Trinitate</u> and has struggled
precisely with the paradox that lies between maintaining the Trinitarian distinction of <u>personae</u> while affirming the radical self-identity
of the Divine Essence. It was no mere accident that occasioned William
of Saint-Thierry to entitle his <u>ex professo</u> study of this paradox the
<u>Aenigma fidei</u>. Certainly, the enigma of faith or fidelity centers on
the apparent contradiction involved in positing distinctive relations,
while simultaneously asserting indivisible unity, in God, and the
consequent difficulty inherent in any attempt to form meaningful
statements about God.

But there is another dimension to the enigma which concerns the
mutual compenetration and ultimate unification between Archetype (God)
and image (man) on the deep level of the self as well as on the level
of <u>personae</u>. The provisional model for this compenetration remains
inextricably bound up in William's God-talk, such that what he states

about God essentially details a descriptive ontology of man. At the
very least, God-talk, in that it emerges out of and is formulated by
the human psyche, must be construed as providing a phenomenology
descriptive of the critical possibilities indigenous to the psyche.
To rest there, however, would be to remain only on the level of clinical
psychology precisely when a philosophy is demanded. But where man is
axiomatically understood to be an image, a translational grammar is
provided simultaneously grounding philosophical discourse about God
and a phenomenology of psychic depth structures. William's whole discourse on the interpersonal relations in the Trinity, and the coextensivity of the Trinitarian _Personae_ with Divine Self-Identity, takes
its peculiar shape from the _a priori_ intentional structure of the
image, that is, from the fact that to be an image is always to be
an image _of_.[1] Once the existentially intentional status of the image
is granted, it follows rigorously that the unifying structural character of the image synchronistically unconceals the very structural
identity of the Archetype and that the transformational character
of the image necessarily consists in directionality, reciprocity,
and communicability. The enigma of faith, inasmuch as it distinguishes
between Self-Identity (the Divine Essence) and distinctive, reciprocating _Personae_ "mediating," as it were, that Self, must also describe
a fortiori the critical difference between self and _persona_ on the
part of the image. In effect, William's God-talk has a double

directionality: one may proceed by excavating the depth structures
of the image to provide a descriptive grammar of the Archetype, or one
may begin with an analysis of the Archetype as paradigm to provide an
onto-phenomenological grammar of the image.[2]

If, therefore, it should seem that William spends far too much
time with God-talk, it is because the Trinity provides the constructive model or paradigm for what interpersonal relations can and ought
to be, and because the unity of the Divine Essence or Self-Identity
provides the model for locating the center of one's own self. In
order that such language function properly, what is needed, from
William's viewpoint, is a notion of persona that can be said to be
true both in the case of God and in the case of man' the definition
employed must disclose the proper character of persona qua persona
without philosophical ambiguity. Failing to locate the critical
notitia of the person, applicable to both the Divine and the human,
would effectively destroy the end of asceticism itself, that is, the
realization of interpersonal compenetration of Archetype and image,
and would eventually entrap philosophical discourse, understanding
God-talk as a paradigmatic language, in epistemological agnosticism.

SED CONTRA BOETHIUM

The spiritual psychologists of the twelfth century were not
especially enamoured of Boethius' definition of the person: rationalis
naturae individua substantia, and for good reason.[3] If Boethius is

correct, then talk of "person" in God is philosophically impossible

precisely because his definition can in no way be understood to apply

to the Personae of the Trinity. The Trinitarian Personae are not

three distinct individuals, since there exists no numerical discrete-

ness.

> But my soul's foolish way of picturing things sees
> and regards the Trinity in such a way, that she fondly
> thinks that there is number in the simple Being of the
> Godhead which, itself beyond all number, made all that
> is by number and by measure and by weight. And she
> thinks of the several persons of the Trinity as having
> each his place, and prays to the Father, through the
> Son, and in the Holy Spirit, as though she passed from
> one to the other through the third. And so my mind,
> befogged by the one, is scattered through the three,
> just as if there were three bodies to be differentiated
> or to be made one.[4]

William again rejects association of "person" with "individual" in

the Aenigma fidei:

> And so the notion of number, if it be number, was used
> in application to the very Nature which created every-
> thing--which created weight, measure, and the ordinal .
> sequence by which all that is created is also disposed.
> What is this number? What sort of number is it? It
> does not augment nor diminish, it does not separate nor
> unify, it is neither distinct nor is it muddled. For
> this reason it is wrong to think of the Trinity on the
> same order that one would think of a trinity composed
> of three men....Indeed, when you say: "Father, Son,
> and Holy Spirit," you seem to count three; but, really,
> there is no number here at all.[5]

Thus, critical in formulating a proper notion of persona is the

exclusion of quantitative discreteness denoted by the concept of

individuality.[6] Furthermore, identification of persona with individuality. would place the formal character of the person within the

category of mass or extension, and would consequently entail properties

of inertia, incommunicability, and anonymity. Certainly, by defining

persona as substantia, Boethius identified it as an incommunicable

predicament.[7]

In the same text, Boethius also offered a description of persona

drawn along etymological lines:

> For the word person seems to be borrowed from a differ-
> ent source [than the previous definition], namely from the
> masks [personis] which in comedies and tragedies used to
> signify the different subjects of representation. Now
> persona "mask" is derived from personare, with a circum-
> flex on the penultimate. But if the accent is put on the
> antepenultimate the word will clearly be seen to come from
> sonus "sound," and for this reason, that the hollow mask
> necessarily produces a larger sound. The Greeks, too, call
> these masks   from the fact that they are placed over
> the face and conceal the countenance from the spectator....
> But since, as we have said, it was by the masks they put
> on that actors played the different characters represented
> in a tragedy or comedy--Hecuba or Medea or Simon or Chremes,
> --so also all other men who could be recognized by their
> several characteristics [quorum certa pro sui forma esset
> agnitio] were designated by the Latins with the term persona
> and by the Greeks with   .[8]

A similar description of persona is found in the Aenigma fidei:

cujus pro sui forma, certa sit agnitio, the sure recognition of which

lies in the distinctive appearance (or substitute: role) of oneself.[9]

Syntatic similarity does not establish semantic identity; so, if Willia

means differently than does Boethius, which is positively evidenced

from context, it is quite beside the point to argue that William's

definition of persona may well have its verbal source in Boethius
when, in fact, its use and especially its meaning necessarily has
a non-Boethian source. What is important is that William carefully
avoids reference to Boethius's identification of persona with the
function of a mask, the purpose of which is to conceal; the omission
is clearly not just casual. That the persona-role could be construed as a concealing mask, which would reduce the identity of the
agent to anonymity, is diametrically the opposite of, and repugnant
to, William's use of the term. In effect, William stands against
everything Boethius has made of persona: Boethius had judged that
the persona is an individual, that is, indivisible, that it is a
substance, that is, incommunicable, and in the second definition that
it is a mask, that is, entails anonymity--thereby contaminating the
philosophical, and a fortiori the ascetical, notion of the person.
From the clinico-ascetical, psychological viewpoint taken by William
the person has, as its proper character, the attribute of communicability and reciprocity, and it receives its propria notitia from its distinctive positionality in relation to other personae by the reciprocity
of consciousness (agnitio, or recognition) enabling it to transcend
anonymity and solitude. There one finds William's notion of persona
qua persona.

PERSONA AS RECIPROCATING CONSCIOUSNESS

For William, the persona qua persona is formally constituted by

what may be construed as positional consciousness, that is, positionality of consciousness ad aliud or ad aliquid.[10] This generic char-
acterization of the persona qua persona, wherein the meaning of its
"to be" consists in conscious recognition of, for, and towards
another positional consciousness, establishes the fundamental and
common aspect of persona as an existential intentionality. In such
a theory, the persona is necessarily to be identified with the consciousness role. So much for persona qua persona. The far more important question focusses on how a positional consciousness may be so constituted as to permit distinctive recognition of persona qua Pater,
qua Filius, qua Spiritus Sanctus or, for that matter, of persona qua
Guillelmus, qua Bernardus, or qua Petrus Abelardus. The critical differentiation of one persona from another, designated by a nomen proprium
simply cannot be understood in generic terms of a relation ad aliud; the
differentiation must be indigenous to the very structure of a conscious
attitude-situation as distinct from any other conscious role. If
there is to be any discrimating differentiation of the person qua
Pater, it would have to consist in a distinctly recognizable positionality of consciousness that exhibits the constitutive role of Paternity;
likewise, the person qua Filius would have to consists in a clearly
recognizable positional consciousness exhibiting the constitutive role
of Filiation. Thus, the persona of the Father would consist in and
be disclosed by a consciousness the character of which is to paternally

envision the Son; the Father is the very consciousness-role which can be identified by its distinctive paternal positionality toward another consciousness-role, and the latter can be identified by its distinctive filial positionality toward the first. The key to distinguish one persona from another, once individuality or numerical discreteness has been rejected as a viable factor in the constitution of the person, lies precisely in the clearly recognizable intentionality structure or directionality of reciprocating consciousness-roles. One must, in effect, capture the ownmost internal character structure any given conscious envisioning takes or the peculiarities of its active seeing, and one must account for the peculiar inscape given by and within that envisioning consciousness to whatever appears there, especially where it concerns the unconcealed configuration of another consciousness-role. What matters importantly is the distinctive, peculiar "shape" of a certain "seeing" and a certain "being seen." Here is discovered the basis for distinguishing between persons qua Pater, qua Filius, or even qua Guillelmus. In terms of Father and Son, William states the point succinctly:

> "No one sees the Father but the Son, nor does anyone
> see the Son but the Father." The reason for this is
> that, for the Father to be [Father] consists in
> seeing the Son, and for the Son to be [Son] consists
> in seeing the Father.11

PERSONA as MEDIUM

Given William's concise formulation, the constitutive principle
of the persona clearly lies in reciprocity of consciousness; but a
relation of this sort can only exist where the process of interiorizing
is either a radical possibility, as in the case of the image, or is
an accomplished fact, as in the instance of the Archetype. The intentional and common character of persona-consciousness as relation ad
aliud must, by that very token, mean esse in alio, that is, not a relation at all but a compresence of mutually involuted consciousness-
roles. Consequently, if the persona is to be understood as a positional intentionality, vis-à-vis its distinctive identity-role qua Pater
or qua Filius, then it must also be construed as the very medium in
quo another persona becomes absolutely unconcealed and, by definition,
authentically exists. By this mutual involution of personae, where
they may be understood to be thoroughly coextensive consciousness-
roles, a total reciprocity of consciousness is effected which excludes
the slightest possibility of anonymity, solitude, or untruth.[12] Such
an "I-Thou" situation, whereby the Father is wholly in the Son and the
Son wholly in the Father, marks the moment of liberation from solitude
when the persona ceases to be capable of being mistaken for a mask.
Here persona is anything but a relation; it would seem that William
actually wanted to move away from the language of relation in describing
the persona inasmuch as the category of relation still retains the

notion of exteriority. Rather, the constitutive role and structure
of the persona is to be understood to consist primarily in a reciprocal
and absolutely internalized presence of mutually indwelling conscious-
nessses.

This would effectively characterize the persona or particular
consciousness-role as an interior and convergent locus of I-conscious-
ness and Thou-consciousness. There are indeed passages where William
civily bows to the traditional scheme of the processions of the Trinitarian Persons, which would place primary emphasis on the relatio
character of the person.[13] When William considers the Persona of the
Holy Spirit, however, he clearly construes the Persona-role as the
interiorized mediation of the Person of the Father and the Person of
the Son; the Person of the Holy Spirit is, in truth, collective consciousness. Two passages of William illustrate this point:

> ...The very Unity of God the Father and the Son--Their
> Kiss, Their Embrace, Their Affectivity...this...is the
> Holy Spirit.[14]

> For through him [the Holy Spirit], who is the love of
> the Father and the Son, their Unity, their Joy, their
> Good, their Kiss, their Embrace, and whatever may be
> shared by both in that absolute Unity of unconcealment
> and unconcealment of Unity....[15]

In effect, the Persona Spiritus Sancti details decisively the identification, in William's thought, between persona and a consciousness-
role communitarian in structural identity. The proper ethos-identity

of the Holy Spirit is characterized as the single I-Thou conscious, I-Thou willing situation of Father-Son, of an absolutely mutual alius in alio. The persona, therefore, cannot be understood as "individual over-against individual," or alius ad aliud, but as a collectivity by reason of its identification with intentional consciousness and affectivity. The critical structure of the persona is indigenously intersubjective, and the Persona-role called the Holy Spirit says as much. What all this does is to move the center of concern, on the entire question of the person, from relational paradigms (alius ad aliud) to a situational model (alius in alio), and consequently to shift emphasis from the question of the procession of Personae, which involves metaphors of separation and otherness suggested by categories of relationship, to the question of the meaning of Self-Identity demanded by the model of mutually indwelling Personae-roles, none of Whom can be construed to have any individual status or to subsist on the order of substantial terms of relation. Personae are not, in such theory, selves per se, but only in alio. In a communitarian God-paradigm, as opposed to a unitarian one, the concept of personal fulfillment in God becomes a distinct possibility; but such a paradigm raises the crucial question: if the person is not to be identified with the self, where is the self to be located?

On Locating Self

One will find the concept of the "self" in the unicity of the
Divine Essence. Self and essence are taken to be equivalent, at least
on the level of the archetypal paradigm. In order to anticipate any
possible scholastic object to this identification, it should be noted
that essence does not signify "whatness," quiddity, mode of limitation,
substantiality, nor numerical oneness; as such, it cannot be construed
even as a substrate any more than can persona. Designating the Divine
Essence or Self-Identity as aeternitas, that is, absolute presence to
oneself, William construes self as communitarian centreity, as the
self-same axis of personae manifestations. There is no point whatever,
in William's thought, of trying to solve how from one three can be
derived, or how one can accrue from three. Rather, it is by the sheer
fact that the critical character of the persona is to be in alio that
it becomes possible to speak of an ipsum se or of a "relation" ad se--
and, for that matter, ex se, in se, per se,[16] In the first place,
self must, for William, be seen as the unitive, communitarian
realization of personae who are unconceal in aliis, that is, as the
deep identity absolutely coextensive with mutually indwelling personae-
roles. Persons are not derivatives of the self, nor is the self a
product of persons. The matrix of self-identity is always present as
the structural center of reciprocating consciousness-roles, that is,
as the essence of a communitarian "we," where mutual indwelling of

personae becomes so perfect and complete as to achieve unicity.

> Truth proclaims...that the very essence [self-
> identity] of God is nothing other than three
> perons, and three persons are nothing other than
> the essence [self-identity] of God.[17]

Recalling that the self is not a substance, what then could it

be? It may be suggested that the self, progressing to the second

step, can be nothing other than the absolute unicity of consciousness

and affectivity, which finds its explicit configuration in the *persona-*

role of the Holy Spirit, Who is the one Thought and the single Will

of the Father and the Son. There is, in effect, only one activity

of all three persons; consequently, in all three one should under-

stand a single operation without dissimilarity whatever and conse-

quently, a single center of action.[18] Where no separation or dis-

tinction of activity exists, we have a single communitarian Self-

Identity.

> All degrees of existence excluded...the Trinity is
> undivided in action, unanimous in will....The insep-
> arable identity of essence guarantees the unity of
> *personae*....[19]

Self-Identity lies in the critical notion of *esse in alio*, and, as

such, must be understood to be a single situation coterminous with

absolute coextensivity of consciousness and will. The proper

consciousness-roles which *personae* are would then be construed as

mediations, by reason of absolute coextensivity and absolute involu-

tion, of Self-Identity; by their internalized compresence and co-

eternity, they locate the precise depth center of unified action.

This perfect indwelling of personae is understood to be exactly the
unicity of intentional consciousness coextensive with each persona,
and the unicity of this action (as well as the unicity of will) designates Self-Identity or the Divine Essence. Where personae are
not individuals nor substances, and where the self cannot be correctly
taken as a monad or substance, the self must be construed as the communitarian singleness of consciousness and all other psychologically-
metaphored operations. As mentioned, this unicity of self is revealed
in the Persona of the Holy Spirit.

> That knowledge which the Father and Son have of each other
> is their very unity; and this unity is the Holy Spirit.
> This mutual consciousness is nothing else but the very
> essence in which they are who they are.[20]

There is another illuminating passage from the Aenigma fidei, which
finalizes the analysis of personae and self on the paradigmatic level
of the Archetype.

> Human words fail us in this matter, so we move on
> quickly to the words of the Word himself. When our
> Lord was speaking to the Jews about himself and his
> Father, they asked him: "Where is your Father?" It
> is as if they were asking: you talk of two, you and
> your Father, but we see only you. Where, then, does
> your Father exist? Then the Lord told them: "We, I
> and my Father, are One." It is as though he had
> said: "One" because I am God with my Father, and "We
> are," since I and my Father are two persons.
>
> ...In effect, the Father and the Son is not One....
> They are One. This Self-Unity is not numerical;
> it is a unity of nature, which means an existing
> wholly integrated in Self without partition. In all
> that the Self is or possesses, it has its integrity

wholly--if one can properly use the terms "whole,"
"total," and "integral" where no numerical parts
exist....In the Trinity, Who is God, the three
Persons are really one Self..., i.e., of one Nature
and of the same Essence. In effect, to predicate a
single Essence implies the perfect identity of the
subject. Where, therefore, someone inquires about
the Persons--the Father, the Son, and the Holy Spirit
by asking: what are these three? the best reply...
is to say (and it agrees with the truth) that They
are one Self.[21]

John Carroll University

NOTES

1. On the intentional status of the image see my article: "The Three Theological Virtues as Modes of Intersubjectivity in the Thought of William of Saint-Thierry," Recherches de Théologie ancienne et médiévale 38 (1971) 89-120, and "William of Saint-Thierry Against Peter Abelard: A Dispute on the Meaning of Being a Person," Analecta Cisterciensia 28 (1972) 6-14.

2. John Scotus Eriugena, "For they assert that God and man are paradigms of each other" De divisione naturae et S. Maximi scholia in Gregorium Theologum (Oxonii, 1681), ch. 8 of the scholia.

3. Contra Eutychen, III. The edition of Boethius used is that of H. F. Stewart and E. K. Rand, Boethius: The Theological Tractates (London, 1926).

4. William, Meditation 2.7, from On Contemplating God; Prayer; Meditations (trans. Sr Penelope, CSMV; Spencer, Massachusetts, 1971). Unfortunately, translations in this volume often betray lack of philosophical awareness of Neoplatonic key notions.

5. M.-M. Davy (ed.), Deux Traités sur la Foi: Le Miroir de la Foi; L'Enigme de la Foi (Paris, 1959) pp. 118-20, no. 32. Translation mine.

6. Meditation 2.8.

7. Aenigma fidei; Davy, p. 124, no. 38.

8. Contra Eutychen, III.

9. Ibid., no. 138.

10. Davy, Aenigma fidei, p. 154, no. 71; see also p. 156, no. 75.

11. My translation of Meditation III, from the Latin text of M.-M.
    Davy, Meditativae orationes (Paris, 1934) p. 80: "Nemo autem
    videt Patrem nisi Filius et Filium, nisi Pater; quia hoc est
    esse Patri, quod videre Filium; et hoc est esse Filio, quod
    videre Patrem."

12. Davy, Aenigma, p. 166, no. 86, and p. 152, no. 69.

13. Ibid., p. 160, no. 78.

14. J.-M. Déchanet (ed.), Exposé sur le Cantique des Cantiques (Paris,
    1962) pp. 112-14, no. 30. Translation mine.

15. M.-M. Davy (ed.), Un Traité de la Vie Solitaire: Epistola ad
    fratres de Monte Dei (Paris, 1940) p. 146, no. 108. Translation
    mine.

16. See Davy, Aenigma fidei, p. 140, no. 55; p. 156, no. 74; Disputatio
    adversus Petrum Abaelardum, PL 180:253BD.

17. Aenigma fidei, p. 136, no. 52.

18. Ibid., p. 140, no. 56.

19. Ibid., p. 166, no. 86.

20. Davy, Speculum fidei, p. 80, no. 68. The text continues: "By this
    consciousness, 'no one knows the Father but the Son; and no one

knows the Son but the Father, and he to whom They wish to make Themselves known.'...They do, in fact, reveal Themselves to some, namely, to those They will; They become known to those to whom They freely give the Holy Spirit, Who is Their common will. Those to whom the Father and the Son reveal each other know the Father and the Son just as They know Themselves, for such persons possess within Their mutual consciousness; they also have within themselves the mutual unity, will, or love of the Father and the Son, namely, the Holy Spirit."

21. Davy, _Aenigma fidei_, p. 122, nos. 34 and 35.

THE CORRESPONDENCE OF WILLIAM OF ST THIERRY

M. BASIL PENNINGTON, O.C.S.O.

Any of us who have done work in the field of Cistercian studies
have grateful thoughts of Leopold Janauschek and his successors,
Jean de la Croix Bouton and Eugène Manning, for the excellent and
most useful tool they have put at our disposal: the Bibliographia
Bernardina.[1] We have also gratefully employed Don Anselm Hoste's
Bibliotheca Aelrediana.[2] It is not surprising, then, as plans were
shaped for a publishing venture to commemorate the millenium of the
Benedictines at St. Thierry, one that would center on that monastery's most notable abbot, William of Liége, that the program would
include a similar bibliographical tool for the study of William.[3]
It has been in the course of the preparation of that bibliography
that I have come to interest myself in the correspondence of William
of St. Thierry.

For a number of his contemporaries, such as his closest friend,
Bernard of Clairvaux, and his somewhat alienated confrere in Black,
Peter the Venerable, we have rather substantial collections of letters.[4] This is due in part to the zeal of the authors themselves,
as well as devoted secretaries.[5] In William's case we are not so
fortunate. Undoubtedly during his fourteen years as abbot,[6] not to
speak of the years before and after that service, many epistles went

out bearing his name and seal. And yet there remains to us a very
meager collection indeed, and most of this is found within the
corpus of the Bernardine writings.

THE BERNARDINE CORRESPONDENCE

It has often been asserted that William was, as it were, lost
in the shadow of his great friend. But that must be seen, at least
in part, as a protecting shadow. For much of William's literary
heritage--and it is largely from that that we know him--has come
down to us, thanks to the patronage of St Bernard. Several of his
treatises were ascribed to the Abbot of Clairvaux,[7] and most of what
we know of his correspondence comes from Bernard's letters to William. Let us then look first at William's correspondence with Bernard.

The earliest surviving letter is one that was not included in
Bernard's own collection. Indeed, it is not certain that it was
addressed to our William. But Dom Jean Leclercq, who first published this letter in Revue Bénédictine in 1951[8] and later in volume one
of his Recueil d'études sur saint Bernard et ses écrits,[9] hold that
it is more probably addressed to William of St Thierry.[10] And
Father Stanislaus Cegler seems to take it for granted.[11] Cegler, who
brings to his study of the chronology of William all the sagacity and

pertinacity of a Sherlock Holmes, dates the letter from the first days

of 1121, before William became abbot of St Thierry, and places the

discussion it refers to, during Advent or, more probably, during the

octave of Christmas 1120.[12]   In the letter Bernard goes over an ex-

planation of the Gospel of the Circumcision and Purification which

he recently shared with Frater G. (Guillelmo), to whom he addresses

the letter, and domino episcopo[13] whom both Leclercq and Ceglar con-

jecture to be William of Champeaux.[14]   Bernard does not want William

to write out the explanation before they can confer on it again--or,

if he has already written it out, not to let anyone read it before

Bernard sees it.[15]   We may have here a hint of how the Brevis

commentatio[16] would later originate.[17]   It betrays an eagerness on

the part of William to write down and share what he received in his

treasured conversations with Bernard. Bernard's concern here was

that they were so intent on the moral sense that in some cases they

erroneously departed from the truth of the letter.[18]   It tells us

something of Bernard's use of Scripture in his meditations and teach-

ing, a concern frequently expressed in his writings, most notably

in the retractation he prefixed to his treatise, On the Steps of

Humility and Pride.[19]   The concluding lines express Bernard's re-

spect and care for William, as he expresses his regret that William

slipped away without the escort that had been promised him.[20]

In a note appended to William's incomplete life of Saint Bernard, Abbot Burchard of Balerne indicates that Bernard had written
"many letters" to William.[21] The same statement is found in the <u>Vita</u>
<u>antiqua Willelmi</u> edited by Poncelet in 1908.[22] In the next letter
we have--if it is the next letter--Leclercq dates it vaguely "around
1125"[23] --Bernard himself admits that William has written him many
letters. He actually says "I have not yet once answered your many
letters to me,"[24] so perhaps Leclercq's dating is late and this letter should be placed before even the preceding one and thus dated
1120. Ceglar has placed William's meeting with Bernard in the spring
of this year or perhaps some months earlier.[25] Considering the tremendous impression that Bernard made on William at that first visit,[26]
a spate of letters could well have followed.

Yet this letter, unlike the preceding, is addressed to the "Lord
Abbot William,"[27] and so perhaps Bernard's statement has to be taken
in a more relative sense and this letter dated somewhat later. William probably assumed his office as abbot of Saint Thierry around
Easter 1121,[28] although there has been some conjecture about his
being abbot elsewhere prior to his coming to Saint Thierry.[29]

From Bernard's letter we catch a glimpse of the content of William's latest. He complains, and Bernard quotes him here, "My affection for you is greater than yours is for me."[30] Under a post-

script he avers that Bernard's messengers pass by his gate without

ever stopping in with some token of Bernard's love.[31]   To this pet-

ulant lover Bernard gives a long involved response, concluding:

"I love you as much as I can according to the power which is given

to me."[32] Bernard goes on to say, "that little preface which you ask

to be sent you, I have not got by me at the moment. I have not yet

had it copied, because I did not think it worthwhile."[33] Bruno

Scott James identifies this preface as the letter which in some

editions precedes the Apologia, Bernard's Epistle 84 bis.[34] If this

is so it would justify dating this letter "around 1125," but there

is little more here than conjecture.

The next letter,[35] one of the most crucial letters William re-

ceived from Bernard, can be dated quite accurately. It was written

on September 9, "almost certainly" in 1124. Ceglar admits it "could

have been a year or two earlier, although this is very unlikely."[36]

Bernard had received a letter the day before from William with the

greeting: "To his friend, all that a friend could wish," and he

makes the greeting his own in reply.[37]   As we can see from Bernard's

response, William had written about a certain fugitive Black Monk,

inquired for the nth time about Bernard's health and, most important-

ly, laid before Bernard his desire to resign and join him at Clair-

vaux. Bernard's reply is full of love and pastoral concern--love and concern in regard to the poor fugitive whom he had sent off and

who had taken refuge with William. He was to be scolded and sent on

home, but not without a letter to his abbot on his behalf -- love and

concern in regard to William. If they followed their hearts, William

would be immediately welcomed at Clairvaux. But, says Bernard,

> it is safer for me and more advantageous for you if I advise
> you as I think God wishes. Therefore I say, hold on to what
> you have got, remain where you are, and try to benefit those
> over whom you rule. Do not try to escape the responsibility
> of your office while you are still able to discharge it for the
> benefit of your subjects. Woe to you if you rule them and do
> not benefit them, but far greater woe to you if you refuse to
> benefit them because you shrink the burden of ruling them.[38]

The deep affection that bound these two men was validly based

on diving love and faith. William took Bernard's words to heart and

continued to rule for another eleven years. Thanks to this decision,

we have further correspondence between the two monks, some of which

was to have far-reaching effects.

APOLOGIA

Not long after this exchange of letters, perhaps a few months

or half a year, William wrote one such letter. The content is known

from Bernard's reply, Epistle 84 bis, sometimes placed as a preface

to the Apologia.[39]   William laid a heavy charge upon his friend.

Relations between the Cluniacs--and remember that William was abbot

in a house which, while not directly subject to Cluny, yet followed

Cluniac observances--and the Cistercians were rapidly deteriorating.

For a number of reasons Cluniac venom was centering on William's
friend Bernard. And so William urged him to act to remove this scandal
from God's kingdom, convince those who complain that the Cistercians
are slandering the Order of Cluny that the malicious tale which they
believe and spread abroad is not true and at the same time condemn the
Cluniac excesses in food, clothing, and other areas.[40] It is unfortunate
we do not have this letter, for Bernard says: "I have read and reread
your beautiful letter -- with ever more enjoyment, since it does not
pall with repetition.[41] William was a good writer.

In his reply Bernard gave what was to be in fact the outline of
the _Apologia_: "Perhaps I could say first that the Order [of Cluny]
itself is quite praiseworthy, and that those who censure it should themselves be censured, and then go on to condemn the excesses present in
it."[42] Bernard's responsiveness to William--one might say, his dependence on him--is striking: "Tell me frankly if this is what you want,
or whether you think a different approach is called for. Do not hesis-
tate to tell me what you want, and I will do it."[43] This is all the
more striking, because Bernard was as yet a young abbot and controversy
was not yet his common experience. His previous writings had been
largely the spiritual teachings of a father abbot. He went on to
frankly express his feelings to William: "At the same time you should
be aware that I find this sort of writing rather distasteful. It means
a great loss of devotion and an interruption of prayer...."[44]

In the Bernardine corpus we find another letter, Epistle 452, addressed "to a certain abbot," which is undoubtedly a variant on this particular letter, almost identical to it except for some amplification in the first paragraph.[45]

When Bernard's _Apologia_ was finally published it was addressed to William: "To the Reverend Father William..."[46] and Bernard lets it be known that it is written at William's request.[47] Bernard's Epistle 88 to Oger makes clear the role William also had in editing the text for publication.[48]

There is another letter of Bernard's to an unnamed recipient, Epistle 446,[49] which Ceglar judges was "almost certainly to William."[50] In fact, by means of rather ingenious reasoning he is able to date it as precisely as the first week of Advent 1125.[51] That it is to William he argues from the inscription _Quid-quid sibi_--not unlike that used by Bernard in other letters to William[52] --and the circumstances. Bernard has just recovered from a grave illness and is replying to a friend who had been at his bedside in this crisis--William describes such a circumstance in his _Vita Bernardi_[53] -- and after leaving wrote of his continued concern.[54] Bernard spoke of his gradual recovery and his desire to see his friend.[55]

One thing stands out very clearly in this correspondence: Bernard had a very high regard for William as a guide and editor, especially in the area of theology. We have already noted William's role in the preparation of the Apologia. In 1128 Bernard addressed his theological treatise, On Grace and Free Will to William and in the prologue asked him to evaluate the work and correct it, if need be, or return it to himself for correction.[56] Finally in the famous or infamous Abelard controversy, William played a key role.

However, before this last exchange an event occurred which has left some epistolary traces. By 1135, William felt he had reached the point where he had done all he could be expected to do for the monks of Saint Thierry, and he quietly slipped off to the Cistercian Abbey of Signy. He evidently did this without Bernard's approval, and when Bernard next wrote he spoke of William's new-found leisure. Perhaps William's sense of guilt caused him to read something into Bernard's words, for he wrote back defensively, expressing the fear that their old friendship was not surviving William's somewhat impetuous move. All this we gather from Bernard's reply "To his friend Wi" which was first published by Hüffer in 1886[57] and which is Epistle 506 in the new Leclercq-Rochais edition. The ascription is not absolutely clear, but Ceglar holds the letter was "almost certainly addressed to William" and dates it at the end of 1135 or early 1136.[58] After assuring Wi of the abiding nature of their friendship and just what he meant by his remark about leisure--that holy leisure zealous for good and fruitful for eternity, of which he himself was envious, though unworthy--Bernard speaks of some sermons that had been requested: "The sermons you ask for are not yet ready, but they shall be got ready and you shall have them."[59] Ceglar conjectures these are the first sermons on the Song of Songs,[60] which may well be the case, as William was to be engaged with this book for some years to come. This would tie in with the date of the letter, for Bernard first started his famous series in 1135.[61]

There is another letter, Bernard's Epistle 422 addressed "to a certain Abbot"[62] who Ceglar says "quite probably" is William.[63] The letter must date then from some time before 1135. It tells us little new. Bernard excuses again the brevity and aridity of his letters which displease the recipient. This short note is to send on a candidate who was from the recipient's own area.

THE ABELARD CONTROVERSY

Perhaps the least needs to be said of the correspondence between the two friends concerning the Abelard affair, for it has been widely studied and by masters in the field.[64] Recently Leclercq has published an edition of William's letter,[65] the first extant letter of William to Bernard that we have if we discount the dedication of his treatise On the Sacrament of the Altar, or On the Body and Blood of the Lord,[66] which William addressed to Bernard in 1128. William lays aside the loving labors of his holy leisure to rouse Bernard and Geoffrey of Lèves.[67] He sends along a list of the errors he has found in Abelard's writings,[68]   and goes on to prepare his own response.[69]   In his response

Bernard gives a summary commendation of William's work and calls for

a meeting as soon as possible, but after Easter, to discuss the whole

affair, for, says Bernard, "I am not in the habit of trusting much in

my judgment, especially in such grave matters," and "I know little or

nothing at all of these things."[70]   Ceglar dates both letters in Lent

of 1140, depending on a well worked out and precise chronology of the

whole course of events leading up to the Council of Sens.[71]

AN ABELARDIAN DISCIPLE

Perhaps encouraged by the effective role he was able to play

through Bernard--there are those who think that Bernard depended wholly

on William for his knowledge of Abelard's theological errors--not long

after, William again addressed a letter to Bernard, a call to action,

this time in the face of the errors of William of Conches. It was

probably in 1141 that William wrote this long letter which was also

recently edited by Jean Leclercq.[72]   William of Conches was a disciple

of Abelard, coming from the school of Chartres.[73]   He published a

Philosophia[74]   which, as William put it, revived and aggravated Abelard's

theories on the Trinity and on the Holy Spirit as the world-soul.[75]

William's letter displays a certain antagonism. Although there was

no personal acquaintance between them, so far as we know, a certain

flippancy in the way William of Conches spoke of God rubbed our William

the wrong way. Yet his refutation remains a well reasoned thing and it
exemplifies William's own attitude toward the writings of the Fathers
and his views of the relation between the intellect and faith. We have
no record of action taken by St Bernard, but William of Conches soon
retired from Chartres to take up a post at the Norman court. In his
later works he exercised greater care and sought a formal cause for
the cosmos in some created force called "nature."[76]

RUPERT OF DEUTZ

Besides these exchanges with Bernard, we have only two other samples
of William's correspondence. Possibly around 1126,[77] though there is
no sure way of dating the letter, he wrote to a Black monk named Rupert,
the abbot of Deutz.[78] This is a lengthy letter[79] involved in a careful theological critique of Rupert's treatise De Officiis.[80] In main
it seeks to show the error of Rupert's contention that the Body of
Christ present in the Eucharist lacked "animal life." But what stands
out in the letter is its warmth and affection, the truth of its charity -
and the charity of its truth. Rupert, his frater in Christo charissimo,
could not question William's attestation that he in no way doubted the
integrity of his faith but wrote only out of loving solicitude for him.

This letter to Rupert has always been closely associated with
William's treatise On the Body and Blood of the Lord,[81] which, as we
have noted above, was addressed to Bernard. In his brief prologue,[82]

William returns Bernard's confidence in him as an editor, calling

upon Bernard to now correct his work.   The reason he gives is signi-

ficant: "so it can be both our work" -- et meum opus et vestrum sit.[83]

But, he notes, the ideas and even the very words he uses are, by pre-
                                        84
ference, those of the Fathers.

THE GOLDEN EPISTLE

The final letter we have to consider, the last extant from

William's pen, has, rightly indeed, been dubbed by Mabillon The Golden
          85
Epistle.   The treatise, which sums up the whole of William's spirit-

uality, is well known.   It is more the prefatory letter addressed to

Prior Haymon and an unknown H. that interests us here.   It is found in
                                        86
two forms, both probably authentic,   the fruit of an evolution, as is
                    87
the treatise itself.   The letter is especially precious for what it

tells us of its author.   First of all, it contains an authentic list

of his writings, some of which, including even the accompanying treatise,
                                        88
were long accredited to others.   Again, it exemplifies William's

monastic ideals, his pastoral and paternal solicitude, his special love

and concern for the young.   And finally, it betrays a certain humble

sensitivity: "I prefer that if my writings be found of no use they

should be delivered to the avenging flames by my friends, acting not

as judges but as counselors, rather than suffer the malicious assaults
                    89
of detractors."

A SPURIOUS LETTER

Before concluding we might note a curious case of "even Homer nods" twice. In his classic work on William, Déchanet speaks of a spurious letter of William to Bernard cited in Manrique's Annales Cistercienses.[90] However, when we consult the cited text we find that Manrique is speaking of a letter not from William to Bernard but from Bernard to William.[91] However, when we consult Manrique's citation we find the text, indeed, but that the letter is from Bernard to Abbot Geoffrey of St Medard.[92] So it is not a spurious letter; there is just a little confusion as to who is writing to whom.

CONCLUSION

Our study of the correspondence of William of St Thierry has not unearthed anything really new; it has made no startling discoveries. In fact, we have relatively little. Bringing it all together in the context of his life may be of some service. It fills in a little more some of the lines and shadows of a very attractive personality. Certainly it portrays a warmth and integralness in the humanity of this twelfth-century monk and his closest friend that belies some of the harshness that stereotypes have projected. If these two monks are typical of the kind of spiritual fathers who formed the Cistercians of the mid-twelfth century--and we have every reason to believe they are--we can readily understand why it was indeed a golden age.

As we see the interplay of these two great personalities in this
fragmentary correspondence, we are fascinated; we would like to see
much more. Many questions come to our minds. Who was indeed the
master of whom--or has love so made them equal that such a question is
without meaning? Can we hope to find yet other letters? I doubt it.
But I do not think we have yet begun to mine fully the richness of
these few we have. May their publication in the new Latin editions
and in English translation facilitate such a rewarding undertaking!

St. Joseph's Abbey
Spencer, Massachusetts

NOTES

1. L. Janauschek, <u>Bibliographia</u> <u>Bernardina</u> (<u>Xenia</u> <u>Bernardina</u>, pars quarta; Wien, 1891, reprint Hildesheim, Olms, 1959); Jean-de-la-Croix Bouton, <u>Bibliographie</u> <u>Bernardini</u>, 1891-1957 (<u>Commission</u> d'Histoire <u>de</u> l'Ordre <u>de</u> Cîteaux, 5; Paris, 1958); E. Manning, <u>Bibliographie</u> <u>Bernardini</u> (<u>1957-1970</u>) (<u>Documentation</u> <u>Cistercienne</u> 6; Rochefort, 1972).

2. Anselm Hoste, <u>Bibliotheca</u> <u>Aelrediana</u> (<u>Instrumenta</u> <u>Patristica</u> II; The Hague, 1962).

3. See M. B. Pennington, "St. Thierry: The Commemoration of a Benedictine Millennium," Cîteaux 23 (1972) 118-22.

4. <u>Op</u>. <u>S</u>. <u>Bern</u>. 7-8. Peter the Venerable, <u>Opera</u> <u>omnia</u>; PL 189:61-486; <u>The</u> <u>Letters</u> <u>of</u> <u>Peter</u> <u>the</u> <u>Venerable</u> (ed. G. Constable; Cambridge, 2 vols., 1967).

5. See J. Leclercq, "Lettres de s. Bernard: histoire ou littera-ture?" <u>Studi</u> <u>Medievali</u> 12 (1971) 1-74; "Recherches sur la col-lection des épîtres de saint Bernard," <u>Cahiers</u> <u>de</u> <u>civilisation</u> <u>médiévale</u> 14 (1971) 205-217.

6. According to the catalog of abbots of St. Thierry as cited by Mabillon, PL 182:207, note 255. See S. Ceglar, <u>William</u> <u>of</u> <u>Saint</u> <u>Thierry</u>: <u>The</u> <u>Chronology</u> <u>of</u> <u>his</u> <u>Life</u> <u>with</u> <u>a</u> <u>Study</u> <u>of</u> <u>his</u> <u>Treatise</u> On the Nature of Love, <u>his</u> <u>Authorship</u> <u>of</u> <u>the</u> Brevis Commentatio, <u>the</u> In Locu, <u>and</u> <u>the</u> Reply to Cardinal Matthew

(Ann Arbor, 1971) ch. IV: The Beginning and the End of William's
Tenure as Abbot of Saint Thierry, pp. 131-58.

7. William's treatises, On Contemplating God, On the Nature and
Dignity of Love and the Golden Epistle are to be found in the
fifth tome of Mabillon's edition of S. Bernardi opera omnia
(PL 184:307-408) because they had been ascribed to Bernard.

8. J. Leclercq, "Saint Bernard et ses Secretaires," Revue Bénédictine 61 (1951) 208-229.

9. J. Leclercq, Recueil d'études sur saint Bernard et ses écrits
(Roma, 1962) I, 10-11.

10. Ibid., p. 9.

11. Ceglar, p. 156.

12. Ibid.

13. "Fratri G. frater B. de Claraualle dictus abbas, salutem. Ex-
planationem illam quam nuper una cum domino episcopo tecumque
conferendo super historiam evangelicam texuimus...." Leclercq,
Recueil 1:10-11.

14. Ibid., p. 10, n. 1; Ceglar, p. 156. Bernard had frequent contacts during the first years of his abbatiate with William of
Champeaux, the bishop of Châlons. The bishop died on January
21, 1121. This fact is used in proposing a date for the letter.

15. "I do not want you to write out that explanation until you
first confer with me again about it. But if perchance you have

already written it out, do not give it to anyone to read before me." Leclercq, Recueil 1:11.

16. Brevis commentatio in Cantici canticorum priora duo capita; PL 184:407-436.

17. See Mabillon, PL 185:259; Leclercq, Etudes sur saint Bernard, ASOC 9 (1953) 106-107, 216; Ceglar, ch. IX: William's Part in the Brevis Commentatio, pp. 350-79.

18. "...Deprehendi nos dum moralibus adinueniendis sensibus nimis intenti essemus, nonnullis in locis a veritate litterae per errorem exorbitassi." Leclercq, Recueil 1:11.

19. Op. S. Bern. 3:15; trans. Ambrose Conway, Cistercian Fathers Series (Hereafter referred to as CF) 13:5.

20. "De caetera noueris multum nos contristatos quod ita a nobis absque conductu qui nobis promissus fuerat discessistis...." Leclercq, Recueil 1:11.

21. "...Plures epistolas idem sanctus [Bernard] scripsit ad illum [William]." PL 185:266.

22. "Vita Willelmi. Vie ancienne de Guillaume de Saint-Thierry," (ed. A. Poncelet; Mélanges Godefroid Kurth; Liége, 2 vols., 1908) 1:90. Trans. David N. Bell, "The Vita Antigua of William of St Thierry" Cistercian Studies XI (1976) 246-255.

23. Op. S. Bern. 7:30, n. 1.

24. Ep. 85:2, ibid., p. 221.

25. Ceglar, ch. II: William's First Meeting with St. Bernard, pp. 28-54.

26. "It was about this time that I [William] myself began to be a frequent visitor to him [Bernard] and his monastery....Going into the hovel which had become a palace by his presence in it, and thinking what a wonderful person dwelt in such a despicable place, I was filled with such awe of the hut itself that I felt as if I were approaching the very altar of God. And the sweetness of his character so attracted me to him and filled me with desire to share his life amid such poverty and simplicity, that if the chance had then been given to me I should have asked nothing more than to be allowed to remain with him always, looking after him and ministering to his needs." S. Bernardi vita prima I, vii, 33; PL 185:246: trans. G. Webb and A. Walker, St. Bernard of Clairvaux (Westminster, Maryland, 1960) p. 56.

27. "Domno abbati Guillelmo, frater Bernardus, charitatem de corde puro, et conscientia bona, et fide no ficta." PL 182:206. Leclercq omits this salutation in his edition; Op. S. Bern. 7:220.

28. Ceglar, p. 135.

29. See Gallia christiana 9:187; Lecuy, "Guillaume de St. Thierry," in Michaud, Biographie Universelle ancienne et moderne (Paris, 45 vols.) 18:170; A. Adam. Guillaume de Saint-Thierry, sa vie et ses oeuvres (Bourge, 1923) p. 34.

30. Ep 85:1; Op. S. Bern. 7:221; trans. B. S. James, The Letters of Saint Bernard of Clairvaux (Chicago, 1953) [hereafter referred

to as Letters] Letter 87, p. 125.

31. Ep 85; Op. S. Bern. 7:221; Letters, p. 126.

32. Ep 85:4; Op. S. Bern. 7:222; Letters, p. 127.

33. Ibid.

34. Op. S. Bern. 7:219; Letters, p. 127, n. 1; PL 182:895-98.

35. Ep 86; Op. S. Bern. 7:223-24.

36. Ceglar, p. 114.

37. "To his friend all that a friend could wish, from Brother Bernard of Clairvaux. It was you who gave me this formula of greeting when you worte, 'To his friend all that a friend could wish.'" Op. S. Bern. 7:223; Letters, Letter 88, p. 127.

38. Op. S. Bern. 7:224; Letters, p. 128.

39. Op. S. Bern. 7:219; trans. CF I:5-6; see Mabillon, PL 182: 895-98.

40. This is evident from the text of St. Bernard's letter:

I am quite prepared to undertake the task you have enjoined on me for the removal of scandal from God's kingdom,... and I understand that you want me to convince those who complain that we are slandering the Order of Cluny, that the malicious tale which they believe and spread abroad is not true. However, it seems contradictory to me, having done just this, to turn around and condemn their excesses in food and clothing and the other areas you mention." Ibid.

41. Ibid.

42. Ibid.

43. Ibid.

44. Ibid.

45. PL 182:643.

46. Op. S. Bern. 3:81; trans. M. Casey, CF 1:33.

47. "Prior to this, if you had asked me to do some writing, I would not have agreed, or if I had agreed, it would have been reluctantly....Now that the situation has become really serious, my former diffidence has vanished. Spurred on by the need for action, mine is the painful position of having no alternative but to comply...." Ibid.

48. "Do not hesitate, I beg you, to find an opportunity of going to see him [William], and do not on any account allow anyone to see or copy the aforesaid booklet [The Apologia] until you have been through it with him, discussed it with him, and have both made such corrections as may be necessary, so that every word may be supported by two witnesses. I leave to the judgment of both whether it shall be published, or shown to only a few, or to no one at all. I also leave to you both to decide whether the preface you have put together out of my other letters will stand or whether it would not be better to compose another." Ep 88; Op. S. Bern. 7:234; Letters, Letter 91, pp. 136-37.

49. PL 182:639-40; <u>Letters</u>, Letter 464, p. 519.

50. Ceglar, p. 32.

51. <u>Ibid</u>., p. 118.

52. Ep 75: "Quidquid vel tibi vel amicis tuis recte vis, qui dedit velle, det et perficere" (<u>Op</u>. <u>S</u>. <u>Bern</u>. 7:223; <u>Letters</u>, Letter 87, p. 127) which spells out the full meaning of the greeting; Ep 422 (PL 182:629-30; <u>Letters</u>, Letter 453, p. 515). However, the argument is not too strong for Ep 422 is to an anonymous abbot who Ceglar holds, is "quite probably" William (p. 32) for the same reason, and at the same time he grants the Ep 450 (PL 182: 642; <u>Letters</u>, Letter 460, p. 520) which has a similar salutation (<u>idem</u> <u>quod</u> <u>sibi</u>) is not addressed to William.

53. PL 185:258-59; Webb and Walker, <u>St</u>. <u>Bernard</u> <u>of</u> <u>Clairvaux</u>, pp. 74-75.

54. See Ceglar, pp. 105-106.

55. "On the First Sunday of Advent I was able for the first time to approach the altar of God for the reception of the Sacrament without anyone helping me; and I have written this letter with my own hand. From these two signs you will be able to gather how much better I am, by the goodness of God, in both body and mind. I would be glad to see you, if it could be arranged conveniently and without any bother." Ep 466; PL 182:640; <u>Letters</u>, p. 519.

56. "You please read it first....Then, should you judge it useful
    to be read publicly, if you notice something obscurely stated
    which, in an obscure subject, might yet have been more clearly
    expressed, without departing from due brevity, do not hesitate
    either to amend it yourself or else to return it to me for
    emendation...." Op. S. Bern. 3:165; trans. Daniel O'Donovan,
    CF 19:3.

57. G. Hüffer, Vorstudien ze einer Darstellung des Lebens und Wir-
    kens des heiligen Bernhard von Clairvaux (Münster, 1886) p.
    213; trans. Letters, Letter 89, pp. 128–29.

58. Ceglar, pp. 148–51.

59. Letters, p. 129.

60. Ceglar, p. 150.

61. See Leclercq, Saint Bernard Mystique (Paris, 1948) Appendix II,
    La date des premier sermon sur les Cantiques des cantiques, pp.
    480–83.

62. PL 182:629–30; Letters, Letter 453, p. 515.

63. Ceglar, p. 32.

64. J. Leclercq, "Les formes successives de la lettre-traité de
    saint Bernard contra Abelard," Revue Bénédictine 78 (1968) 97–
    105; "Les lettres de Guillaume de saint-Thierry a saint Bernard,"
    Revue Bénédictine 79 (1969) 375–91; Edward Little, The "Heresies"
    of Peter Abelard (Diss., Montréal, 1969); "Bernard and Abelard

at the Council of Sens, 1140" in <u>Bernard</u> <u>of</u> <u>Clairvaux</u>: <u>Studies</u> <u>presented</u> <u>to</u> <u>Dom</u> <u>John</u> <u>Leclercq</u> (CS 23; Washington, 1972) pp. 55-71; "The Sources of the <u>Capitula</u> of Sens (1140)" in <u>Studies</u> <u>in</u> <u>Medieval</u> <u>Cistercian</u> <u>History</u> <u>II</u> (CS 24; Kalamazoo, 1975) 96-100.

65. Cited in the previous note.

66. PL 180:343-46.

67. "There is also <u>Against</u> <u>Peter</u> <u>Abelard</u>, and it was this which prevented me from completing the preceding work (<u>Exposition</u> <u>on</u> <u>the</u> <u>Song</u> <u>of</u> <u>Songs</u>) for I did not think I was justified in enjoying such delightful leisure within doors while outside he, with naked sword, as they say, was ravaging the confines of our faith." <u>The</u> <u>Golden</u> <u>Epistle</u>, Pref. 10; ed. R. Thomas, <u>Lettre</u> <u>aux</u> <u>frèses</u> <u>du</u> <u>Mont-Dieu</u> (<u>Pain</u> <u>de</u> <u>Cîteaux</u>, 33; Chambarand, 1968) p. 28; trans. T. Berkeley, CF 12:6.

68. Leclercq, "Les Lettres de Guillaume..." pp. 377-78. PL 182:552.

69. <u>Adversus</u> <u>Petrum</u> <u>Abelardum</u>, PL 180:283-332.

70. Ep 327, PL 182:553; <u>Letters</u>, Letter 236, p. 315.

71. Ceglar, pp. 172-87.

72. Leclercq, "Les lettres de Guillaume...," pp. 382-91; there is an earlier edition in PL 180:333-40.

73. See P. Delhays, "William of Conches" in <u>New</u> <u>Catholic</u> <u>Encyclopedia</u> (New York, 14 vols., 1967) 14:923-24.

74. PL 90:1127-78, 172:39-102.

75. Leclercq, "Les lettres de Guillaume...," pp. 382-83; PL 180:333.

76. Delhays, *loc. cit.*

77. J.-M. Déchanet, Oeuvres choisies de Guillaume de Saint-Thierry (Paris, 1944) p. 47; William of St. Thierry: The Man and His Work (CS 10; Spencer, 1972) p. 33, n. 87.

78. Rupert (d. 1129), a monk of Saint Laurence of Liége, where he received his education, became abbot of Deutz (Tuy) in 1120. He was well known for his literary style and knowledge of Scripture, leaving extensive writings (PL 167-170). His principal work, De divinis officiis, which William criticises, was completed in 1111. While he lived he was a figure of continual controversy, challenged by such notables as William of Champeaux and Anselm of Laon, but after his death he received little attention until the Reformation, when his imprecise language on the Eucharist caused him to be accused of teaching "impanation." See P. Séjourné, "Rupert de Deuts," Dictionnaire de théologie catholique (Paris, 15 vols., 1930-1946), 14:169-205; B. S. Smith, "Rupert of Deutz," New Catholic Encyclopedia, 12:723.

79. PL 180:341-44.

80. PL 170:9-332.

81. PL 180:345-66.

82. PL 180:343-46.

83. PL 180:345-46.

84. Ibid.

85. Jean Déchanet, ed., Lettre aux fréres du Mont-Dieu (Lettre d'or), Sources chrétiennes 223 (Paris, 1975).

86. J.-M. Déchanet, "Les manuscrits de la Lettre aux Fréses du Mont-Dieu di Guillaume de Saint-Thierry et le problème de la 'preface' dans Charleville 114," Scriptorium 8 (1954) 236-71, especially 264-68.

87. See J.-M. Déchanet, "Les divers étates des texte de la 'Lettre aux Frères du Mont-Dieu' dans Charleville 114," Scriptorium 11 (1957) 63-86.

88. See note 7 above; also D. Massuet, PL 184:299-308. William's Meditations were also attributed to St. Bernard by various editors and his Commentary on the Song of Songs drawn from St. Ambrose to Anthony de Mouchi (Déchanet, Oeuvres choises, pp. 41-42). See also A. Wilmart, "La série et la date des ouvrages de Guilluame de Saint-Thierry," Revue Mabillon 14 (1924) 157-67; "Les écrits spirituele des deux Guiges, la Lettre aux Frères des Mont-Dieu," Revue d'Ascétique et de Mystique, 5 (1924) 127-58.

89. S Ch 223:140; CF 12:7.

90. CS 10:17, n. 53.

91. A. Manrique, Annales Cisterciences (Lyons, 4 vols., 1642; reprinted Westmead, 1970) 1:130.

92. PL 182:174; Op. S. Bern. 7:162.

THE CISTERCIAN ABBOT IN MEDIEVAL IRELAND

COLUMCILLE S. Ó CONBHUI

In the following paper I shall be considering the Cistercian abbot in medieval Ireland, and it is necessary to state in the beginning that the abbot here depicted is not the ideal abbot whose character is delineated in the Rule of St Benedict, but the very human and often very imperfect abbot revealed to us in the historical and juridical documents of Church and State in Ireland in so far as such documents are available to us. The great drawback of such documents, of course, is that they depict primarily the public life of the abbot and have very little to say, except by inference, of the abbot as ruler of his monastery and father of his community. These documents tell us practically nothing of his work as the wise physician of souls depicted by St Benedict--the master chosen for his wisdom of doctrine, learned in the law of God, whose duty it was to teach and instruct his disciples not merely by word of mouth but more especially by the good example of his own life. The picture we get from contemporary historical and legal documents whether of Church or State is necessarily one-sided, and that fact must be borne in mind when reading this paper.

The surviving documents show clearly that the medieval Irish abbot figured prominently in the public life of his time. This involvement of the abbot in public affairs had already begun before the

close of the twelfth century and was to continue and even to increase
right up to the dissolution of the religious orders in Ireland under
Henry VIII in 1539. The Cistercian reform, as we know, aimed at a
return to the primitive simplicity of the Benedictine Rule, and that
rule lays down in no uncertain terms the kind of man the abbot ought
to be, as well as his position in the monastery. In the second chapter of the Rule of St Benedict it is stated that the abbot is believed to hold the place of Christ in the monastery. Elsewhere (Chapter 63) he is reminded that he is called Lord and Abbot, not because he
has taken it upon himself, but out of reverence and love of Christ.
He is told, therefore, to be mindful of this and show himself worthy
of such an honour. In treating of the election of the abbot St Benedict reminds the brethren that he who is to be appointed should be
chosen for the merit of his life and the wisdom of his doctrine
(Chapter 64). He is to be learned in the law of God that he may
know whence to bring forth new things and old; he must be chaste, sober
and merciful, ever preferring mercy to justice that he himself may
obtain mercy. He is to hate sin and love the brethren, and even in
his corrections he should act with prudence and not go too far lest,
while he strives too eagerly to rub off the rust the vessel be broken.
He is warned to keep his own frailty ever before his eyes and remember
that the bruised reed must not be broken. This does not mean that he
should suffer vices to grow up, but that prudently and with charity he
should cut them off in the way he shall see best for each. In all he

commands, whether concerning spiritual or temporal matters, he is to
be prudent and considerate. In the works he imposes he is to be dis-
creet and moderate so that he may not cause his flock to be overdriven
(Chapter 64). He is to be both a father and a shepherd and should
follow the example of the Good Shepherd who, leaving the ninety-nine
sheep on the mountains, went back to see the one which had gone
astray, on whose weakness he had such compassion that he deigned to
place it on his own sacred shoulders and so carry it back to the
flock (Chapter 27).

St Benedict leaves his disciples in no doubt as to who is the
master in the monastery. The abbot is the master both as a teacher
and a disciplinarian. He is the master who is to teach more by the
example of his life than by word of mouth; but he is also the master
who must be obeyed and who must sometimes show "the dread character
of the master" in reproving, correcting and chastising the negligent,
the undisciplined and the hard of heart. The abbot stood at the head
of the community and his power was supreme, subject only to the Rule
and the law of God. Because of the responsibility which power brings
and the grave temptation to abuse power, especially when it is absolute, the abbot is warned to remember always the name by which he is
called and to make his actions correspond therewith. He is warned
not to lead the brethren by his own example to do what he had told
them was unlawful lest, while preaching to others, he himself should
become a castaway. His power, then, though great, was not to be

abused nor was it to be used in an arbitrary manner. He was to strive
to be loved rather than feared, and should remember that it befitted
him rather to make himself useful to his brethren than to rule over
them. Even in giving orders he was to be considerate, showing dis-
cretion and kindness; and he was so to arrange all things that strong
souls might strive to do more while the weak might not be discouraged.
Finally, he is reminded more than once that he must give an account
to God of all his deeds and judgements and warned that he himself
must observe the rule in all things.

Although the Cistercian reform was based on a return to the
primitive observance of the rule the reformers, drawing on the experience of centuries, deliberately limited the abatial authority, taking
from the abbot much of the power placed in his hands by St Benedict.
The experience of history had shown that such powers could be and,
indeed, had been abused. Moreover, the early Cistercians found that
in order to preserve the spirit it was necessary to make certain
changes in the letter of the rule. Although the abbot was still
supreme in his own house his power was no longer absolute, for he himself was subject not only to the limitations imposed by the rule of
St Benedict but also to the constitutions of the new order as laid
down in the Carta Caritatis as well as to the decrees and definitions
of the General Chapter. He was, besides, subject to an annual visitation of his house by the abbot of the mother house, and although his
term of office was nominally for life he could be and often was

deposed by the General Chapter or the abbot of the mother house if
he abused his powers or failed to rule his house in a satisfactory
manner. Despite all these precautions to curb the absolute power of
the abbot and to make him amenable to regular discipline, and notwithstanding the vigilance of the General Chapter, the abbot developed
in the course of time on lines not envisaged either in the Rule of
St Benedict or in the Carta Caritatis and, influenced perhaps by the
part played by St Bernard in the public life of his time, came
eventually to play an important role in the public affairs of both
Church and State.

In Ireland this development had already begun before the close of
the twelfth century. Within a decade of the foundation of Mellifont,
the first house of the order in Ireland, its abbot, Gilla Críst Ó
Conairche, had become the first of a long line of Irish Cistercian
bishops. He had been created bishop of Lismore in 1150 by Pope
Eugenius III who had been his fellow novice at Clairvaux where both
had been trained by St Bernard. Consecrated by Eugenius himself and
appointed by him permanent legate a latere for all Ireland, he returned to Ireland with Cardinal Paparo with whom he presided over the
great Synod of Kells in 1152. This synod, which seems to have opened
at Kells and concluded at Mellifont,[1] gave the Irish hierarchical
system the form it has substantially retained to the present day.
The part played by the abbot of Mellifont in that synod shows that
already the new order was making itself felt in the public life of

the Irish Church. Before the close of the same century ten Cistercian
bishops had occupied Irish sees, and with the invasion of the country
by the Anglo-Normans we find the Cistercian bishops foremost in supporting the new regime which, incidentally, had the wholehearted
support of the pope. Once again Gilla Críst presided over a national
synod, this time the Synod of Cashel, convened by Henry II of England.
Closely associated with Gilla Crist was Ralph, Cistercian abbot of
Bildewas in England, who was one of the three English representatives
sent by the king to call the bishops of Ireland together and to assist
at their deliberations. He was also the Father Immediate of the Abbey
of the Blessed Mary near Dublin. Thus the English as well as the
Irish Cistercians were represented at this synod which among other
measures forced the Irish Church to abandon its ancient observances
and adopt those of the Church of England while at the same time con-
firming the Anglo-Norman conquest of Ireland and swearing fealty to
the king of England as lord of that land.

Within the decade following the synod Gilla Críst Ó Conairche had
resigned his see and retired to the abbey of Kyrie Eleison in Kerry
where he died in 1186. Another abbot, Finn Mac Gormain, who had been
appointed bishop of Kildare had already died in 1160. In the meantime
five other Cistercians had been appointed to Irish sees between 1150 and
1182[2] while three more sees came into Cistercian hands between 1182 and
1199.[3] Thus, between 1150 and 1199 ten Irish sees were ruled for a
longer or shorter period by Cistercian bishops, namely, Clogher in the

province of Armagh; Ferns, Kildare, Leighlin and Ossory in the province

of Dublin; Clonfert and Elphin in the province of Tuam; and Cashel,

Emly and Lismore in the province of Cashel or Munster. Of the ten

Cistercians thus appointed nine were abbots[4] when chosen to be bishops.

The status of the tenth is not known, but it is very likely that he

too was an abbot. Three of the bishops had been abbots of Mellifont,

two had been abbots of Boyle and one each abbot of Baltinglass, Jer-

point, Monasterevan and Newry. The first Cistercian archbishop of

Cashel, Muirgheas Ua hÉnne, who was made papal legate in 1192, had

later fallen into disgrace and retired to the abbey of Holy Cross

where he died in 1206.[5] It is not improbable, therefore, that he was

originally a monk of that house and may even have been abbot there be-

fore his appointment to the episcopacy. At that period a simple monk

would scarcely have been sufficiently well known to merit appointment

to such an important post in the ecclesiastical hierarchy.

The prominent part played by Cistercians in contemporary ecclesi-

astical affairs is strikingly illustrated by the fact that from at

least 1185 until 1238 four successive archbishops of Cashel were

Cistercian monks,[6] and though the Cistercian succession was temporarily

interrupted by the election of the Dominican friar David mac Cellaigh

Ua Gillapátric in 1238, he was succeeded in 1253 by another great

friend and benefactor of the order, David mac Cearbhaill, who himself

took the Cistercian habit in 1269 and ruled for the last twenty years

of his life as a Cistercian bishop. He it was who brought the

Cistercians from Mellifont to Cashel in 1272 thus becoming the founder of the last daughter house of Mellifont. Of the seven archbishops who ruled Cashel from 1200 to 1300 all but two were Cistercians; and it was largely due to the vigorous efforts of these Cistercian archbishops in bringing to the notice of the Holy See the wrongs inflicted by the Anglo-Norman administration on the Irish Church and people that the pope was moved to issue a scathing denunciation of the iniquitous customs introduced by the Normans with the aim of discriminating against the native Irish. Writing to his legate, the pope commanded him to see that these customs were completely abolished and to compel the English, even by ecclesiastical censure if needs be, to allow the Irish to enjoy equal rights with themselves.[7]

During the whole of the thirteenth century the Irish Cistercians were active in the affairs of the Church and no less than thirty monks of the order ruled over Irish sees between 1200 and 1300. These Cistercian bishops included men of Anglo-Norman as well as of Irish race. Apart from the bishops the abbots themselves were now beginning to take a leading part in public life, and their involvement in public affairs did not stop at the religious sphere. Wedded as it was to the cause of ecclesiastical reform the order was used by the pope to carry out papal policy and thus were abbots brought more and more into prominence in public life. This involvement, though confined at first to ecclesiastical affairs, gradually extended to secular life and led eventually to the involvement of the abbots in the whole feudal system.

By the end of the century the Cistercian abbot had become a feudal
lord and by the middle of the following century had in many cases come
to take his place in the parliaments and councils of the king as a
peer of the realm in Anglo-Norman Ireland. Not all Cistercian abbots
were summoned to parliament, and the grounds on which any of them were
summoned are far from clear. It has been stated that only those prelates who were tenants in chief of the king and held their lands of
him in barony (or part of a barony) were bound to attend the Curia
Regis and were vested with the dignity of parliamentary barons.[8]
Since the Cistercians held their lands not in barony but in frankal-
moign--in free and perpetual alms--they should not strictly have been
bound to attend parliament at all.

Our knowledge of the summoning of Cistercian abbots to parliament
before 1375 is slight. We know, however, that the abbot of Owney did
attend before that year. From 1375 onwards we have evidence that a
number of Cistercians, not exceeding eleven at any time,[9] were so summoned, but it seems certain that no abbot of a purely Irish house was
summoned. It is true that among the abbots summoned from time to
time were those of such Irish foundations as Mellifont, Bective, Baltinglass, Maigue, Jerpoint and possibly Monasterevan, all of which had
been founded by or with the aid of Irish kings and princes, and four
of which had been founded before the coming of the Normans to Ireland;
but it must be noted that when these abbots were first summoned to
parliament the houses named had passed under English control and had

become outposts of English culture in Ireland. We cannot be sure how
many abbots of the order were actually summoned to parliament at one
time or another. We know that the abbot of Owney had been so summoned
before the period 1323-1326 for a record exists of a fine imposed upon
him during that period for failing to attend a parliament to which he
had been summoned earlier.[10] In 1375 writs were issued to the abbots
of Dublin, Dunbrody, Mellifont, Baltinglass, Jerpoint, Tintern, Duiske,
Tracton and Maigue,[11] and we know from a list compiled from earlier
sources by Sir James Ware in the seventeenth century that the abbots
of Monasterevan and Bective were also among those called to parliament
at this time.[12]

Whatever about the honour attaching to the dignity of a baron of
parliament it is quite certain from the available evidence that many
if not indeed most of the abbots on whom the duty of attending parliament devolved considered it a burden rather than a privilege, and many
sought to be excused from attending. It was, of course, an expensive
privilege and often entailed absences from the monastery on the part
of the superior which led to the neglect of his monastic duties. In
1375 the abbot of Jerpoint asked to be excused on the grounds that the
abbot of Baltinglass, his Father-Immediate who himself attended the
parliament, represented his daughter house as well as his own.[13] On
this occasion the abbot's plea was accepted and he was freed in perpetuity from the obligation of attending parliament. Nevertheless,
we find the abbot of Jerpoint again summoned to parliament in the year

1382.[14] The number of abbots attending **parliament** continued to drop with the passing of time. The **abbot** of Duiske does not seem to have been summoned in 1378 while the abbot of Tintern as well as the abbots of Duiske and Jerpoint were missing from the list in 1380. Although the abbot of Jerpoint was back again in 1382 the attendance continued to drop, for by then the abbot of Maigue had ceased to attend.[15] During the course of the fifteenth century the attendance decreased still further until at last only the abbots of three houses--Dublin, Mellifont and Baltinglass--continued to attend, and these last three seem to have continued to sit in parliament until the final suppression of the religious houses in the sixteenth century.

The absence of the abbot from his house during sessions of parliament was occasionally availed of by refractory monks to organize a conspiracy against him with a view to ousting him from office. A case in point is the attempt by a Welsh monk with the connivance of certain Irish abbots and a disaffected monk of Mellifont to remove the abbot of that house from office by means of a pretended "visitation" of the monastery while the abbot, Richard Contour, was attending a parliament in Dublin. The abbots of Jerpoint and Tintern issued a summons ordering the abbot of Mellifont to present himself before them on 29 May 1533 at a visitation to be held by them at Mellifont. At the time they issued this summons they were well aware that the abbot could not come owing to his parliamentary duties; they were also aware of the fact that the regular visitation of the abbey of Mellifont had already been

carried out by the abbot of Bective at Easter. In the event, they
came to Mellifont and there, under the pretext of a visitation, "deposed" the abbot and "appointed" in his place the Welsh monk Lewis
Thomas who had some six years earlier assisted the abbot of Bective to
make a canonical visitation of Mellifont. The two abbots purported
to depose Abbot Richard Contour notwithstanding the fact that the
latter had appealed to the abbot of Cîteaux against the action of the
pretended visitators. The deposed abbot then sought letters of protection from the archbishop of Armagh.[16] The outcome of this curious
affair was that Richard's title to the abbey was upheld and confirmed
by an ecclesiastical court of inquiry held in the following year.[17]

An even more extraordinary case was that of the abbot of Dunbrody
who, when summoned by writ to come to parliament was reluctant to do
so because of the danger of the ways. He did, however, send his proctor to answer for him in parliament and the latter was received and
admitted in due course. On the eve of the session, however, the abbot
underwent a change of heart and decided that he would after all attend
the parliament despite the fact that he had already sent his proctor.
The rest of the story is best summarized from the Statute Rolls of
Ireland. The abbot, we are told,

> peaceably reposing himself in his chamber the night
> before he should begin his journey to the said parliament,
> one Dom John Balle, Dom Thomas Sutton, Dom Nicholas Fur-
> long, apostates, William Robertson Sutton and William
> Davyson Sutton of the county of Wexford, and Thomas
> Comerford of Waterford, with divers others unknown,
> with force and arms against the peace of our sovereign

lord, entered the chamber of the said abbot and there
took him prisoner, and the goods and chattels of the
said abbot out of the said abbey to the value of forty
pounds took, and carried the said abbot with them to
Waterford, and there detain him as prisoner with great
duress, in contempt and derogation of our sovereign lord
and his parliament aforesaid, and intolerable hurt and
prejudice of the said abbot; and also to the very bad
example of others in time to come if it shall not be
remedied at this time.

To make a long story short the parliament issued a proclamation

against the kidnappers of the abbot ordering them to set him at

large and to restore to him the goods and chattels they had taken from

the abbey. This was to be dome within eight days on pain of for-

feiture of all their lands, rents, possessions, goods and chattels to

the king.[18]

By the middle of the fourteenth century the Cistercian abbot in

Ireland had become a great temporal lord exercising secular as well

as ecclesiastical jurisdiction over great tracts of land. The abbot

and convent had their tithes, altarages and other feudal revenues or

sources of revenue. They had their tenants and their courts. These

courts were of various kinds. In the first place there was the manor-

ial court to which the tenants and vassals had to come to plead and

receive judgment. Here justice was administered and disputes between

tenants and vassals of the lord abbot were settled; for the abbot, as

lord of the manor, was judge over all his vassals and presided over

the manorial court, otherwise called the court baron, either in per-

son or by his steward, the court being composed of all the free tenants

or freeholders of the manor. When, as sometimes happened, the possessions formed a seignory of several manore held under one lord,
this seignory was known as the honour and had an honorial court.
Many of the larger monasteries were, in fact, composed of several
such manors. One of the earliest functions of the court baron was
the view of frank-pledge and its attendant jurisdiction. By frank
pledges were meant the free men who were mutual pledges for the good
behavior of one another. The jurisdiction attendant on the view of
frankpledges was concerned with the preservation of peace and various
offences against the common good, and when exercising these powers the
court-baron came to be known as the court-leet. The court-leet was
held within the manor once a year and it was a court of record, that
is to say its proceedings were officially recorded and it had the
right to fine and imprison. It had not only the right but the duty
to present by jury all crimes committed within the jurisdiction and to
punish the same. Besides the courts-baron and the courts-leet, monasteries which had acquired the right to hold a fair had also what was
known as the court-merchant which was used both for the settling of
trade disputes and for the trial of strangers. All these courts per-
tained to the abbot's function as a feudal lord charged with adminis-
tering feudal justice. But the abbot was not merely a secular lord;
he was also endowed with ecclesiastical jurisdiction over his religious
subjects and in this capacity had his ecclesiastical court to which
his lay vassals were not subject. Since monks and clerics were not

generally subject to secular courts in medieval Ireland they had to
be brought before ecclesiastical courts even when charged with offences
against the civil law.[19] If a monk charged with an offence should
happen to be brought before a secular court he could plead exemption
from the jurisdiction of such a court and would, on the fact of his
exemption being proved, be delivered to his abbot to be dealt with by
the abbot's court. Cases of this kind are on record and two instances
concerned with Cistercian monks may be mentioned here.

In 1277 two monks of St Mary's Abbey near Dublin who at the time
were dwelling on the abbey grange at Portmarnock, were arrested and
brought before the Chief Justiciar charged with the murder of Elias
Comyn, lord of Kinsealy. During the trial in Dublin Castle the abbot
appeared before the court and demanded that the monks should be handed
over to him as his subjects. When it was proved to the satisfaction
of the court that they were indeed the abbot's subjects they were delivered to him to be tried in his court. In the event, they were con-
victed of the murder and sentenced to perpetual imprisonment in the
monastic prison, in chains and on bread and water.[20] Monasteries
like Mellifont and Dublin had two prisons: one for delinquent monks
and the other for delinquent lay people. All abbeys might not have
a secular prison, but the prison for the religious was regulated and
provided for by the General Chapter itself. A strong and secure
prison was ordered to be erected in each abbey of the order for the
incarceration of thieves, incendiaries, forgers, murderers and other

criminals.[21] These prisons were used not only for the incarceration
of criminals but also for the insane, and the abbey of Dublin provides
us with an example of the treatment of the insane at the period while
recording another clash between secular and ecclesiastical jurisdiction
in which the abbot on the one hand and the king's officials on the
other were involved. We give here a summary of the facts.

A certain Brother William who had been showing some signs of
mental aberration for about two months became completely insane one
day and, entering the choir of the sick during vespers, stripped himself of all his clothing and then, dagger in hand, entered the choir
of the monks where he stabbed and mortally wounded the sacristan and
another monk. William was committed to the abbey prison, but when news
of the occurrence spread abroad the coroner and other officials of the
city of Dublin came to hold an inquest on the bodies of the slain
monks. The abbot objected to this on the grounds that the abbey was
not within the city of Dublin. The inquest was held despite the
abbot's protest and resulted in the king's chief sergeant demanding that
the abbot should deliver Brother William to him as a felon. The abbot
resisted, claiming that Brother William as a monk and his subject
should be detained in the monastic prison, but the king's sergeant
insisted and the outcome was that William was delivered up by the abbot
under protest. The case eventually came before the Chief Justiciar in
Dublin Castle where the abbot appeared in person to claim William as
his subject. The claim was allowed and the justiciar directed that

the accused monk should be transferred from the prison of Dublin
Castle to that of St Mary's Abbey.[22]   This was done, and the unfortunate
Brother William spent the remainder of his life in chains in the monas-
tic prison.

With the growing involvement of the Cistercian abbot in public
life he ceased to live as heretofore in the midst of his monks.   In
the monastery itself it became the recognized custom for the abbot
to have his own quarters as well as his own household or establishment of servants and retainers, and the income of the monastery was
divided between the community and the abbot.   This gave rise to
many evils, for the status of the abbot as a great secular lord made
the abbatial office a rich and tempting prize to be striven for and
won by worldly and ambitious men who had little or no concern for
religion except as a means of worldly advancement.   And in fact by
the middle of the fifteenth century the order in Ireland (and elsewhere) was plagued by the activities of such men.   Not that such men
formed the majority of monastic superiors at any time, but in general
the lord abbot of the late medieval period was far removed in tempera-
ment and outlook from the abbot of St Bernard's day.   Only too often
he was a man in whom spiritual fervour was sadly lacking, even though
in his secular role he might be a talented administrator and an ener-
getic promoter of the material well-being of his community.   Of course
it could, and sometimes did happen that an abbot could be at one and
the same time a fervent religious man and an able administrator of

the monastic property while occupying a prominent position in public
life. Such an abbot, for instance, was Walter Champfleur, abbot of
St Mary's Abbey outside the walls of Dublin, whose office as Treasurer
and keeper of the great Seal under Edward IV and Richard III did not
prevent him from working hard and perseveringly in the cause of
monastic reform during the period of his abbacy.[23] But this was
exceptional.

A report sent by John Troy, abbot of Mellifont, to the abbot of
Cîteaux some time after January 1498,[24] describes what he terms "the
ruin and desolation" of the entire order in Ireland at that time.
The report makes sad reading. Among the causes of the ruin which had
overtaken the order in Ireland the abbot enumerates the ceaseless
wars waged between the two races arising from the hatred begotten in
consequence of the original conquest; the system of provisions and
commends by the Holy See; the excessive oppression practiced by the
nobility; the pensions and tributes paid by the monasteries for the
support of provisors and commendatory abbots contrary to the rights
of the incumbents, as well as similar pensions and tributes for the
support of the said incumbents against the provisors and commendatory
abbots. In consequence of such exactions the order was in straitened
circumstances. In many cases laymen had seized on the monastic revenues so that the monks were compelled to wander abroad in search of
the very necessities of life. Divine worship was largely neglected,
hospitality no longer practiced, and if the abbot of Mellifont is to

be believed there was scarcely a monastery in the entire country in which the divine office was sung according to note or the monastic habit worn; the only exceptions were, he claimed, Mellifont and Dublin.

The general state of affairs disclosed by this report is confirmed to a great extent by the information contained in the papal registers, the statutes of the General Chapter, the Statute Rolls of Ireland, the Irish Annals and other authentic documents of the period. In some cases the evidence shows that the bad state of certain monasteries was due to internal mismanagement or even to the quarrels of rival abbots or aspirants to the abbacy.[25] Complaints were made that the abbot did not reside in person in his monastery; in one case he was said to have spent the revenues of the house on his sons and daughters and other laymen. The abbot in this case was the abbot of Duiske and the year was 1459.[26] His house appears to have been much impoverished and the situation did not improve with time for in 1468 two chalices and a bible were pawned by the monks[27] and had not yet been redeemed in 1471.[28] Rival claimants to an abbey had no hesitation in enlisting the support of armed laymen--often their own kinsmen--to promote their interests,[29] and freely granted such allies leases, pensions and tithes for terms of years to the grave loss of the community.[30] References to the ruinous and dilapidated state of the monastic buildings as well as of properties and buildings held by the monks in outlying districts are commonplace in the papal registers of the

period. Various causes are mentioned as responsible for this among
which may be noted the impoverishment of the monasteries by war and
other calamities,[32] the abundant hospitality given to all without
distinction,[33] the excessive exactions of the nobility[34] who compel
the abbot and convent to pay them feudal dues, private subsidies, and
even "protection money," while from the abbot's tenants and vassals
they extort "illegal and detestable exactions...demanding as their
right provision and lodgings for themselves and their servants and
their horses...and all kinds of delicacies...which they expect to be
given...to them for nothing, and which they extort from the same
tenants and vassals against their will and despite their resistance by
means of threats, terrorism,...savage floggings of men and women and
other devilish and unchristian ways."[35]

Probably the greatest scourge of the Irish Cistercians during the
late middle ages was the _provisor_. This was the name given to the
abbot appointed by papal provision instead of by the free choice of
the community as required by the rule. The system of papal provision
began to operate in Irish Cistercian houses for the first time during
the great schism (1378-1417) and by the end of the fifteenth century
had superseded the elective system in most of the Irish houses. These
provisors were to become the curse of the order and letters written
by the abbots of Dublin and Mellifont to the abbots of Cîteaux and
Clairvaux were loud in their complaints on this subject. The abbot
of Dublin, indeed, complaining of the provisions made by the Holy

See, asked that representations should be made by the superiors of the order to put an end to the system, otherwise, he states quite bluntly, "the little glimmer of religion that remains in Ireland will very likely be extinguished."[36] Many of the provisors were prepared to go to any length in order to obtain the abbey of their choice and were not too scrupulous in the means they used to oust their rival. Some of these provisors were themselves Cistercian monks, some were monks or friars of other orders, others again were secular priests or clerics[38] and many were mere laymen.[39] We have not anything like a full list of the abbatial succession in most of the medieval Cistercian monasteries in Ireland. As far as can be ascertained the total number of Cistercian abbots of whom there is record from 1400 to the dissolution of the monasteries in 1539 is two hundred and fifty-three. Of these abbots, thirty-five were abbots in commendam, eighty-five were provisors, twenty-one were said to be intruders of one kind or another, while 133 had been elected and confirmed in the regular way. Thus the number of abbots elected according to the rules and constitutions of the Cistercian Order during the period in question formed a minority of the total number of whom there is record during the period. It should be noted also that the number so elected gradually decreased until at the end of the fifteenth century most of the abbots present at a regional council could be described by the abbot of Mellifont as men who owed their promotion to provisions made by the Holy See,[40] men, to use the words of the same abbot, who took no care of the goods of the house except to plunder them for their own use.[41]

As we have already seen a number of Cistercian abbots took their seats in the parliament of the pale as peers of the realm. Some were also justices of the peace--charged among other duties with supervising the erection on the frontiers of the pale of defences against the incursions of the "Irish enemy"[42] --while others acted as agents for Crown officials of the highest rank. Two of the abbots of Dublin, as has been noted, attained to the highest position in the Anglo-Irish state under the Lord Deputy, that of Keeper of the Great Seal, while part of the state archives was actually housed in their monastery,[43] and the King's Council is said to have met and deliberated in the Chapter House which, by the way, is still in existence.[44] It was there that Silken Thomas, son and heir of the earl of Kildare, threw down the sword of state and went into open rebellion against the English crown on hearing the rumor that his father who had been imprisoned in the Tower of London by order of the king had been executed. The rumor, in fact, was false, but the rebellion resulted in the attainder and death of the unfortunate Silken Thomas himself and the fall of the house of Kildare, the most powerful of all the Anglo-Irish families.[45]

The abbot's close involvement in the public life of the period sometimes led him into devious political courses as happened in 1487, when the abbots of Mellifont and Dublin rallied to the support of Lambert Simnel, a pretender who was believed by the mass of the Anglo-

Irish to be Edward, earl of Warwick, legitimate male heir to the English
throne. On May 24, 1487, he was crowned by the archbishop of Dublin
in the presence of the great Anglo-Irish lords (with the notable exception of the Butlers of Ormond) and the clergy of the Pale, the two
abbots mentioned above taking a prominent part in the proceedings.
Mustering an army, the Anglo-Irish nobility landed in England where,
unfortunately for their cause, they were completely overthrown by
the forces of Henry VII. Many of the leaders lost their lives and
Simnel himself was captured. In the following year the new lord deputy sent to Ireland by the king received the fealty and homage of
the discomfited supporters of the Yorkist cause and proclaimed a full
pardon to all Simnel's supporters. Among those pardoned were Walter
Champfleur and John Troy, the abbots respectively of Dublin and Mellifont. Indeed the fealty and homage of the former rebels had been received and full pardon proclaimed under the Great Seal by Sir Richard
Edgecumbe in Walter Champfleur's own abbey of St. Mary's.[46] It is
quite certain that the two abbots, like the vast majority of the Anglo-
Irish and English of Ireland really believed that Simnel was, in fact,
the earl of Warwick. In supporting his coronation, therefore, they
did so in the belief that they were aiding in the coronation of the
true king of England in opposition to the usurper who then occupied
the throne.

Abbot Butler, in his work on Benedictine Monachism has painted a
picture of the feudal abbot which is as true of the medieval Cistercian

as it is of his Black Benedictine brother.

> Naturally and inevitably [he writes] they were caught
> up into the feudal system and became great feudal lords,
> exercising the functions, enjoying the privileges, bearing
> the burdens, sharing the rank of the feudal barons. They
> had their courts; they attended parliament, and consequent-
> ly had their London houses; they frequently were engaged
> on business with or for the king. The popes commissioned
> them to hear ecclesiastical cases and appeals...and the
> king employed them on missions to the Holy See and to
> other sovereigns. At the abbey too they had their own
> quarters separate from the community, and their own es-
> tablishment; and the income of the monastery was divided
> in fixed proportions between abbot and community, each
> having their own obligations towards the upkeep of the
> house. The abbot was not a "Lord Abbot" for nothing.
> This was no courtesy title. The "Lord Abbot" was not
> only a lord of parliament, but was as truly a lord of the
> serfs and vassals, the tenants and retainers throughout
> his abbey lands, as the baron and earl who were his peers
> and next-door neighbours.[47]

Although Abbot Butler is speaking specifically of the Black

Benedictine abbot in the passage quoted above, the description in most

particulars is literally true of the Cistercian abbot in medieval

Ireland. This applies particularly to those abbots who ranked as

lords of parliament. But the process had begun even before the coming

of the Normans; the fact that in the early years of the invasion the

abbot of Mellifont was selected by the last Ard Rí (High King) of

Ireland, Ruaidhrí Ó Conchubhair, to go on a mission to the pope in

1172 shows that even under the Gaelic dispensation the abbot was a

personage of considerable importance in the public life of the country.

After the conquest he took an even more active part in public affairs

and the abbot of Mellifont in the course of time had a house in Dublin

and another in Drogheda in which he lodged with his retainers when
summoned to attend parliaments held in those towns. These Cistercian
abbots were, for the most part, lords of vast domains—that of Mellifont exceeded fifty thousand acres, that of Baltinglass thirty thousand
that of Dublin twenty thousand. And this vast domain was populated
by tenants and vassals of various degrees as well as serfs, and contained castles, houses, farms, cottages, and, needless to say, the
abbot and convent drew a large rental from the numerous tenantry. The
abbot of those days might even exercise his lordship over a number of
towns and villages, holding the power of life and death over his
secular subjects of which the manorial pillory and gallows were grim
reminders. These latter powers formed part of the very extensive
liberties, immunities and privileges of a secular nature with which
some of the greater abbots were endowed by the kings of England in the
period between the Anglo-Norman conquest of Ireland and the destruction
of the Irish monasteries in the sixteenth century.

One of the most extensive grants of this kind was that made by
Edward III to the abbot and convent of Mellifont on September 28, 1348.
By this charter[48] the monks were granted in perpetuity free warren in
all their demesne lands in Callan, Ballymascanlan, Salterstown, Culboyg
Grangegeeth, Monknewtown, Ballyfeddock, Fernaght, Sleubroght, and their
granges of Oldbridge, Staleen, Rosnaree, Knowth, Doe, Gulboyde and New-
grange in the counties of Meath and Oriel. They were also permitted to
build a prison at their own expense in any one of their manors in

County Meath, wherever they should deem it most expedient, to have and to hold in perpetuity to themselves and their successors. In this prison were to be confined malefactors and felons indicted in the monks' lands as well as such of the king's enemies as might happen to be apprehended in the marches of the same lands, there to be detained until justice could be done on them according to the law and custom of those parts. They were to have in all their lands and fees various privileges including Infangthef (the privilege granted the lord of the manor to judge thieves captured on his own lands) and Outfangthef (the privilege whereby the lord of the manor was empowered to bring to judgement in his own court any man dwelling in his manor and taken for felony in another place out of his fee). And in the towns of Callan, Ballymascanlan, etc., as well as in the granges already mentioned--amounting in all to ten different places in the counties of Meath and Louth--the abbot was empowered to have a gallows, a pillory and a tumbrill, and all the other liberties already enjoyed by the abbot and convent of St Mary's Abbey near Dublin. Besides having custody and assay of weights and measures in their own lands the abbot and convent were given permission to acquire a house in Dublin and another in Drogheda or in the suburbs thereof as a dwelling and residence for the abbot and his successors and his (or their) household in coming to parliaments or other councils or assemblies which might be summoned or held there.

In view of all the privileges, liberties and immunities recorded above the reader will scarcely be surprised to learn that by the year

1479 the abbot of Mellifont had, or claimed to have "all manner of
ecclesiastical jurisdiction and the correction of whatsoever persons,
as well ecclesiastical as secular, within the precincts of the lands
and possessions belonging to the aforesaid house,"[49] and the king in
the following year (out of love for the Cistercian Order as the Statute
Roll records) granted to the abbot and his successors the right of ap-
prehending excommunicated persons such as was wont to be exercised by
bishops.[50] This meant in practice that should anyone be excommunicated
by the abbot and not make satisfaction to God and Holy Church within a
month after such excommunication, then, if the abbot certified this
fact to the chancery, a writ should be directed to the sheriff or to
another royal official to seize the excommunicated person and keep him
in prison without bail until due satisfaction should have been made.
Eight years later, be a decree dated September 28, 1487, Pope Innocent
VIII granted to all the abbots of the order jurisdiction over all their
tenants, vassals, subjects and servants, even to the extent of freeing
their said subjects from all jurisdiction, superiority, correction,
visitation, subjection and power of archbishops, bishops and their vicars
etc., and subjecting them immediately to himself and to the Holy See.
This was the apex of the abbot's power.[51] The ascent (if so it may be
termed) had been a gradual process extending over centuries. The descent was rapid. Half a century later came the quarrel between Henry VII
and the pope culminating in the breach between England and Rome and the
dissolution of the religious orders on England and Ireland. The

Cistercian communities were suppressed with the others; the abbots were pensioned off, the monks dispersed, and the vast landed possessions of the order confiscated. <u>Sic</u> <u>transit</u> <u>gloria</u> <u>mundi</u>!

Mhainstir Mhellifont, Ireland

NOTES

1. Aubrey Gwynn, S. J., "The Centenary of the Synod of Kells, 1152," IER LXXVII (1952) 161-76, 250-64.

2. The five were: Peadar O Mordha, abbot of Boyle (bishop of Clonfert 1150-1166), Floirint Mac Riagain O Maelrunaidh (bishop of Elphin 1175-1195), Charles O Buachalla (bishop of Emly, 1177) Felix O Dulaney Dulaney (bishop of Ossory, 1178-1202), Muirghes or Matha O Henni (archbishop of Cashel, 1182-1206). I here follow the generally received opinion that Felix O Dulaney, who was "abbot of Ossory" before being appointed bishop of the diocese of that name was a Cistercian abbot. I think it more probable, however, that he was a Benedictine abbot before his elevation to the episcopacy. For a discussion of this question see "The Origins of Jerpoint Abbey Co. Kilkenny" in CCC XIV, 4 (1963) 293-306.

3. These were the sees of (1) Ferns the Cistercian bishop being Ailbhe O Maelmhuaidh who had been abbot of Baltinglass and who was bishop from 1186 to 1222, (2) Mael Isa O Maelciarain (bishop of Clogher, 1192-1196), and (3) Leighlin, the bishop of which from 1198 to 1201 was John, abbot of Monasterevan.

4. The abbots were: Gilla Crist O Conairche, of Mellifont; Finn mac Gormain mac Gormain mac Tiarnain of Newry; Peter O Mordha of Boyle; Floirint mac Riagain O Maelruanaidh of Boyle; Charles O Buachalla of Mellifont; Felix O Dulaney of Ossory and possibly of Jerpoint

(but if so, before that monastery became affiliated to the Cistercian Order; it is, of course, possible that after Jerpoint became Cistercian the bishop also became a member of the order); Ailbhe O Maelmhuaidh, abbot of Baltinglass; Mael Isa O Maelciarain of Mellifont, and John, abbot of Monasterevan.

5. The archbishop had been suspended by the pope "pro multis et magnis excessibus." In the year 1202 the papal legate had written to the pope informing him that the archbishop, while desiring to be absolved, had by then become so incapacitated by old age that he was unable to proceed in person to Rome to beg the benefit of absolution. Despite this, the pope, rather harshly, we may think, refused the request and insisted that the archbishop should fulfil the terms of the suspension placed upon him. [*Reg. Vat. 5 ff 47r-48r*]. This letter of Innocent III to John cardinal priest of St Stephen in monte Coelio and legate of the Apostolic See has been printed and critically edited by Maurice P. Sheehy in his collection of medieval papal chancery documents concerning Ireland: *Pontificia Hibernica, vol. I, no. 52, pp. 120-121.*

6. The archbishops were: Muirgheas O Henni (1182-1206), Donatus (Domhnall) O Longargain II (1206-1215), Donatus (Donnchadh) O Longargain III (1216-1223) and Marianus (Mael Muire) O Briain (1224-1238). Muigheas was probably a monk of Holy Cross to which monastery he retired after being suspended by Pope Innocent III

for "many and great excesses" c. 1200. He died, according to the

Annals of Innisfallen, in 1206. Donatus O Longargain III became

a Cistercian while actually archbishop. Having visited Cîteaux on

his way to Rome he had been taken seriously ill,and, believing him-

self to be on the point of death, took the Cistercian habit. He

recovered and continued on his way to Rome. He returned to Ireland

with letters from the pope to the clergy and people of Cashel in-

forming them that the fact that the archbishop was now a monk was

all the more reason they should accept him as their pastor. His

successor, Mael Muire O Briain, had been bishop of Cork before his

translation to Cashel and was certainly a Cistercian monk at the

time of his appointment as archbishop. The fact that on his resig-

nation from the archbishopric in 1236 he retired to the abbey of

Inishlounaght suggests that he had originally been a monk of that

house. He died there in 1238 according to the Annals of Inisfallen.

7. Theiner, A., *Vetera Monumenta Hibernorum et Scotorum Historiam*

   Illustrantia, nos. 36 and 38, p. 16.

8. William Lynch, 166-68, and see Gearoid Mac Niocaill, *Na Manaigh*

   Liatha in Eirinn, *1142-c.1600* (Baile Atha Cliath: Clo Morainn,

   1959) p. 37.

9. Lynch, pp. 315-38 and see H. G. Richardson and G. O. Sayles,

   The Irish Parliament in the Middle Ages (Philadelphis, 1952).

10. This is the earliest known reference to the summoning to parliament

    of an Irish Cistercian abbot. It is contained in the *Report of the*

Deputy Keeper of the Public Records in Ireland no. 42 (1911)
p. 73.

11. Richardson and Sayles.

12. Sir James Ware, Coenobia Cisterciensia Hiberniae (1626) p. 74. This
is in the Bodleian Library, Oxford, but it has been reprinted by Sir
John Gilbert in his Chartularies of St Mary's Abbey Dublin [CSM]
(London, Dublin, 2 vols. 1884) II.

13. Ball, W., and E. Tresham (edd.) Rotulorum Patentium et Clausorum
Cancellariae Hiberniae Calendarium [Rot. Pat.], I, pars 1 (1928)
no. 166, p. 94b, and see Parliaments and Councils of Medieval
Ireland I, edd. H. G. Richardson and G. O. Sayles for Irish Manuscripts Commission (Dublin: Stationery Office, 1947) pp. 78-9.

14. Rot. Pat. no. 123, p. 118b.

15. Ibid.

16. L. P. Murray and A. Gwynn (edd.) [Calendar of] "Archbishop Cromer's
Register," Journal of the County Louth Archaeological Society (1943)
122-23 and see the next note.

17. Papers of Marquis of Drogheda in National Library of Ireland. This
report has been printed in full by Gearoid Mac Niocaill in Na
Manaigh Liatha, Aguisin E., 207-16.

18. Statute Rolls of the Parliament of Ireland. Reign of King Henry VI.
Henry F. Berry, ed. (Dublin: HM Stationery Office, 1910) pp. 129-30.

19. Despite this we find monks arraigned before secular courts and not
infrequently abbots themselves were indicted on various charges.

For examples of such charges see The Story of Mellifont by the
present writer (Dublin: M. H. Gill and Son, 1958) pp. 108, 110,
112-13.

20. Gilbert, CSM I, 1-2.

21. Monasticon Cisterciense, ed. Hugues Sejalon (Solesme, 1892) pp. 320,
    423, 511; and see notes on p. 320.

22. Gilbert, CSM I, xxx, 67.

23. In passing it may be noted that the office of Treasurerehad also
    been held by one of Abbot Walter's predecessors--Stephen Roche
    (1383-1410) who incidentally had been one of the inspectors of the
    expenditure of the amount granted by King Richard II for the repair
    of the bridge at Dublin (CSM I, xliv). He was appointed Sub-
    Treasurer of Ireland in 1395 but resigned the same year (Ibid., p. 378).

24. A copy of this report is preserved in the Public Library, Armagh in
    Octavian's Register, fol. 121a-122b. This, with other Cistercian
    documents from the same register and two letters from the Archives
    de la Côte d'Or (Fonds de Cîteaux) has been edited with a commentary
    by the present writer in Seanchas Ard mhacha II, 2 (1957) 286-92.
    These documents will be cited as Irish Cistercian Documents or in
    abbreviated form ICD.

25. Calendar of Papal Letters I-XIV (1986-1956) cited henceforth as
    CPL: VIII, 194 (Abbehshrule); X, 297-98, 595, 678 (Abbeyowney);
    300, 391 (Chore); 300, 306 (Duiske); 389-90 (Dunbrody); 389 (Holy
    Cross); 464-65 (Fermoy); 510-11 (Tracton); 596-97 (Baltinglass);

XI, 218 (Abbeydorney); 481 (Boyle); 509 (Inishlounaght); 264-65
(Knockmoy); 53 (Fermoy); xii, 92 (Abbeyowney); 53, 179 (Chore);
309-310 (Inishlounaght); 87 (Knockmoy); XIII, Calendar of Justiciary Rolls, Ireland (CJRI), I, 134, 136; II, 350, 351; III, 1.
SRI II, 97-99; III, 685-87.

5. CPL XII, 13 (Duiske).

7. Register of St Saviour's Waterford, ed. Gearoid Mac Niocaill in
Analecta Hibernica, no. 23, pp. 149-50.

8. Ibid., p. 192.

9. CJRI II, 350-51; III, 1 (Maigue); CPL, 300, 391 (Chore); 391 (Maigue),
194 (Abbeyshrule); SCG IV, 1411:7; (Jerpoint).

0. CPL X, 678 (Wotheny, that is, Abbeyowney); XII, 92-93. SCG IV,
1411:75 (Jerpoint). SRI III, 831ff. (Mellifont).

1. CPL IX, 248 (Jerpoint), 458 (Kilcooly); XII, 271 (Fermoy); 378, 509
(Hore Abbey); XIII, 99 (Abbeyowney); 531 (Inishlounaght); EIM, 126
(Baltinglass); 181 (Jerpoint); 213 (Mellifont); Archives de la Côte
d'Or 11 H 20 in ICD 271.

2. CPL XII, 275 (Fermoy); EIM 136 (Abbeyleix); 143-4 (Tracton); 145
(Fermoy); 150 (Chore); 151-2 (Abbeymahon); 194-6 (Duiske), 213-17
(Mellifont); ICD 271, 289-92. For the occupation and destruction
or partial destruction of monastic buildings by one or more of the
warring armies which from time to time devastated various regions
see Annals of Loch Ce sub annis 1202, 1235 (Boyle); 1392, 1398
(Assaroe) and Miscellaneous Irish Annals sub anno 1164 (Newry); see

also CSM II, pp. 417, 421, and SRI II, pp. 97-99, (Tintern).

33. CPL XII, 180 (Tracton). This may have been an exceptional case, for the abbot of Mellifont in his report on the state of the order in Ireland already quoted asserts that hospitality was no longer practiced in most of the monasteries, "hospitalitas deficit..." ICD, no. 10, 290.

34. CPL X, 497-98 (Duiske), 499 (Abbeydorney); XII, 274 (Abbeydorney); Register of John Swayne 114 (Newry); "Seven Documents from the Old Abbey of Mellifont" ed. Fr. Colmcille, O. Cist. in LAJ XIII, 1 (1953): 55-60 (no. 5).

35. Ibid., pp. 56 and 58. The other side of the coin is revealed in the "Presentments of the Gentlemen, Commonalty and Citizens of Carlow, Cork, Kilkenny, Tipperary, Waterford and Wexford" made in the reigns of Henry VIII and Elizabeth printed from the originals in the Public Record Office London under the title of The Social State of the Southern and Eastern Counties of Ireland in the Sixteenth Century, and edited by Herbert J. Hore and the Rev. James Graves. Among the presentments we find that "the Abbot of Jerrypoins, th'Abbot of Kyllcole...th'Abbot of the Holly-crosse, th'Abbot of Duske...do (in lyke manner) charge ther tenauntes with coyne and lyverye" (p. 120); while of the abbot of Inishlounaght they state inter alia that "James Butler, Abbot of Inislonaght and deane of Lysmore...useth coyne and lyvery..." (1537). They also present that in the districys in question the "spirituall Bysshopes, abbottes and

Pryors...do charge their tenauntes with codyes* and cosshyes** as
often as they will, and pay no thing therefor" (121). That these
abuses were of long standing and were not confined to the south of
Ireland is certain; and indeed they are referred to in the letters
of protection given by the archbishop of Armagh and his suffragans
to the abbot and convent of Mellifont in 1495 and published in ICD
no. 5, pp. 56 and (in translation) 58. An Inquisition taken at
Cashel in the reign of Henry VIII (Exchequer Inquisitions Tipperary,
Henry VIII, PRO Dublin, 1a.48.85) quotes a charter of the former
abbot of Inishlounaght, James Butler, dated 10th December 1519, by
which, with the consent of his chapter, he granted the grange of
Loghkyraghe with all its appurtenances to Thomas Butler, layman, for
a term of sixty years from term to term, on condition that the said
Thomas should construct there a church or chapel in honour of
Blessed Mary, paying annually (a rent of) 13s.4d. and the refection
of twenty-four men on the feast of Christmas or 6s.8d. and sixteen
men on the feast of Easter, or 4s.3d. and certain other items
which are included under the name of Caynogly. *Codyes stands
for the Irish Cuid oíche--a night repast or supper. **Cosshyes
probably renders the Irish Cóisri, plural of cóisir, a feast or
festive party, generally referred to in contemporary Anglo-
Irish sources as "cosherings."

36. Archives de la Côte d'or (Fonds de Cîteaux) 11 H 20 printed in ICD
no 1, p. 271.

37. C̲P̲L̲ V, 23 (Kilbeggan); IX, 129 (Knockmoy); 570 (Maigue); XII, 186 (Inishlounaght); I̲M̲E̲D̲, 232 (Abbeyowney).

38. De Annatis Hiberniae, I: Ulster transcribed by M. A. Costelloe, M. A., O. P. ed. Ambrose Coleman, O. P. (Dundalk: Tempest, 1912); 262, 265, 277, 281 (Assaroe); C̲P̲L̲ VII, 133 (Corcumroe), 61 (Knockmoy); 493 (Assaroe); VIII, 99, 145 (Kilbeggan); XII, 99, 136, 358 (Macosquin); XIII, part 1: 323 (Corcumroe); 531 (Inishlounaght); 601 (Newry); 681 (Jerpoint); 754 (Monasterevan); 849 (Mascoquin); XIV (Galley Proofs in National Library of Ireland, Dublin) SD-39, Vatican Regesta vol. DCCLXV 8 Innocent VIII, 19 May, 1492 (Inishlounaght). I̲M̲E̲D̲, 73 (Holy Cross).

39. I̲C̲D̲ no. 10, 290, 291.

40. I̲C̲D̲ no. 11, 293.

41. I̲C̲D̲ no. 10, 290.

42. S̲R̲I̲ II, 45-7 (Tintern); 315, 367, 403-5 (St Mary's Abbey Dublin); 503-5, 541 (Mellifont); 757 (St Mary's Abbey Dublin). S̲R̲I̲ III, 139 485, 517-19. R̲o̲t̲. P̲a̲t̲. 99 (no. 275); 239 (no. 117).

43. C̲S̲M̲ I, XXXIX.

44. In Meeting House Lane, off Mary's Abbey, Dublin.

45. The Irish Historie by John Hooker (London, 1586) p. 89, quoted by Gilbert C̲S̲M̲ II, XXV-VI.

46. Pat. Roll. Hen VII 25 May, 1488. See C̲S̲M̲ II, XXI citing Edgcumbe's narrative.

47. Dom Cuthbert Bulter, O.S.B., Benedictine Monachism, 2nd edition

(London: Longmans, Green and Co., 1924), p. 195.

48. Edited with translation and notes by the present writer in LAJ XIV, I (1957):1-13. The confirmation of earlier charters and the very extensive privileges with which the monks were endowed on this occasion appear on pp. 5-7 with translation and notes on pp. 7-11.

49. SRI IV, p. 847.

50. SRI IV, p. 849.

51. Privilegia Ordinis Cisterciensis, p. 179. Although the Nomasticon Cisterciense (editio nova, emendata et usque ad tempora nostra deducta a R. P. Hugone Sejalon [Solesmes: MDCCCXCII]) states that the privileges granted to the order before the Council of Trent remained entire and inviolate after that council and were renewed and confirmed by many popes from 1563 to 1729, the claim by the Cistercian abbots in the seventeenth century that they were completely exempt from the diocesan bishops in all that concerned visitations, correction, convocation to synods, approbation to hear confessions and entire and absolute episcopal jurisdiction of every kind, and that they held these rights over all parish churches and chapels formerly belonging to the order, was hotly contested by the Irish hierarchy. In 1633 the Congregation of Propaganda came out in favour of the bishops by issuing decrees for the Irish Church which declared that the provisions of the Council of Trent and the Constitution of Gregory XV which abolished such extensive privileges were binding on the Irish Cistercians. Notwithstanding this un-

equivocal declaration the Irish Cistercian abbots clung obstinately
to their privileges which they declared were not abrogated so that
even after 1633 recurring complaints were made by the bishops to
Rome in this connection. This bitter controversy lasted almost to
the end of the century, for as late as 1673 we find Archbishop Brennan
of Cashel complaining to Monsignor Cerri, Secretary of Propaganda of
a "Bernardine abbot" named James Stafford residing in the diocese of
Ferns who continued to grant dispensations notwithstanding that he
had been forbidden to do so.

ABBREVIATIONS USED IN NOTES

CCC   Citeaux Commentarii Cistercienses

CJRI   Calendar of Justiciary Rolls Ireland i, ii, ed. James Mills. Dublin: H. M. Stationery Office, 1905-14; iii ed. Margaret C. Griffith. Dublin: Stationery Office, 1956.

CPL   Calendar of Papal Letters, 1896 seq.

CSM   Chartularies of St Mary's Abbey, Dublin, i-ii, ed. John T. Gilbert. London and Dublin, 1884.

EIM   Extents of Irish Monastic Possessions, 1540-41, ed. Newport B. White. Dublin: Stationery Office, 1943.

LIFB   A View of the Legal Institutions, Honorary Hereditary Offices, and Feudal Baronies established in Ireland during the Reign of Henry the Second, by William Lynch, F.S.A. London: Longman, Rees, Orme, Brown and Green, 1830.

ICD   Irish Cistercian Documents in Octavian's Register, Armagh, ed. An tAth. Colmcille, O.C.S.O. in Seanchas Ardmhacha, ii, 2 (1957): 269-94.

IMED   Irish Monastic and Episcopal Deeds A.D. 1200-1600, ed. Newport B. White, Dublin: Stationery Office, 1936.

IER   Irish Ecclesiastical Record.

LAJ   Journal of the County Louth Archaeological Society, 1904 seq.

IPMA   Irish Parliaments in the Middle Ages, H. G. Richardson and G. O. Sayles, Philadelphia, 1952.

Rot. Pat. <u>Rotulorum</u> <u>Patentium</u> <u>et</u> <u>Clausorum</u> <u>Cancellariae</u> Hiberniae

Calendarium, vol. i, pars i, Hen. II - Hen. VII. Ed. W. Ball

and E. Tresham, 1828.

SCG <u>Statuta</u> <u>Capitulorum</u> <u>Generalium</u> <u>Ordinis</u> <u>Cisterciensis</u> i-vii.

Ed. J. M. Canivez, O.C.R., 1933-1939. (Louvain).

SRI <u>Statute</u> <u>Rolls</u> <u>of</u> <u>Ireland</u> arranged as follows:

i. <u>Statutes</u> <u>and</u> <u>Ordinances</u> <u>and</u> <u>Acts</u> <u>of</u> <u>the</u> <u>Parliament</u> <u>of</u>

<u>Ireland</u>. <u>King</u> <u>John</u> <u>to</u> <u>Henry</u> <u>V</u>. Ed. Henry F. Berry

(Dublin: HMSO, 1907).

ii. <u>Statute</u> <u>Rolls</u> <u>of</u> <u>the</u> <u>Parliament</u> <u>of</u> <u>Ireland</u>. <u>The</u> <u>Reign</u>

<u>of</u> <u>King</u> <u>Henry</u> <u>VI</u>. Ed. Henry F. Berry (Dublin: HMSO, 1010)

iii. <u>Statute</u> <u>Rolls</u> <u>of</u> <u>the</u> <u>Parliament</u> <u>of</u> <u>Ireland</u>. <u>First</u> <u>to</u>

<u>Twelfth</u> <u>Years</u> <u>of</u> <u>the</u> <u>Reign</u> <u>of</u> <u>King</u> <u>Edward</u> <u>the</u> <u>Fourth</u>.

Ed. Henry F. Berry (Dublin: HMSO, 1914).

iv. <u>Statute</u> <u>Rolls</u> <u>of</u> <u>the</u> <u>Parliament</u> <u>of</u> <u>Ireland</u>. <u>Twelfth</u> <u>and</u>

<u>Thirteenth</u> <u>to</u> <u>Twenty-first</u> <u>and</u> <u>Twenty-second</u> <u>Years</u> <u>of</u> <u>the</u>

<u>Reign</u> <u>of</u> <u>King</u> <u>Edward</u> <u>IV</u>. Ed. James F. Morrissey of the

PRO (Dublin: Stationery Office, 1939).

MEDIEVAL NETHERLANDIC VERSIONS OF THE <u>EXORDIUM</u> <u>MAGNUM</u>*

ELEVENTH CONFERENCE ON MEDIEVAL STUDIES

PHILIP E. WEBBER

Allow me to open this paper with a few facts which may help
orient my colleagues working outside the field of Netherlandic
manuscripts.

In 1970, one hundred and twenty-five manuscripts, from more than
fifty European and American collections, found their way to The Royal
Library, Brussels, for inclusion in what is generally considered to
have been the most monumental exhibition of medieval Netherlandic
vernacular manuscripts ever held.[1] It is noteworthy that, among the
items carefully selected for display, we find within the distinguished
circle of texts the <u>Exordium</u> <u>magnum</u> represented not by one manuscript,
but indeed by two separate exhibition entries.[2]

Despite such obvious recognition of its significance, however,
the Netherlandic <u>Exordium</u> <u>magnum</u> has enjoyed little scholarly attention.
In his very fine articles for the 1970 Brussels exhibition catalogue,
Jan Deschamps draws together all previous literature on the vernacular
text: apart from catalogue and acquisition notices, this consists entirely of a helpful notice, with sample texts, in de Vooys' literary-
historical <u>Middelnederlandse</u> <u>legenden</u> <u>en</u> <u>exempelen</u>, and an unannotated
edition (discussed below) of a partial text.[3] It need hardly be
stressed that the <u>Stand</u> <u>der</u> <u>Forschung</u> is such that I would welcome

additional information from my colleagues.

My own interest in this topic was aroused by Deventer, Stads- of
Athenaeumbibliotheek Ms. I, 37 (101 D 18), from the Buusken House
(Common Life) in Deventer, and by the pair Ms. I, 38 (101 D 8)--Ms. I,
39 (101 D 9) from Brandes House (also Common Life), also in Deventer.
The oldest of these bears a colophon identifying the copyist:

Gescreuen van johan henricsoen scoelmeyster . ende gheeyndet

op sunte Appolonien dach . In den iaer ons heren M. cccc. ende

lxix. Bidt voer hem een Aue maria . om god.

Our copyist may be the person of the same name who (re)emerges
in documents dated 1484-1519, invariably in juridicial and trustee
actions, usually in association with the nuns of Ter Hunnepe, the only
Cistercian establishment in the area of Deventer.[4] At first I believed
that I could show Henricsoen as an intermediary and purveyor of texts
between Ter Hunnepe and the Common Life houses in Deventer. Incomplete evidence has forced me to lay this hypothesis aside, at least
temporarily. This may prove to have been a fortunate turn of events,
for in placing into abayance my investigation of Johan Henricsoen,
I have been forced to face some questions whose answers shall, I believe, be of far broader significance both to our own and to other
disciplines. How many Netherlandic <u>Exordium magnum</u> manuscripts are
there? Where did these texts originate, and what is their geographic
proliferation? Who--in particular, what orders--actually produced
and used these texts? Is there anything noteworthy about the pattern

of Common Life provenance established by the three Deventer manuscripts?

I am aware of fifteen extant manuscripts of the Netherlandic Exordium magnum, apart from selections in Dirc van Herxan's First and Second Dietse kollatieboek. Table 1 presents a checklist of known manuscripts of what appears to have been the most widely proliferated version of our text.[5] An interesting comparison is presented by Table 2, showing similar data for a second, somewhat more Southern and Eastern version.[6] While there is some work left to be done on exact classification of versions, the information on origin may be considered fairly definitive. The Deventer manuscripts appear to be typical in date (late fifteenth century), in geographic origin (Northeast Netherlands and immediately adjacent Westphalia), and also in having been produced in houses whose affiliations (primarily Common Life and Windesheim) are associated with the spiritual ferment which has long made the study of this period and area so captivating.

Two other manuscripts come from the Northern Netherlands. One of these, Leiden: University Library, Letterkunde 1031, may be safely identified on linguistic evidence as coming from the Northeast Netherlands. It is ironic that this manuscript, which differs from the others in consisting of thirty-four selections taken from throughout the Exordium magnum, is the only one to have been edited.[7] The unannotated edition by A. Greebe was to have initiated a series, Bydragen tot de geschiedenis der Cisterciensers in: [sic] Nederland.[8] The other manuscript is Weesp, Gemeentearchief, III B 1, our only text from the Northwestern Netherlands. It was completed in 1468 by

the copyist Peter Swaninc for the sisters of the Tertiary Convent of

St John the Evangelist at Weesp.[9] The versions of both the Leiden

and Weesp manuscripts bear further investigation.

Turning to the Southern Netherlands we find two manuscripts:

one, a fragmentary piece, now in Vienna, Austrian National Library

15.458 (Suppl. 2642), appears related to the very complete translation

of 1457 preserved in Brussels, The Royal Library, Ms. 12.166.[10]

Our earliest ownership notice associates this manuscript with Bethany,

near Mechelen, a cloister belonging to the Chapter of Windesheim.[11]

Finally, we find four excerpts from the Exordium magnum in Dirc

van Herxen's First Dietse kollatieboek (Utrecht, University Library,

Ms. 3 L 6, dated 1445, and Leiden, University Library, B.P.L. 2231)

and eight excerpts in his Second Dietse kollatieboek (Amsterdam,

University Library, I G 47).[12] An excerpt from the Exordium magnum

also appears in Leiden, University Library, Letterkunde 336, a manu-

script containing, among various other texts, five epitomes on Saint

Augustine taken from the First Dietse kollatieboek.[13]

What conclusions may we draw from this body of data?

1. The vernacular Exordium magnum must be regarded as a signi-

ficant text in the spiritual literature of the late medieval Nether-

lands, deserving of far more scholarly attention than has hitherto

been accorded it. My own intended contribution along these lines is

to be a more thorough textual study of the several versions in relationship to one another and to the Latin original.

2. We may safely conclude that the centers of textual activity for the Netherlandic Exordium magnum lay primarily in or adjacent to the Northeast Netherlands, and that the greatest propagation of texts occurred during the second half of the fifteenth century. A glance at maps of Cistercian establishments in the Low Countries in the Atlas de l'ordre cistercien, and those of Common Life and Canons Regular establishments in Post's The Modern Devotion, reveals that the geographic and chronological concentration of manuscript production described here coincides strikingly not with the concentration of Cistercian establishments, but rather with the concentration of Common Life and Canons Regular (and in particular the Chapter of Windesheim) establishments, whose members were, as we have seen, the chief producers and users of the Netherlandic Exordium magnum.[14] I personally suspect, although the hypothesis bears further close investigation, that the Netherlandic Exordium magnum arose in an atmosphere such as the one which must have prevailed at the Zwolle Brotherhood House under the rectorship of Dirc van Herxen (1409-1457), himself a prolific translator, writer and compiler, in whose Dietse kollatiekoeken we find the earliest extant material of the text in question. (I by no means discount the possibility that Dirc van Herxen himself translated the major version of our text. He was remembered in the following terms: "Insuper valde egregius et planus translator fuit et expositor de latino in teutonicum, nam multas

materias de viciis et virtutibus scripsit et transtulit, item passiones

sanctorum et multa utilia."[15])

3. The production and use of the Exordium magnum by Windesheimers

and affiliates of the Common Life can hardly be overstressed. If one

hears much at all about Cistercians in the era and area associated

with the birth of the Devotio moderna, one notices that a number of

monasteries were reformed by missionaries from Windesheim, or that

Geert Groote cautioned his disciples regarding the strict rule and

regimen of the Cistercians.[16] Such information, while documented,

nevertheless tends at times to look at only one side of the coin.[17]

I find it inaccurate, for instance, to suggest that no fifteenth-

century monastic worth his salt, living around the busy hub of the

Devotio moderna, would admit deference to the Cistercians, who were

by then woefully sunken--we are asked to believe--in hopeless degener-

ation. Such claims are familiar from, among others, a school which

once claimed that Thomas à Kempis could not possibly have written the

De imitatione Christi, since this work openly praises the rigor of

Cistercians and Carthusians.[18] According to such a theory, we are

asked to believe that the Cistercians lost esteem in the Northeast

Netherlands as the fifteenth century wore on. The textual history of

the Exordium magnum (which must, of course, be taken in conjunction

with other evidence) suggests exactly the opposite.

It is my sincere hope that this paper may prove instrumental in

a reevaluation of the contribution of Cistercian ideals, as conveyed

in the Exordium magnum, to spiritual life in the late medieval Netherlands. In so saying, I complete the lap which I have run as a textual
scholar, and pass forward the baton to my colleagues in spiritual
history.

Central College

Pella, Iowa

Table 1

* Aachen, Bischöfliches Diözesanarchiv, Ms. 184 (2761).	Paper, 314 fols.	Dist. 1 - 6	(late) 15th century (Xanten?) (Brigittines)
Deventer, Stads- of Athenaeumbibliotheek, Ms. I, 37 (101 D 18).	Paper, 319 fols.	Dist. 1 - 6	1487 Deventer, Buusken House (Common Life)
- - -, Ms. I, 38 (101 D 8).	Paper, 200 fols.	Dist. 1 - 3	1469 Deventer, Brandes House (Common Life)
- - -, Ms. I, 39 (101 D 9).	Paper, 193 fols.	Dist. 4 - 6	1474 Deventer, Brandes House (Common Life)
* Nijmegen, University Library, photocopy of olim Gaesdonck, Ms. 61.		Dist. 4 - 6	early to mid-15th century Arnhem, St Agnes House (Common Life, after 1459 Windesheim)
Utrecht, University Library, Ms. 1016 (5 D 6).	Paper, 323 fols.	Dist. 1 - 6	1491 Neerbosch (Windesheim)
Vienna, Austrian National Library, Cod. s. n. 12.844.	Paper, 190 fols.	Dist. 4 - 6	circa 1470 Northeast Netherlands

* Indicates particular need for further work on classification of the version.

Table 2

oblenz, Landeshaupt- archiv, Best. 701, Nr. 147.	Paper, 200 fols.	<u>Dist</u>. 1 - 6	late 15th century Northeast Netherlands
armstadt, Hessische Landes- und Hoch- schulbibliothek, Ms. 106.	Paper, 233 fols.	<u>Dist</u>. 1 - 6	15th century bound at Cologne by the Brothers of the Common Life
trasbourg, National and University Library, Germ. 722.	Paper, 223 fols	<u>Dist</u>. 1 - 6	15th century Rheinberg, St Barbara's Garden
rier, Stadtbibliothek, Ms. 1236 (604).	Paper, 294 fols.	<u>Dist</u>. 1 - 6	1466 (Eberhardsklausen?) (Windesheim)

NOTES

*This paper represents a report of research in progress and a projection
of proposed work; the author wishes to point out further, subsequent
work which updates data presented here in 1976. Cf. footnote 8.

1. J. Deschamps, Middelnederlandse handschriften uit Europese en
    Amerikaanse bibliotheken [Exhibition Catalogue for The Royal
    Library, Brussels, October 24 - December 24, 1970], 2nd ed. (Leiden,
    1972).

2. J. Deschamps, Middelnederlandse handschriften, entries 62, 63.

3. C. G. N. de Vooys, Middelnederlandse legenden en exempelen,
    2nd ed. (Groningen and The Hague, 1962), pp. 15 - 20. [Cf. also
    footnote 7.]

4. Tijdrekendundig register op het Oud-Provincial Archief van
    Overijssel, ed. J. I. van Doorninck, 6 parts (Zwolle, 1857 - 1875),
    entries passim as listed in the index. The possibility that
    several persons having the same name are involved must not be dis-
    counted. Our copyist may also be the same Johan Henrikszoon who
    entered Albergen (evidently as a young cleric) in 1434. If so,
    it is unlikely that he is the Johan Henrickszoon mentioned as
    late as 1519.

5. For information on the Aachen manuscript I am indebted to the
    Diocesan Archive for copies of its unpublished notes. For the
    data on the Deventer texts I wish to thank Drs. Bonnie Rademaker
    for helping me take copious notes during a research trip to

Deventer, sponsored by the American Philosophical Society, during the summer of 1974. Cf. much shorter entries in the Catalogus der handschriften berustende op de Athenaeumbibliotheek te Deventer, ed. J. C. van Slee (Deventer, 1892). For an earlier report on the Nijmegen manuscript, see C. Borchling's "Vierter Reisebericht" in Nachrichten der Königlichen Gesellschaft der Wissenschaften zu Göttingen, Philologische-historische Klasse, 1913, Beiheft, pp. 127 - 128. For information on the Utrecht manuscript I am indebted to Drs. K. van der Horst for extensive correspondence. Cf. Catalogus codicum manuscriptorum Bibliothecae Universitatis Rheno-Trajectinae, 2 parts (Utrecht and The Hague, 1887 - 1909), part I, pp. 246 - 247, and Gregor Hövelmann, "Die Handschriften der Klosterbibliothek Gaesdonck," Gaesdoncker Blätter 21 (1968), pp. 74 - 75. For information on the Vienna manuscript I am indebted to Dr. Jan Deschamps, Brussels, for sharing his notes with me, and to Mr. István Németh, Vienna. Cf. the entry for this manuscript in vol. 3 of H. Menhardt's Verzeichnis der altdeutschen literarischen Handschriften der Österreichischen Nationalbibliothek, 3 vols. (Berlin, 1960 - 1961).

6. I am indebted to the Landesarchiv, Coblenz, for pointing out and updating the description of their manuscript by C. Borchling, "Vierter Reisebericht," pp. 39 - 40. The Hessische Landes- und Hochschulbiliothek kindly shared their unpublished notes on Ms. 106; regarding the binding, see Hermann Knaus, "Die Kölner

Fraterherrn, Handschriften und Einbände aus ihrer Werkstatt,"
Gutenberg Jahrbuch, 1958, pp. 334 - 357, esp. p. 348 and note 22.
For the Strasbourg manuscript, see the Katalog der Kaiserlichen
Universitäts-und Landesbibliothek in Strassburg. Die deutschen
Handschriften . . ., ed. Adolf Becker (Strasbourg, 1914) pp. 119-
120. For the Trier manuscript, see the Verzeichnis der Hand-
schriften der Stadtbibliothek Trier, Heft 7 (Trier, 1911), entry
1236 (604), and Heft 8 (Trier, 1914), entry 495 (1236).

7. Bydragen tot de geschiedenis der Cisterciensers in: [sic]
   Nederland. Deel I. De Middelnederlandse vertaling van het
   Exordium magnum volgens het handschrift der universiteitsbiblio-
   theek to Leiden (Mij. Ndl. Letterk.) 1031, ed. A. Greebe
   (Achel, 1932).

8. I wish to openly thank P. Edmundus Mikkers, Achel, for his exceptional generosity in forwarding to me A. Greebe's notes on,
   inter al., Deventer, Stads- of Athenaeumbibliotheek, Ms. I, 37;
   it appears from these notes that the Deventer manuscript was to
   have been next in line for publication in this series.

9. See J. Deschamps, Middelnederlandse handschriften, entry 63, and
   the literature cited by him.

10. For data on the Vienna manuscript, I am indebted to Dr. Jan
    Deschamps, Brussels, for sharing his notes with me. For the
    Brussels manuscript, see J. Deschamps, Middelnederlandse hand-
    schriften, entry 62, and my unpublished notes on this manuscript.

11. J. Deschamps, Middelnederlandse handschriften, entry 62, and literature cited.

12. For the Dietse kollatieboeken, see J. Deschamps, Middelnederlandse handschriften, entry 90, and the literature cited, especially Deschamps' "De Dietse kollatieboeken van Dirc van Herxen (1381-1457), rektor van het Zwolse fraterhuis," Handelingen van het XXIIIe. Vlaams Filologencongres (Brussels, 1959), pp. 186 -193.

13. Bibliotheca Universitatis Leidensis. Codices Manuscripti. V. Codicum in finibus Belgarum ante annum 1550 conscriptorum qui in bibliotheca universitatis asservantur. Pars I. Codices 168 -360 societatis cui nomen Maatschappij der Nederlandsche Letterkunde, ed. G. I. Lieftinck (Leiden, 1948), p. 180.

14. Frédéric van der Meer, Atlas de l'ordre cistercien (Amsterdam and Brussels, 1965), Map III; R. R. Post, The Modern Devotion [Studies in Medieval and Reformation Thought, III] (Leiden, 1968), maps 1, 2 ad fin.

15. Jacobus Traiecti alias de Voecht, Narratio de incohatione domus clericorum in Zwollis, ed. M. Schoengen [Werken uitgegeven door het Historisch Genootschap, III, 13] (Amsterdam, 1908), p. 236.

16. Among abundant literature on these subjects, see, for the question of reform, sources such as those cited by A. Hyma, The Christian Reformation, 2nd ed. (Hamden, Connecticut, 1965), in footnote 57 to Chapter III, pp. 383 - 384; for the statement of Groote, with appropriate commentary, see ibid., pp. 564 - 565.

17. Reforms, of course, were by no means unilateral. For a more composite treatment of Groote's views, see R. R. Post, The Modern Devotion, "Groote's Attitude to Monasteries," pp. 51 - 66, and especially the latter part of this section.

18. See A. Hyma, The Christian Renaissance, Chapter V, "The 'Imitation of Christ'," pp. 158 - 190, esp. pp. 180 - 181, and the supplemental chapter, "The Original Version of the 'Imitation of Christ'," pp. 543- 581, esp. pp. 558 - 559.

EXEGESIS AND CHRISTOLOGY IN THE SERMONS
OF HUGH OF PONTIGNY

NICHOLAS GROVES

Hugh, first abbot of Pontigny, was a contemporary of St Bernard.
Born sometime between 1080 and 1085, he was abbot of Pontigny from
its foundation in 1114 until his election as bishop of the diocese
of Auxerre in 1137. Our main sources for his life are the accounts
given of him in the Vita prima of St Bernard and a short biography
in a collection of lives of the twelfth-century bishops of Auxerre.
Unfortunately, neither of these sources tells us much about Hugh as
abbot of Pontigny. The Vita prima tells of Hugh as a friend of Bernard, whom Bernard "converts" to the monastic life, while the Auxerre account gives us information on Hugh as bishop.[1] Our only
source for Hugh as abbot of Pontigny is a collection of sermons.
There is only one complete text of these that has so far been discovered, a manuscript in the Austrian monastery of Zwettl. There
are also a few individual sermons which appear in other collections
of sermons (Angers, Bibl. munic., 303 ff. 129-43; Paris, Bibl. nat.,
lat. 3301 C, ff. 11-16v, 34-37, 38-41v, 49v-50, 77-79, 87-89v; Bibl.
nat. lat. 2569, ff. 237-41; Orléans, Bibl. munic. 198, pp. 330-34;
Monte Cassino, Bibl. de l'abbaye, 410 LL, pp. 191-93; Evreux, Bibl.
munic., 9, ff. 160v-61).[2] I am presently working on the preparation of a critical edition of the sermons. From a study of the

sermons, it is possible for us to see something of Cistercian thought outside of the abbey of Clairvaux between 1114 and 1137.

The purpose of this paper is to discuss briefly the scriptural exegesis and christology of Hugh of Pontigny. These themes are immense, and we can only briefly outline them here. Yet they are important for our understanding of Hugh, and are interrelated. They are important because Hugh, though what we might call a "minor" author, does give significant indications of Cistercian spirituality of his period and is known to have been a close friend of St Bernard. They are interrelated because in Hugh's view the purpose of scriptural interpretation is to lead us to a deeper understanding and appropriation of the life of Christ to ourselves. In this he shows his adherence to the tradition of <u>sacramenta</u> Scripturae so prevalent in the twelfth century, in which the Scriptures serve as "signs" which reveal Christ.[3] Thus in describing Jesus as a young boy Hugh says:

> While he was still a little boy, since he was born under
> law, he fulfilled the precepts of the law, and now as a
> man he became a lawmaker and unravelled the holy secrets
> of all the Scriptures. For now he was hanging on the
> cross, he who made Moses hide his face, and the veil of
> the temple was rent and the holy of holies was revealed
> so that the <u>sacramenta</u> of Scripture might be understood.[4]

Hugh's purpose in expounding the meanings of Scripture was to make his monks into *viri spirituales*, as he frequently says in the sermons.[5] We shall concentrate here on two elements of Hugh's exegesis and christology: his treatment of Christ as prefigured in the Scriptures and the contrast Hugh loves to emphasize between Christ's divinity and humanity.

The Prefiguring of Christ in the Old Testament

One of the oldest forms of scriptural interpretation in the Christian tradition is typology, seeing Christ foreshadowed in the events and personalities of the Old Testament. Hugh of Pontigny makes abundant use of typology, and it is integral to both his exegesis and his spirituality. In this he is following a long and highly developed tradition. Although there is uncertainty as to how much typology appears in St Paul and other New Testament authors, we do find it clearly established by the time of the Epistle of Barnabas and the writings of Justin Martyr. The purpose of typology was to a large extent apologetic, that is, to show unbelievers, particularly Jews, that Christ was indeed the Messiah, the fulfillment of the Old Testament.[6] Thus in the Epistle of Barnabas the "good land" described in Exodus 33:1, 3 is seen as Christ in the flesh.[7] Barnabas also understands the Temple as a prefiguring of the Messiah:

Further, I will tell you about the Temple, how deceived
were the miserable people who put their hope in the
building, and not in their God who made them to be the
real temple of God.[8]

Justin Martyr is one of the most important individuals in the
development of typology. He begins a number of themes which will
continue throughout the scriptural exegesis of the Fathers and the
monastic authors. One such theme is that of Noah as prefiguring
Christ. Justin explains this typology in this way:

Christ who was the first-born of all creation also became the beginning again of another race, reborn by him
through water and faith and wood, since he brought the
mystery of the Cross, just as Noah also saved by wood,
riding on the waves with his family.[9]

This theme is taken up by countless medieval authors and becomes a
part of a common tradition. So Hugh can describe Noah in one of the
poems which follow his sermons:

Adam producitur de limo nascitur Christus de virgine
Archam ingreditur Noe concluditur Deus in homine.[10]

The purpose of comparing these patristic texts with Hugh is not
to suggest "direct" influence. Barnabas and the works of Justin
would not have been available to him directly. But the themes which
began to be of importance in early patristic exegesis and typology

continued to be used and developed by authors such as St Augustine, Ambrose, and Gregory with whom Hugh would have been quite familiar. These are the authorities Hugh directly identifies at various points in his sermons.[11]

The basic significance of typology as a way of understanding the Scriptures was first systematically developed by Origen. He took the earlier traditions of typology and made them into a "science" of scriptural interpretation. To various degrees this method of interpretation was adopted by Ambrose, Augustine, and Gregory the Great.[12] At the heart of this understanding of Scripture was the idea that Christ was hidden or foreshadowed in everything, even in the actions of people who did not consciously recognize him, as in many Old Testament figures. All of Scripture was an expression of Christ, and thus all of it created a harmony which Origen compared to the strings of a lyre.[13] Christ, in Origen's exegesis, spoke through the prophets, the psalms, and even such natural events as the flood, because Christ was incarnate in Scripture:

> We see in a human way the Word of God on earth, since
> He became a human being, for the Word has continually
> been becoming flesh in the Scriptures in order that
> He might tabernacle with us.[14]

To Origen and those who were to follow the model of scriptural interpretation he set forth the Word was Sacrament. This idea became

the basis for the popular medieval theme of <u>sacramenta</u> <u>Scripturae</u>
which we discussed earlier.[15] It was only in the early development
of scholastic theology [16] shortly after Hugh that theologians began
more carefully to define certain rites as "sacraments" in the sense
we understand them.

In one passage Origen observes that the prophets spoke to three
audiences at once: their contemporaries, others who came later, but
most of all those who could penetrate to this meaning of Christ in
some event that occurred before Christ's advent into the world. This
principle Origen describes as comparing spiritual things to spiritual:

> It is only a person who is wise and truly in Christ who
> could give as a connected whole the interpretation of
> the obscure passages in the prophets by "comparing
> spiritual things with spiritual" (1 Cor. 11:13) and
> by explaining each phrase he found in the text from
> the common usage of that phrase elsewhere in scrip-
> ture.[17]

This theme of Scripture as the record of the revelation of Christ
is one of the most constant and fully developed ideas in the sermons.
It is the basis of Hugh's exegesis and of his theology. For Hugh,
Scripture is the medium through which God reveals his Word, who is
Christ. Even the creation of the world is a prefiguring of the In-
carnation:

Behold in the beginning of the world is prefigured the
beginning of man's restoration. For man's restoration
·is the incarnation of the Word.[18]

Hugh, though often a tedious preacher, becomes most eloquent
when he describes the prefiguring of Christ. We can sense his enjoyment in the working out of these themes:

He therefore entered into a house (Wr. 10:38) when he

revealed the signs of his Incarnation to the faithful

ones. He entered into a house in Abraham, in Isaac,

in Jacob, in the paschal lamb, in the manna, in the

red calf, and in the bronze serpent. He therefore

is Abraham, he is Isaac, he is Jacob, he is the lamb,

he is the manna, he is the red calf, he is the bronze

serpent.[19]

Hugh can create a poem of descriptions of the prefigurings of Christ
as he does at the end of the collection of Sermons on the text Pa-
terne glorie splendorem hodie sacra puerpera gignente patuit quod
clausum latuit diu sub littera.[20] His prose becomes eloquent:

Blessed are those whom Christ restores because they will

not hunger or thirst again (Rev. 7:16). In order that

they may never hunger He is the living bread, in order

that they may never thirst He is the source of life.

He indeed is the tree of life in the middle of Paradise

(Gen. 2:9) shading those striken with heat with its
branches, attracting those seeking it by its scent,
enticing those looking on it by its beauty, restoring those enjoying it with its sweetness. Its shadow is a spiritual cooling, its scent is balm, its
beauty the brightness of eternal light, its fruit
eternity, its enjoyment health.[21]

Hugh admits that he is following the tradition of the sancti
doctores in seeing Christ and Christian doctrines prefigured in
the Old Testament. Thus he sees Abraham's reception of the angels
as a prefiguring of the Trinity:

Hence in the coming of the three angels, in preparation for them Abraham killed a bull. By the bull is
to be understood stubbornness. The immolation of the
bull is thus the humiliation of a proud heart. To
such the three angels appeared because to the humble
God gives grace through which a knowledge of the
Trinity is poured out. As indeed the holy doctors
say these three angels are the Father, the Son, and
the Spirit. These were first seen by Abraham in the
valley of Mambre, next by Jacob, in Bethel; by Abraham as they were coming down the road, by Jacob as
they came down a ladder.[22]

For Hugh, the significance of this method of viewing Scripture is that it makes of Scripture a revelation of Christ, and Hugh invites his monks to make of this revelation a personal experience of conversion, an encounter with the living Christ. Revelation, and an understanding of revelation, demands a personal response. After describing Christ as the tree of life in the garden (Gen. 2:9) Hugh says that the purpose of Christ's refreshing us is to invite us to himself. The tone is unmistakeably Cistercian:

> With such delights the table of the King of Kings is
>
> filled to which Jesus now invites us. Let us run
>
> therefore by our labors, let us hasten by our love,
>
> let us hurry by our behaviour, let us pass through
>
> our desire, seeing that with the living Saviour him-
>
> self we merit to come to it, striving to enjoy and
>
> possess him.[23]

Because the revelation of Scripture is a direct invitation to know Christ, it is important for us to examine how Hugh describes Christ. His exegesis leads us to his christology.

The Nature of Christ According to Hugh of Pontigny

A thorough discussion of Hugh's christology would take us far beyond the bounds of this paper. In our present discussion we emphasize the ways in which Hugh understands the nature of Christ. During the first half of the twelfth century--that is, during the

time Hugh was abbot of Pontigny and later bishop of Auxerre--there
were lively debates about Christ's nature and the meaning of his re-
demptive act. The most celebrated and controversial of these involved Abelard (1141) and Gilbert of Poitiers (1148). In both the
Cistercian presence in the person of St Bernard proved crucial.
While we cannot expect of Hugh the precision of theological vocabulary of an Abelard or a Gilbert, we can derive some idea of his
view of Christ from the important place of christology in the sermons.

In his article "The Case of Gilbert de la Porrée Bishop of
Poitiers (1142-1154)," Nicholas Häring outlines the three theories
of the hypostatic union held in Gilbert's time.

Häring outlines the three basic types of twelfth-century Chris-
tologies in this manner:

> The crucial issue is their concept of person and per-
> sonal union. With the eyes of their mind trained on
> the Boethian definition of person as naturae ration-
> abilis individua substantia, they made numerous and
> hardly successful efforts to explain the undisputed
> truth of faith that the second trinitarian Person
> assumed human nature. . .the first theory held that,
> in the Incarnation, a man's substance became God; the
> second opinion denied this and reduced both the divin-

ity and humanity to natures entering into the composition of Christ's single substance, which led to
the logical conclusion that Christ's humanity as
such is not a substance or person but a substantial
principle or nature; the third theory denied the
idea of substantial components, declared that Christ's
humanity is related to the second trinitarian Person
as a _habitus_ is related to a substance, and agreed
with the second theory in the sense that in Christ's
humanity body and soul were never so united to one
another as to form a substance which would have made
it a person.[24]

According to this outline, I believe, we can say that Hugh
accepted the second option, that Christ's humanity was a "substantial principle or nature." I say "basically" because Hugh's language is never so consistently methodical that we can identify a
Christology in the manner Häring does. Although Hugh frequently
employs the phrase _assumptus homo_ in speaking of Christ, we can say
that he places the greatest emphasis on God's action in assuming
human nature rather than on how a man's substance could become God.
The emphasis throughout is on Christ's single substance. Hugh describes Christ's nature in sermon 14:

On account of this God took up (_assumpsit_) from man all

that was man's, except for sin, and bestowed on man all

that was God's. He took up humble things, he gave man

heavenly things, and thus he said to man "Stand upon

the heights." Behold how in the newest Adam is fulfilled

what was first said by God, "Behold Adam was made as one

of us." Stand in awe of the Son of God and of man who be-

cause of the taking on (assumptionem) of flesh is called

Adam. The nature which he assumed (assumpsit) he deified

and lifted into the glory of the being like to God, and in

those who share with him in this he keeps his word truly,

saying that we are sons of God and shall be like him. God

in giving this honor to man, in man standing in the mirey

clay says to man, "Stand upon the heights."25

As Häring maintains, this second christological explanation emphasizes that:

Christ did not become a person but was a person from all

eternity. In the incarnation. . .He only became a man's

person and thus a "composit person."26

St Bernard expresses a similar christology in his second sermon
on the Nativity. Speaking of the failure of the "work" that was human nature Bernard describes how God planned to repair this by send-
ing his Word into the world:

He said, "I shall make a new mixture (commixturam) where

more expressly and strongly I shall place an image
(sigillum) that is, him who is not just made in my
image, but is the image itself, the splendor of the
glory and the figure of the substance, not made, but
born before all ages. . .The Word that was "in the
beginning with God and was God," the soul which was
created from nothing and before which was not, and
the flesh from the mass of corruption without any
corruption by the divine action made like no other
flesh, came together into unity in an indissoluble
person.[27]

This sounds very much like Häring's second option. Bernard is
here expressing not only a christology but an anthropology as well.
It is the anthropology much favored by Cistercians of this time who
taught that man was made up of three elements: rational ability,
the soul, and the flesh.[28] In describing Christ's nature Bernard
parallels it to the nature of man.

Hugh stresses that although both the divine and the human enter
into the make up of Christ, there is an "inseparable union" or, as he
expresses it in sermon 17, "Dei et hominis inseparabilis unio," and
that this union comes when Christ the Word assumed humanity:

The Son assuming humanity as wax with the imprint of
the divine likeness united it humanity to himself

who "truly is the figure of the substance of God."[29]

If Hugh lays emphasis on the divinity of Christ in his theological descriptions, in his devotion Hugh stresses Christ's humanity.
Although he can return repeatedly to the theme of an eternal Christ
prefigured in Scripture, the corollary of this throughout the sermons is that Christ became man, and took on himself the nature of
man in order that man might become one with God.

There are two very important patristic sources here. The first,
and the one that influenced Hugh most directly, was the Chalcedonian
document of St Leo, the Tomus ad Flavianum. Leo expresses there the
contrast between Christ's divine and human natures:

> *Salva igitur proprietate utriusque naturae,*
>
> *Et in unam coeunte personam,*
>
> *Suscepta est a maiestate humilitas, a virtute infirmitas*
>
> *Ab aeternitate mortalitas.*[30]

The second source, one that would have reached Hugh indirectly
through other patristic authors, was Irenaeus.[31] While Irenaeus
was not the first theologian to develop the idea of deification,
he did give it a systematic expression which influenced later authors. Although we cannot pinpoint with certainty Hugh's source
for this idea, he does sound remarkably similar in some of his language on this point to St Ambrose. There is a marked likeness in
both thought and expression between a passage from one of Ambrose's

scriptural commentaries and sermon 29 of Hugh. Writing of the in-
fancy of Christ, Ambrose says:

> He therefore was a little one, an infant, so that
> you O man could be made perfect; He was wrapped in
> swaddling clothes so that you might be loosed from
> the bands of death; He was in a manger so that you
> might be raised on the altars; He did not have any
> lodging so that you might have many mansions in
> heaven. . .Therefore that poverty is my inheritance,
> and the weakness of the Lord is my strength. He pre-
> ferred to be in need so that He could abound in all
> things. The tears of that child wash me, those tears
> wash away my crimes.[32]

Hugh writes in similar fashion in explaining an allegory in
sermon 29:

> Of these, that is, the lion, the hen, and the lamb,
> that is to say, the word, the soul, and the flesh,
> there is made a union when God and man come together
> in one, so that in this remarkable manner the humble
> might be exalted, the unknown visible, and the undying
> one able to suffer. O wondrous exchange, God is found
> a little child, and weak, and man is made all powerful
> and unbounded.[33]

This is clearly chalcedonian christology. In many other passages of Hugh this christology immediately appeals to our emotions
so that we might be moved to follow Christ's example. Hugh expresses
this idea in a dialogue between Christ and man:

> For this reason Jesus took up human things from man so
> that He might give man divine things. So He says to
> man: "Follow me." And so He says: "I so that I might
> accept you in whom I live came down to you, you truly
> that you can accept me in whom you live forever rise up
> to me." Follow me. Follow me the weak one the strong,
> the mortal one life, the hungry bread, the thirsty
> drink, the tired rest, the beggar a gift, the miser-
> able one mercy.[34]

There are many more examples we could give of Hugh's use of
Christ's divine and human natures as a motive for an affective appeal to his audience. It is certainly one of his favorite ideas
throughout the sermons. The point of all these in Hugh's spirituality is that by Christ's work and example we are brought to be one
with Him. This is akin to Aelred of Rievaulx's image of Christ's
humanity being myrrha mortalitatis eius. This myrrh comforts us
and at the same time leads us to seek Christ:

> Sweet certainly to me is your food and drink taken with
> sinners and publicans, sweeter than the rigid abstinence

of the Pharisees. Surely the odor of your ointments is
better than all other perfumes. How satisfying to the
taste that I know the Lord of majesty showing himself
in bodily form and human affections, not like the
strong, but in the manner of the weak! How this comforts me in my infirmity! Surely this infirmity of my
Lord is the strength and support of my infirmity.[35]

Although the accents are individual in Hugh, Bernard, and Aelred, we can say that Hugh shares with his contemporaries an emphasis on Christ's divinity as the goal, and his humanity as the way.
As Hugh expresses it:

Christ the man is our way, Christ God our homeland.
The way is one of pure actions, the homeland is one
of eternal blessedness. Therefore through the way
we travel so that we might merit to come to this
homeland.[36]

The University of Chicago

NOTES

1. For the Vita Prima, see PL 185, 235ac. For Hugh as bishop of
   Auxerre see the anonymous work in L. M. Duru, ed. Bibliothèque
   Historique de l'Yonne. Vol. I. (Auxerre: Perriquet, 1950) pp.
   417ff. I owe this reference to Ms. Constance Bouchard, a fellow graduate student in history at the University of Chicago.
   Ms. Bouchard has examined the manuscript from which the printed
   edition of Duru was prepared. She informs me that the hand is
   clearly twelfth-century.

2. These mss. were discovered by Dom Jean Leclercq as he was working on his edition of St Bernard.

3. There are many discussions of this theme. See, for example,
   J. de Montclos, Lanfranc et Berengar. La Controverse Eucharis-
   tique du XIe siècle. (Leuven, 1971). Also H. De Lubac. Corpus
   Mysticum; l'Eucharistie et l'Eglise au moyen âge. Etude historique. 2nd ed. rev. et augm. (Aubier, 1949) pp. 23-66.

4. Sermo 15: Cum adhuc parvulus esset utpote natus sub lege legis
   observavit decreta, cum iam vir factus fuisset ut revera legis-
   lator legis et omnium scripturarum propolavit secreta. Eo namque
   in stipite pendente quo facies Moysi erat velata velum templi scis-
   sum est et patuerunt sancta sanctorum it intelligerentur sacramen-
   ta scripturarum."

5. The term <u>vir</u> <u>spiritualis</u> occurs frequently in Hugh's sermons. There is a definition of it in <u>Sermo</u> 1.

   "Avis est vir spiritualis qui supernorum desiderio raptus, celestibus exercitiis est intentus. Qui modo quodam ad volatum cum proficit in Deum."

6. See R. P. C. Hanson. <u>Allegory</u> <u>and</u> <u>Event</u>: <u>A</u> <u>Study</u> <u>of</u> <u>the</u> <u>Sources</u> <u>and</u> <u>Significance</u> <u>of</u> <u>Origen's</u> <u>Interpretation</u> <u>of</u> <u>Scripture</u>. (London: SCM Press, 1959) pp. 97-129.

7. <u>Epistle</u> <u>of</u> <u>Barnabas</u> 6, 8. Quoted in Hanson, <u>Allegory</u>, p. 98.

8. <u>Epistle</u> <u>of</u> <u>Barnabas</u> 16; Hanson, p. 98.

9. Justin Martyr. <u>Dialogue</u> <u>with</u> <u>Trypho</u> 138; 2; Hanson, p. 104.

10. "Adam is made from clay, Christ is born of a Virgin. Noah enters the ark, God is enclosed in man."

11. For example, St Gregory, <u>Moralium</u> <u>Liber</u> <u>XXXV</u>, <u>In</u> <u>Caput</u> <u>XII</u> B. <u>Job</u>; PL 76:765C, quoted in <u>Sermo</u> 9; St Augustine, <u>Ad</u> <u>Maced</u>. <u>Epist</u>. CLV; <u>Operum</u> Vol. 2, c. 703, (1797 edition); PL 33:671, quoted in <u>Sermo</u> 20; St Gregory. <u>Moralium</u> <u>Liber</u> <u>XIV</u>, <u>Cap</u>. <u>LIII</u>; PL 75: 462, quoted in <u>Sermo</u> 22.

12. For St Augustine, see M. Pontet, <u>L'Exègese</u> <u>de</u> <u>S</u>. <u>Augustin</u> <u>Prédi-cateur</u>. (Paris: Aubier), n. d. On the exegesis of St Ambrose see F. H. Dudden. <u>The</u> <u>Life</u> <u>and</u> <u>Times</u> <u>of</u> <u>St</u> <u>Ambrose</u> (Oxford: Oxford University Press, 1935) Vol. II, pp. 558 ff., 576 ff. There are some important essays on aspects of Ambrose's use of Scripture in

the volume <u>Ambroise</u> <u>de</u> <u>Milan</u>. XVIe <u>Centenaire</u> <u>de</u> <u>son</u> élection
<u>episcopale</u>. Yves-Marie Duval, ed. (Paris: Etudes Augustiniennes,
1974).

13. Origen. <u>Philocalia</u> VI. 2, quoted in Hanson, <u>Allegory</u>, p. 199.

14. Origen. <u>Philocalia</u> XV. 19, Hanson, p. 193.

15. Another very basic book here is H. De Lubac. <u>Histoire</u> <u>et</u> <u>Esprit</u>.
<u>L'intelligence</u> <u>de</u> <u>l'Ecriture</u> <u>d'après</u> <u>Origène</u>. (Paris: Aubier,
1950).

16. See P. Damien Van der Eynde. "Les définitions des sacraments
pendant la première période de la théologie scholastique," <u>Anton-
ianum</u> 24 (1949) pp. 183-228.

17. Origen. <u>Contra</u> <u>Celsum</u> <u>VII</u>, <u>11</u>; ed. Henry Chadwick (Cambridge,
1953).

18. <u>Sermo</u> 57: Ecce in exordio mundane conditionis exordium prefigur-
atur humane restaurationis. Humana restauratio Verbi est incar-
natio.

19. <u>Sermo</u> 26: Intravit itaque in castellum quando sue incarnationis
signa premonstravit populo fidelium. Intravit castellum in
Abraham, in Isaac, in Iacob, in agno paschali, in manna, in
vitula russa, in serpente eneo. Ipse igitur est Abraham, ipse
Isaac, ipse Iacob, ipse agnus, ipse manna, ipse vitula russa,
ipse serpens eneus.

20. <u>Sermo</u> 75.

21. Sermo 10: Beati quos reficit Christus quia non esurient, neque
    sitient amplius. Ut nunquam esuriant ipse est panis vivus, ut
    nunquam sitiant ipse est fons vite. Ipse est item lignum vite
    in medio paradisi aestuantes obumbrans foliis, diligentes at-
    trahens odore, pulchritudine contemplantes alliciens, reficiens
    gustantes dulcedine. Eius umbra spirituale refrigerium, eius
    odor infusio carismatum, eius pulchritudo candor lucis eterne,
    eius fructus eternitas, eius gustus sanitas.

22. Sermo 71: "Hinc item in adventu trium angelorum taurum mactavit
    Abraham. In tauro nota cervicositatem. Tauri ergo immolatio
    tumidi cordi humiliatio. Talibus apparent tres angeli quoniam
    humilibus dat Deus gratiam per quam infunditur eius noticia
    Trinitatis. Ut enim sancti doctores asserunt tres illi angeli,
    Pater et Filius et utriusque Spiritus. Qui primo ab Abraham
    in convalle Mambre, postea visi sunt a Iacob in Bethel, ab Abra-
    ham descendentes per viam, a Iacob descendentes per scalam."
    This particular exegesis has a venerable history. Justin Martyr
    uses the visit of the angels to Abraham to explain that God
    appeared in the Old Testament under the appearance of other
    identities than "Maker of the universe." See Justin Martyr. Dia-
    logue with Trypho 56. St Augustine discusses this revelation
    in De Trinitate, Bk. II. 34 (PL 42, 868).

23. Sermo 10: Talibus deliciis mensa Summi Regis cumulatur ad quam

Iesus nos invitat. Curramus itaque operibus, festinemus affectu, properemus moribus, transeamus desiderio, quatinus eodem salvatore vivante ad eam pervenire, pervenientes degustare possidere mereamur.

24. N. Häring, "The Case of Gilbert de la porrée Bishop of Poitiers (1142-1154)," Mediaeval Studies 13 (1951) pp. 28 ff.

25. Sermo 14: Ob hoc Deus ab homine totum quod erat hominis praeter peccatum assumpsit ut totum quod Dei erat conferret homini, assumpsit humilia, contulit sublimia, proinde dixit homini: Sta in excelso. Ecce in novissimo adam completum est quod a Deo de primo dictum est 'Ecce adam quasi unus ex nobis factus est.' Revera Dei et hominis filius qui propter carnis assumptionem dictus est adam naturam quam assumpsit deificavit et divine similitudinis gloria sublimavit in suis participibus prestaret fiduciam veraciter dicendi filii Dei sumus et similes ei erimus (I Io. 3, 2) Hunc honorem conferens Deus homini, in homine stans in limo profundi dixit homini: Sta in excelso.

26. Häring. "The Case of Gilbert," p. 32.

27. St Bernard. Sermo 2 in Nativitate. ed. J. Leclercq. S. Bernardi Opera Vol. IV. Sermones. (Rome: Editiones Cistercienses, 1966) pp. 253-54:

28. For a discussion of Cistercian anthropology see B. McGinn. The Golden Chain. A Study in the Theological Anthropology of Isaac

of <u>Stella</u>. Cistercian Studies Series: No. 15 (1972) pp. 115 ff.

29. <u>Sermo</u> 19: Filius humanitatem assumens quasi quandam ceram sigillo divine similitudinis aptando univit eam sibi qui vere est figura substantie Dei.

30. Therefore through the saving property of each nature coming together into one person, lowliness is taken up by majesty, weakness by strength, mortality by eternity.' Quoted in A. Grillmeir. <u>Christ</u> <u>in</u> <u>Christian</u> <u>Tradition</u>. <u>From</u> <u>the</u> <u>Apostolic</u> <u>Age</u> <u>to</u> <u>Chalcedon</u> (<u>451</u>). (London-New York, 1964) p. 466 -- translation mine.

31. Irenaeus was very important in developing the theology of deification. The significance of this concept, as well as citations from key texts in his writings are shown in Adolf Harnack. <u>History</u> <u>of</u> <u>Dogma</u>. Vol. II. (New York: Dover Publications, Inc., 1961) pp. 239 ff.

32. St Ambrose. <u>Exp</u>. <u>Luc</u>. <u>II</u>: CCL 14, 49 ff -- translation mine.

33. <u>Sermo</u> 29: Horum scilicet leonis, galline et agni, id est, verbi anime et carnis facta est coniunctio quando Deus et homo convenerunt in unum, ut miro modo esset excelsus humilis, incognitus visibilis, athanatos passibilis. O admirabile commercium. Deus inventus est parvulus et infirmus, homo effectus est omnipotens et immensus est.

34. <u>Sermo</u> 52: Ob hoc Iesus ab homine assumpsit humana ut homini commicaret divina. Inde ait illi: "sequere me." Ac si dicat:

"Ego ut a te acciperem in quo transirem ad te descendi, tu vero ut a me accipias in quo permaneas ad me ascende." "Sequere me" infirmus fortem, mortalis vitam, esuriens panem, sitiens fontem, lassus requiem, mendicus munificum, miser misericordem.

35. Aelred, Sermo II in Natali Domini; PL 195:226: "Dulcius certe mihi olet cibus tuus et potus in medio peccatorum et publicanorum, quam rigida abstinentia Pharisaeorum. Certe odor unguentorum tuorum super omnia aromata. Quomodo mihi sapit, quod cerno Dominum majestatis exhibentem se, quantum ad corporalia exercitia, et humanas affectiones, non secundum modum fortium, sed secundum modum infirmorum! Quantum me confortat hoc in infirmitate mea!"

36. Sermo 23: Christus homo via nostra, Christus Deus patria nostra. Via conversationis honeste, patria beatitudinis eterne. Igitur per viam gradiamur quatinus ad patriam pervenire mereamur.

JOACHIM OF FIORE AND THE CISTERCIAN ORDER:

A STUDY OF <u>DE VITA SANCTI BENEDICTI</u>

SANDRA ZIMDARS-SWARTZ

Two primary concerns of the twelfth-century Calabrian abbot and prophet Joachim of Fiore come to focus in the Cistercian Order. One is, as Bernard McGinn has aptly called it, Joachim's "unremitting search for the most perfect form of the monastic life."[1] The other is the abbot's perception of the forward movement of events, and hence his three state (<u>status</u>) schema of history. Although Joachim by no means regarded the Cistercian Order as the fulfillment of his vision of the ideal monastic life or of his schema of history, his views on these matters cannot be understood apart from his critique of the Cistercianism of the twelfth century. In this critique, Joachim sees the Cistercian Order standing at a particularly crucial and creative juncture in the history of salvation.

Until 1188/89, Joachim himself was intimately associated with the Cistercian Order.[2] Under his guidance as abbot, the benedictine monastery Corazzo adopted Cistercian customs and sought full incorporation into the Cistercian Order. But by the time Corazzo had become a daughter house of Fossanova, Joachim had left the Order to establish his own independent monastic community, San Giovanni in

Fiore. Joachim's comments about the Cistercian Order have almost
always been interpreted in the light of his founding of the community at Fiore. Especially Foberti, Buonaiuti, and Russo have been
interested in the Abbot's alleged dispute with the Order and in his
reasons for leaving.[3] A tract sometimes cited in this regard is the
De vita sancti Benedicti et de officio divino secundum eius doctrinam,[5]
which Joachim composed in the years 1186/87, just prior to leaving the
Cistercian Order.[5] Although the tract gives insights into Joachim's
motives for leaving the Cistercians, it is more important positively
as a witness to an early state of his thought about the nature of
monastic perfection.

In 1184 Joachim began work on his three major treatises, the
Liber concordie, the Expositio in Apocalypsim, and the Psalterium
decem chordarum.[6] In the years following, Joachim continued to
work on these, finally satisfied to submit only the Liber concordie
for papal approval in 1200. Reeves believes to be able to trace
something of the development of Joachim's thought in the Liber concordie.[7] A detailed study of this tract, however, indicates that it
is a tightly organized, well-polished composition.[8] Baraut indeed
considers the Liber concordie Joachim's only completed work.[9] To
study the early state of Joachim's ideas, therefore, one must look
to the shorter, unrevised tracts, completed earlier, such as the

De prophetia ignota[10] and the Vita Benedicti. Although Joachim's
mature thought about the perfected monastic life of the third state
is most clearly explicated in the Liber concordie, the Vita Benedicti
provides that detailed analysis of contemporary monasticism which in
a very basic sense underlies his mature and prophetic vision.

The title of the tract, as Baraut observes, is an indication of
its organization. In the first part of the tract, Joachim comments
on certain incidents from the life of St Benedict, as related in
Book II of Gregory the Great's Dialogues. In the second part, he
comments on passages which pertain to the nocturnal celebration of the
divine office, as stated in the benedictine Rule.[11] Yet, Joachim's
concern was always to understand all the events of history specifically in relation to, and in harmony with, the Scriptures. Thus his
task in the Vita Benedicti was not only to explicate the significance
of certain parts of the life and Rule of Benedict, but also to establish their concordance with the Scriptures, and to understand their
significance through that concordance.[12] Benedict's importance for
Joachim is grounded in the fact that he was the founder par excellence
of monasticism and the giver of the Rule for monastic life. But with
regard to Joachim's method of commentary Benedict is also an eschatological type. Thus, the events of Benedict's life are prefigured
by biblical events, and at the same time, in harmony with those

biblical events, they provide the means for understanding present conditions and future direction.[13] It was through this method of biblical commentary that Joachim understood the significance of the Cistercian Order, both with regard to contemporary monasticism and to his schema of history.

Joachim saw the history of monasticism as a movement toward perfection. He considered the monastic life to be of a higher and more spiritual order than the lives of the clerics and laity. Joachim admitted that monastic history up to his own time had generally been rather unexemplary, but nevertheless it had been the context for such exceptional lives as those of Elijah, Benedict, and Bernard of Clairvaux.[14] Joachim conceived of monastic history according to the biblical pattern of the lives of the favored ones who suffer diagrace. Joseph, for example, designates "that most chaste Order of Monks begun by the most blessed Benedict."[15] The time that Joseph spends in slavery in Egypt signifies the many times that the Order of Monks has been enslaved to secular businesses. Joseph's undeserved confinement in prison indicates the difficulty of trying to lead a spiritual life--the attempt may not be in vain, but it will not be without punishment. Nonetheless, just as Joseph was raised up to freedom in Egypt, so the monastic order would be raised up in the Cistercian Order.[16]

Sara and Rachael point to the coming time of the Order of Monks when it will give birth to spiritual sons. Both beloved of their husbands, Sarah and Rachael must remain sterile while their less favored counterparts, Hagar and Leah, bear children. But when their time finally comes, Sarah and Rachael bear favored sons to whom the inheritance passes.[17] So too the Order of Monks has been unfruitful, while the Church has born many sons of the flesh. But Joachim felt that with the coming of the "seed of righteousness, namely the boy Benedict," the monastic order too would conceive and bear spiritual sons.[18]

As Joachim wrote, however, he saw both the Cluniacs and the Cistercians claiming to stand heir to the one order and Rule instituted by Benedict. The Cluniacs held priority with regard to being the elder order. But from Joachim's perspective, they had "carried off Benedict."[19] They imitated the footsteps of Benedict in terms of clothing, but not customs.[20] Like Esau coming burdened to his blind father with game, they were enslaved and they enslaved those who entered their monasteries.[21] The Cistercians, although distanced from Benedict in time, were nonetheless the order in which Benedict "lives and grows."[22] Unlike Esau, they were not bound to a blind father. Joachim observed that the Cisterican abbots like Jacob choose rather to sit next to the gracious mother, delighting

in freedom.[23] And as Scholastica won the favor of God so that an
unwilling Benedict sojourned with her through the night, and as
Rebecca secured the blessing of Isaac for Jacob, so the inheritance
would pass to the Cistercian Order.[24]

That the Cistercian Order would receive the favor of God is
prefigured, according to Joachim, in the twelve tribes of Israel.[25]
In the first state of the world characterized by the Order of the
Laity, five tribes of Israel -- Gad, Judah, Ephriam, Manassah and Ru-
ben, -- were favored over the seven other tribes. In the second state
of the world characterized by the Order of Clerics, five churches received the inheritance: Jerusalem, Antioch, Rome, Constantinople,
and Alexandria. But the inheritance also passes spiritually from
these churches to the seven churches which John the Evangelist
founded in Asia. In the third state of the world characterized by
the Order of Monks, a third harmony would be completed. As Joachim
wrote, he believed that five monasteries were already preferred to
all others: Cîteaux, La Ferté, Morimond, Clairvaux, and Pontigny.[26]
But seven new ones would receive the inheritance. Thus the Cistercian
Order was not destined to keep the inheritance. Monasticism had already moved geographically from Greece to Italy, and from Italy to
France,[27] which as Baraut has noted, corresponds to an inner transformation from basilian to benedictine to cistercian monasticism.[28]

Joachim likened this movement to Israel's descent into Egypt and ascent from Egypt to the banks of the Jordan. One change yet remained to be made: a final move that would leave the Cistercians behind and would take the Order of Monks "from the camps of Moab to the Judean mountains."[29]

The Cistercians, called out from Molesme by God, contained the kernel of a perfect monastic life. They followed the Rule joyfully, knew the value of contemplation and the necessity for silence, and were cognizant of the meaning of inward spiritual freedom.[30] Yet Joachim did not think that the Order had achieved perfection. He saw more concern for the physical increase of some monasteries than for their spiritual growth. With the increase of monasteries, the anxieties and worries about caring for those monasteries began to mount, and involvement with the world increased.[31] Although the Fathers of the Order wisely established rules against monastic involvement in secular businesses such as villas, rents, graves, and altars, Joachim saw many abbeys around him involved in such affairs.[32]

Joachim's criticisms are based on his conviction that the Cistercians were trying to combine the active and contemplative lives. By the active life Joachim meant that preaching in the world and care for the neighbor which had been primarily, but not exclusively, the concern of the Order of Clerics. By the contemplative life he meant that life

of meditation and prayer, directed toward God and carried out in
seclusion from the world, which had been the concern of some members
of the Order of Monks. Even at this early stage in his thinking, the
Calabrian Abbot was quite clear that the two lives could not in fact
be combined. The problems of the world, with which one in the active
life must deal, cannot be mixed with the quiet and solitude needed for
contemplation. Trying to combine the two is like trying to hold together fire and water, so that the water does not extinguish the fire,
and the fire does not consume the supply of water. The water of
action, he claimed, was in great danger of extinguishing the total
grace of contemplation.[33] Joachim thought of the contemplative life
as a poorer life, a high, narrow mountain-top which tolerated few, and
which few in fact could tolerate.[34] For this reason, the Cistercian
Order is symbolized not in Benedict, who can lead a life on the mountain-top, but in Scholastica, to whom Benedict descends compelled by
love, and with whom he must remain, although unwillingly, through the
night.[35]

In the <u>Vita Benedicti</u>, Joachim posed this problem of the incom-
patibility of the two lives with particular sharpness, but he also
began to find a way toward a solution. Precisely the Cistercian
Order's attempt to combine these two lives placed it in an unusually
creative position. Joachim paralled the Cistercian Order to Mary in

its role of being the final point of transition into a new state.
As the bearer of Christ, Mary stands under both law and grace, giving
birth to the higher out of the lower. In this sense she is a media-
trix between them. The Cistercian Order, according to Joachim, stands
in the same position with reference to the second and third state, and
the active and contemplative lives. It stands next to the gracious
mother, bearing spiritual sons who intiate the new state of the full-
ness of grace.[36]

Marjorie Reeves has observed that Joachim was "no esoteric mystic
who locks up the spiritual future within a select group while the
masses perish."[37] Rather, for Joachim, love of God was matched by
love of neighbor. He was concerned that the gleanings of contemplation be spread among the people of God through preaching, and he expected during the third state the conversion of the schismatic
Greeks and of the Jews.[38] The Order of Monks thus bears responsibility for both contemplation and preaching.[39] But because
Joachim believed firmly that these two lives could not be combined,
a peculiar problem arose with regard to the conception of life in
the third state.

The Vita Benedicti shows this problem clearly, and at the same
time shows Joachim's first attempts at its solution. Here it becomes
evident that the active and contemplative lives must be separated in

some manner, but Joachim is not yet clear about the manner of separation. Two different schemata of separation can be identified in the tract, one temporal and the other spatial.

In the schema of temporal separation, Joachim states that the monks emerging from the Cistercian Order would first spend time preaching. Then would come a persecution and a period of contemplation, followed by an outpouring of the Spirit upon the monks, enabling them to complete the final labor of evangelical preaching before the end of the world.[40] Here, then, the tasks of contemplation and preaching are carried out by the same group of men, but are separated in time.

In the schema of spatial separation, however, the contemplative monks (corresponding to Benedict) remain on the mountain-top, descending only as far as the preaching monks (corresponding to Scholastica) to convey to them the word of God. The preaching monks then carry the word out into the world, while the contemplatives ascend the mountain again.[41] Here the tasks are accomplished at the same time, but by two different groups of monks, one leading a contemplative life totally removed from the world, the other leading an active life but observing monastic rule.

Joachim's major writings, especially the <u>Liber</u> <u>concordie</u>, develop a view of the monastic life of the third state corresponding to this

schema of spatial separation in the <u>Vita</u> <u>Benedicti</u>. One particularly
interesting passage in the <u>Liber</u> <u>concordie</u>, upon which the monastery
plan of the <u>Liber</u> <u>figurarum</u> is apparently based, describes a monastery
divided into mansions according to the talents and weaknesses of the
brothers. Here, gathered around the contemplatives, as around a
central focus, are groups of brothers dedicated to God, having
spiritual gifts other than contemplation.[42] Joachim's unremitting
search for the most perfect form of the spiritual life has thus been
united with a desire to bring diverse spiritual gifts into the unity
of the monastery.

A paradigm for such unity can be found already in the <u>Vita</u>
<u>Benedicti</u>. In the closing lines of this tract, commenting on the
reading of the night office, Joachim pictures a unity in diversity,
which can only be achieved in the context of worship:

> He who is zealous for the exercise of the body sings the
> response after the Gospel of Luke; he who embraces the
> virtue of humility and excercises himself inwardly, sings
> the response after the reading of Matthew; he who strives
> to grasp the fortitude of faith and to exclude from him-
> self all idleness of doubt sings the response upon hearing
> the Gospel of Mark; he to whom it is given to penetrate the
> secrets of God through the Spirit, sings not only the res-
> ponse but also the Gloria upon hearing the voice of John.
> Nevertheless, those who began the responses sing also the
> verses, and these they all sing at the same time, for as
> each reading pertains uniquely to an individual, so in
> another manner, they may be common to all.[43]

The University of Kansas

NOTES

1. B. McGinn, "Joachim and the Sibyl," <u>Cîteaux</u> 24 (1973) 104.

2. Some disagreement remains as to whether Joachim first entered the Cistercian monastery Sambucina and there became a Cistercian monk, or whether he entered the benedictine monastery Corazzo and thus was never a full member of the Cistercian Order. For a recent biography which holds to the first position, see C. Baraut, "Joachim de Flore," <u>Dictionnaire de Spiritualité</u> 8: 1179-80; for the latter position, see McGinn, <u>op</u>. <u>cit</u>., pp. 102-107.

3. F. Foberti, <u>Gioacchino da Fiore</u>: <u>Nuovi studi critici sulla mistica e la religiosità in Calabria</u> (Florence, 1934) pp. 48-49, 148-51; E. Buonaiuti, <u>Gioacchino da Fiore</u>: <u>I tempi, la vita, il messaggio</u> (Rome, 1931) pp. 139-47; F. Russo, <u>Gioacchino da Fiore e le fondazioni florensi in Calabria</u> (Napoli, 1958) pp. 49-81. M. Reeves has studied Joachim's later influence in the Cisterican Order in "The Abbot Joachim's Disciples and the Cistercian Order," <u>Sophia</u> 19 (1951) 355-71, and in <u>The Influence of Prophecy in the Later Middle Ages</u> (Oxford, 1969) pp. 145-60.

4. Edited by C. Baraut, "Un Tratado Inedito de Joaquin de Fiore," <u>Analecta sacra Tarraconensia</u> 24 (1951) 33-122.

5. For dating of the tract, see Baraut, *op*. *cit*., p. 39; and H. Grundmann, "Zur Biographie Joachims von Fiore und Raniers von Ponza," *Deutsches* *Archiv* *für* *Erforschung* *des* *Mittelalters* 16 (1960) 493.

6. *Liber* *Concordie* *novi* *et* *veteris* *Testamenti*,(Venice, 1517); *Expositio* *in* *Apocalypsim* (Venice, 1527); *Psalterium* *decem* *chordarum* (Venice, 1527).

7. M. Reeves, *The* *Figurae* *of* *Joachim* *of* *Fiore* (Oxford, 1972) pp. 13-19. For her discussion of all Joachim's writings, see *Influence* *of* *Prophecy*, pp. 1-27.

8. I hope to explore the exegetical method used in the *Liber* *concordie* in another paper.

9. Baraut, "Joachim de Flore," cols. 1183-84.

10. Edited by McGinn, *op*. *cit*., 97-138.

11. Baraut, "Un Tratado Inedito," p. 35. Joachim comments at length on chapters 8, 9, and 11 of the Rule, and briefly on chapters 10, 12, 13, 15, and 17.

12. Similarly, McGinn observes with regard to *De* *prophetia* *ignota* that Joachim was careful to establish the Sibylline text in question in its harmony with the canonical Scriptures, and gave it authority only insofar as it agreed with those Scriptures; *op*. *cit*., p. 122.

13. The biblical passages Joachim cited in the <u>Vita</u> <u>Benedicti</u> fall
    into a two-fold pattern. In his commentary on the life of Bene-
    dict, Joachim relied heavily on the stories of the Old Testament
    patriarchs found in Genesis. In his commentary on the selections
    from the Rule, Joachim draws mainly from the Book of Daniel and
    the Apocalypse.

14. For the Abbot's general discussions of the history of monasticism,
    see <u>Vita</u> <u>Benediciti</u>, paragraphs 7-11.

15. <u>Ibid.</u>, 1, 16-17.

16. <u>Ibid.</u>, 1, 14-42.

17. <u>Ibid.</u>, 2; 13; 15, 13-18. Joachim uses the figures of Sarah-Hagar
    and Rachael-Leah many times throughout his writings, generally to
    illustrate the distinction between the Order of Clerics and Order
    of Monks, and berween the active and contemplative lives, as for
    example, <u>Liber</u> <u>concordie</u>, 57c, 83b-84a.

18. <u>Vita</u> <u>Benedicti</u>, 2, 1-18.

19. <u>Ibid.</u>, 11, 1-2.

20. <u>Ibid.</u>, 3, 1-8.

21. <u>Ibid.</u>, 3, 12-15; 4, 19-58.

22. <u>Ibid.</u>, 11, 32-33.

23. <u>Ibid.</u>, 3, 17-20.

24. <u>Ibid</u>., 4, 26-54.

25. For a discussion of the numerical significance of "twelve" see Reeves, <u>The Figurae of Joachim of Fiore</u>, pp. 13-19.

26. <u>Vita Benedicti</u>, 7, 15-40; 11, 37-47. A similar statement is found in the <u>Liber concordie</u>, 57d-58c.

27. <u>Ibid</u>., 8, 13-19; 10, 26-31.

28. Baraut, "Un Tratado Inedito," p. 4; "Joachim de Flore," col. 1195.

29. <u>Vita Benedicti</u>, 11, 47-52; see also, <u>Liber concordie</u>, 58b.

30. <u>Vita Benedicti</u>, 3, 17-22.

31. <u>Ibid</u>., 12, 55-60; <u>Liber Concordie</u>, 101b.

32. <u>Vita Benedicti</u>, 15, 41-56.

33. "Non solum autem in his, verum et in universis moribus et constitutionibus suis sic ecclesiastici ordinis formam retinet, ut quasi altera esset canonica, et nichilominus heremitice vite parsimoniam et solitudinem emulari nititur, ita ut apud quosdam non cenobium sed heremum esse videatur. Sed quamdiu simul esse poterunt, cum omnino non sibi conveniant, duo ista? Sicut enim qui librare quereret aquam et ignem, ut nec aqua ignem extingueret, nec ignis aque copiam desiccaret, sed et ignis arderet iugiter et aqua semper in sua quantitate persisteret, sic qui querit temporalibus affluere

et spiritalia non minuere, verbo predicationis insistere et silentio vacare, actionibus servire et contemplationi quiescere, frustra laborat: cedat enim alterum necesse est. Si autem sic necesse, et servare diu simul ambo non possunt, nonne melius est perfectionem querentibus ei parti valedicere que deorsum trahit, et illam totis viribus amplecti que tibi plenam exhibet et servat exhibitam libertatem?" Ibid., 15, 26-41; see also lines 55-56.

34. Ibid., 12, 53-60.

35. Ibid., 13, 17-25.

36. Ibid., 15, 18-26; 3, 17-30. Here are clear exceptions to Gregorio Penco's thesis that for Joachim Mary does not symbolize both the active life and the contemplative life. "Maria, modello della vita contemplativa secundo Gioacchino da Fiore," Benedictina 14 (1967) 51-56.

37. Reeves, Influence of Prophecy, p. 140.

38. Idem. Randolph Daniel discusses the influence of this expectation of the conversion of schismatic Greeks and of the Jews on the concept of missions, in his article, "Apocalyptic Conversion: The Joachite Alternative to the Crusades," Traditio 25 (1969) 128-54; and in the Franciscan Concept of Mission (Lexington, 1975) pp. 14-22.

39. "Apocalyptic Conversion....," pp. 141-42.

40. "Sicut ergo Christus Ihesus, de patriarchis nasciturus, primo,
     glorificavit matrem ex ea carnem assumens, ad extremum baptizatus,
     Spiritu sancto unctus est ut baptizaret in Spiritu, quique col-
     lectis discipulis, mori et resurgere dignatus est, suscitatus
     autem, in celum ascendit, ibique accepta plenitudine Spiritus,
     his quos agregaverat et reliquerat misit, ita Spiritus sanctus,
     qui spiritalibus patribus velut in semine promissus erat, Cis-
     terciensi ordini adveniens, promissa Patris et Filii completurus
     advenit, faciens uterum eius intumescere, dando se mentibus fili-
     orum suorum, inter quos Bernardus primatum tenuit, servans tem-
     pora pacientie Christi, quibus oportet alios succedere, quibus
     visibiliter columba et quasi corporali specie descendere videa-
     tur, quos oportet predicare annis tribus et dimidio, regnante
     cornu illo undecimo et ita duci ad passionem et pervenire ad
     gloriam. Qui autem erunt residui, pennas contemplationis acci-
     pere et scrutari cum Iohanne etiam profunda Dei, et post hec
     descendere super illos plenitudinem Spiritus, et predicari
     evangelium in universum orbem, et sic veniet consumatio."
     Vita Benedicti, 45, 13-30.

41. Ibid., 13, 17-35.

42. Liber concordie, 71c-72a.

43. Vita Benedicti, 46, 13-22.

THE CISTERCIAN STUDIES SERIES

EARLY MONASTIC TEXTS

MONASTIC STUDIES

CISTERCIAN STUDIES

BY DOM JEAN LECLERCQ

CISTERCIAN PUBLICATIONS

Titles Listing

THE CISTERCIAN FATHERS SERIES

THE WORKS OF BERNARD OF CLAIRVAUX

THE WORKS OF WILLIAM OF ST THIERRY

THE WORKS OF AELRED OF RIEVAULX

THE WORKS OF GUERRIC OF IGNY

OTHER CISTERCIAN WRITERS

* Available in paperback
OP Temporarily out of print
† Projected